Music as Social Life

Thomas Turino

Music as Social Life
The Politics of Participation

THE UNIVERSITY OF CHICAGO PRESS   *Chicago and London*

The University of Chicago Press, Chicago 60637
The University of Chicago Press, Ltd., London
© 2008 by The University of Chicago
All rights reserved. Published 2008.
Printed in the United States of America

20 19 18 17 16 15 14   8 9

ISBN-13: 978-0-226-81697-5 (cloth)
ISBN-10: 0-226-81697-4 (cloth)
ISBN-13: 978-0-226-81698-2 (paper)
ISBN-10: 0-226-81698-2 (paper)

Library of Congress Cataloging-in-Publication Data

Turino, Thomas.
   Music as social life : the politics of participation /
Thomas Turino.
       p. cm. — (Chicago studies in ethnomusicology)
   Includes bibliographical references and index.
   ISBN-13: 978-0-226-81697-5 (cloth : alk. paper)
   ISBN-10: 0-226-81697-4 (cloth : alk. paper)
   ISBN-13: 978-0-226-81698-2 (pbk. : alk. paper)
   ISBN-10: 0-226-81698-2 (pbk. : alk. paper)
   1. Music—Social aspects. I Title.
   ML3916.T87 2008
   781'.1—dc22

                                    2007050135

⊗ This paper meets the requirements of ANSI/NISO
Z39.48-1992 (Permanence of Paper).

For Amy,

And all the happiness
That quietly crept in with her.

Contents

CD Track List

1. "Elzic's Farewell" (traditional). Euphor Stringband: Matt Turino fiddle, Tom Turino five-string banjo, Michael Shapiro guitar. This is a three-part (AAB-BCC) old-time fiddle tune in the style we use for dances. The texture is basically homophonic, with the guitar providing chords behind the melody played in unison by the fiddle and banjo. There are some heterophonic moments between the fiddle and banjo when one or the other adds variations to the tune. Banjo is performed here in clawhammer or frailing style, with strumming to add density on the B section. The tune begins with the standard old-time opening formula "four potatoes" played on the fiddle (0.03 on the CD player's time indicator); then the form for the first repetition is as follows: A (0.05), A (0.13), B (0.21), B (0.29), C (0.37), C (0.45), A (0.53) . . .

2. "Home Is Where the Heart Is" (C. Gately, J. Talley). Cletus and the Barnburners: Michael Penque guitar, Phil Weinrobe bass, Nick Aives five-string banjo, Tom Eaton mandolin, Ben Smith fiddle. This is an example of bluegrass style and instrumentation. The form is a verse-chorus structure with the vocal sections being alternated with instrumental solos that provide prearranged contrasts. The texture is basically homophonic, with the banjo playing arpeggiated chords and fills and the mandolin and fiddle playing occasional fills behind the vocals. The Scruggs three-finger banjo style is clearly heard on the banjo solo and should be compared to the frailing style heard on track 1. The timbre of the fiddle is more transparent here and should be compared to the denser fiddle sound on track 1 (used with permission from the band).

3. Carnival Pinkillu (indigenous Andean flute) music. Aymara musicians in the town of Moho, near Conima, Puno, Peru. Ten flute players accompanied by six large snare drums. This example well illustrates dense texture and wide

tuning. The drums add density as well as rhythmic drive for dancing. The form here is AABBCC: A (0.04), A (0.13), B (0.23), B (0.33), C (0.43), C (0.51), A (1.00) . . . The same motive is used at section cadences: (A 0.10), (A 0.20), (B 0.30), (B 0.40), (C 0.49), (C 0.57), illustrating the trait of motivic repetition across sections, discussed in chapter 2 (recorded by author).

4. "Saqsahumanpi/Valicha/Capuliñawi Cusqueñita." Takiy Orqo: Larry Crook *bombo* (drum), Dan Dickey guitar, Tom Turino *kena* (indigenous Andean flute). This is an example of the cosmopolitan folkloric style of Andean music developed for nightclub, folk club, and festival presentational performance. It is a medley of three songs from Cusco, Peru, with a fourth *fuga* (concluding) section and is an example of particularly transparent homophonic texture and planned contrasts, especially between vocal and instrumental sections and among the three melodies. The first text is in the Andean Quechua language and the second is in Spanish. "Saqsahumanpi" (0.09); "Valicha" (1.20); "Capuliñawi Cusqueñita" (1.46); *fuga* (2.22).

5. "Taimbureva," mbira music from Murehwa, Zimbabwe. Emmanuel Chidzere and David Mapfumo mbira, Piyo Murungweni hosho and vocals. This has a four-phrase forty-eight-beat cycle (recorded by author).

6. "Shuramurove," *dandanda* dance-drumming music from Mhembere village, Murehwa, Zimbabwe. This is a cyclical twenty-four-beat piece and an excellent example of dense heterophonic texture recorded in a participatory setting. This vocal performance might be compared to the school choir example (track 8) to get a good sense of the contrasts between participatory and presentational styles in Zimbabwe (recorded by author).

7. "0000," composition for four-channel electroacoustic music (stereo version) by David Psenicka, 2001. Fales's typology of electronic music sounds (chapter 3) ranging from the easily iconic to the anxiety producing might be considered when listening to this studio audio art piece. Although recorded digitally, it opens with sounds that, to my ear, are iconic of the surface noise and scratches one hears on an old vinyl LP, and thus (in my interpretation) it is genre-referential to the history of recording itself (used with permission of the composer).

8. "Shorten' Bread." School choir from Umtali, Zimbabwe (late 1950s). Notice the clarity of texture and diction and the well-arranged harmony and contrasts of voicing and dynamics in this old recording of presentational school singing. Exemplifying middle-class aesthetics, this example could be compared to indigenous participatory dandanda music (track 6). American 'folk' and popular

songs such as this one were often taught by American missionaries to African students (personal collection of the author).

9. "Ewe Dudu." De Black Evening Follies, "concert" ensemble of Zimbabwe. This exemplifies the jazzy Mills Brothers–influenced style of the 1940s, although it was recorded in the early 1960s (personal collection of the author).

10. Jerusarema Dance. Murehwa Jerusarema and Burial Society (recorded by author).

Figures

All photos except for figures 6.1 and 6.2 are by author.

Preface

Around the time that I turned fifty, my approach to teaching the large 'world music' survey classes that I had been doing for seventeen years at the University of Illinois began to change. My son had entered our university as a freshman and complained about the irrelevant, cursory, and rather impersonal quality of some of the large lecture classes that he was required to take, one of which was largely delivered by video. Classes like mine? I wondered. I believe in public universities and have been proud of mine. I accept although I do not like the necessity of large lecture classes. But through Matt's eyes I began to worry that as an institution we were failing our mission to teach critical synthetic thinking, that we were simply continuing the rote learning for standardized computer-graded tests that is coming to dominate in high schools and grammar schools.

I view the large survey classes as one of my primary social functions, the place where I touch the greatest number of people. Although I cannot personally know most of the 240 students who take Introduction to World Music each semester, I periodically try to imagine them as if they were my own sons and daughters. What do I want them to think about? Drawing from the collective work of ethnomusicologists, anthropologists, and social theorists, what can I present that might be meaningful to them over time when fashioning their own lives? Beyond the presentation of case studies from regions where I have studied music, especially Peru, Zimbabwe, and the United States, it seems important to teach analytical concepts and frameworks that would help students explore the key roles of music and dance in social life and spur them to think about music and the nature of social groups in new ways.

I found no texts that synthesized the conceptual frameworks that I wanted to teach in a form that was practical and accessible for assignments. Thus, I began to write materials for the students in which I attempted to draw together key ideas from a variety of social theorists and philosophers as well as my own ideas about society and culture as they pertain to, and are informed by, the arts and expressive cultural practices. I assigned these short unpublished pieces for several years in the 'world music' survey, in undergraduate and graduate seminars, and in the core course for our international arts minor, and they seemed helpful for generating thinking and debate. Several of these articles form the starting point for this project. The same questions that now inform my undergraduate and graduate teaching are the impetus for writing this book: What do I want people to consider about the nature of musical meaning and the crucial roles music plays in social, spiritual, and political life? What conceptual tools can I provide for people to think through these problems and processes for themselves?

Thomas Turino
Urbana, Illinois, 2007

Acknowledgments

Special thanks to Elizabeth Branch Dyson for her continued support and her insightful and frank commentary on an earlier draft; it was just what I needed and what only a great editor and friend would provide. My *comadre* Carol Spindel, a novelist and nonfiction writer, read the same draft and blew on it from other sides, guiding in the same directions. I lived with these two women page by page through the first revision and felt safer for their presence. My wife Amy's questions and gentle comments completed the consensus for shaping the penultimate draft, which was then revised further in light of the generous and intelligent commentary from my anonymous readers. My son Matt has been a longtime reader of parts of this manuscript; he and my daughter Crissy were ever in my mind as members of the audience I wanted to reach. My graduate students James Lea and Tony Perman and I have discussed Peirce's semiotics for so long that I am not always sure whose ideas are whose. Art historian and co–team teacher David O'Brien has added insights and criticism on a number of issues in the book; especially helpful were his requests for clarifying the cultural formation–cultural cohort distinction, which, along with comments from Phil Clark and Ben Smith, spurred further development. Paul Hartley, Abby Lyng, Sara Mosher, Eduardo Herrera, and Joanna Bosse provided excellent arguments and suggestions about the four musical fields that I propose, sharpening my own thinking and explanations. Miriam Larson helped with interviews and research on the local old-time music scene in Urbana and provided insights on the scene more broadly. I would like to express my appreciation to Paul Watkins for allowing me to include his wonderful photos. Finally, I am particularly grateful to all the students, too numerous to name, who have chewed over this material in draft form; their questions, confusions about my confusions, and breakthroughs were guiding inspiration for refinement and for writing the book in the first place.

Material support for work on this book came from the University of Illinois Research Board and a summer grant from the College of Fine and Applied Arts.

1 Introduction
Why Music Matters

Musical sounds are a powerful human resource, often at the heart of our most profound social occasions and experiences. People in societies around the world use music to create and express their emotional inner lives, to span the chasm between themselves and the divine, to woo lovers, to celebrate weddings, to sustain friendships and communities, to inspire mass political movements, and to help their babies fall asleep. Music is the basis of a huge industry and can be an avenue to money and fame. It is also a constant of everyday life, wafting through the dentist's office like sonic wallpaper. A central thesis of this book is that _music_ is not a unitary art form, but rather that this term refers to fundamentally distinct types of activities that fulfill different needs and ways of being human. At a deeper level, I argue that musical participation and experience are valuable for the processes of personal and social integration that make us whole.

The famous European composer Igor Stravinsky is often credited with the idea that music has no meaning beyond itself. He was expressing a notion that is held by some people about music, especially European classical instrumental music, that it is an abstract, socially autonomous art. One reason for this attitude is that it is often difficult to capture or translate musical meaning with words. Like the other arts, musical sounds can be a special kind of communication and experience that draw upon and draw out different parts of the self. This book is a theoretical exploration of some of the ways music is socially meaningful; it is also an introduction to some basic conceptual models that might help illuminate why and how music and dance are so important to people's understanding of themselves and

1

their identities, to the formation and sustenance of social groups, to spiritual and emotional communication, to political movements, and to other fundamental aspects of social life. This chapter sets the stage by introducing some of the basic theoretical ideas that will be developed throughout the book.

Why Art Matters

Although many societies around the world do not have a single concept translatable with the English word *music*, activities akin to what we call music and dance are practiced among people everywhere and have been throughout history. It is worth asking why this is so. The performing, visual, language, and architectural arts are certainly sources of pleasure, but this alone does not explain why human beings everywhere and at all times have been moved to enact dramas, tell and write stories, make musical sounds, dance, paint on cave walls and on canvas, make decorative textiles, wear masks, adorn their bodies, and construct buildings that do far more than simply provide shelter. Pleasure alone does not explain why people of all times and places have gone to great effort to enact elaborate rituals and ceremonies, or why they are universally drawn to sports, games, and more generally to *play*, the English verb used to denote music making.

Some anthropologists have suggested that the arts are central to human evolution and human survival. This can be understood in several basic ways. Music, dance, festivals, and other public expressive cultural practices are a primary way that people articulate the collective identities that are fundamental to forming and sustaining social groups, which are, in turn, basic to survival. The performing arts are frequently fulcrums of identity, allowing people to intimately feel themselves part of the community through the realization of shared cultural knowledge and style and through the very act of participating together in performance. Music and dance are key to identity formation because they are often public presentations of the deepest feelings and qualities that make a group unique.[1] Through moving and sounding together in synchrony, people can experi-

---

1. Over the last three decades, ethnomusicologists have repeatedly documented the special power of music for realizing social identities and cultural subjectivies (e.g., Peña 1985; Feld 1988; Koskoff 1989; Waterman 1990; Turino 1993; Stokes 1994; Sugarman 1997; Radano and Bohlman 2000b; Turino and Lea 2004; Feldman 2006; Buchanan 2006).

ence a feeling of oneness with others.[2] The signs of this social intimacy are experienced directly—body to body—and thus in the moment are felt to be true. Social solidarity is a good and, in fact, necessary thing. We depend on social groups—our family, our friends, our tribe, our nation—to survive emotionally and economically and to belong to something larger than ourselves. In cases where in-group solidarity supports the dehumanizing of other groups—that is, overvaluing difference and undervaluing the basic sameness of people—survival can once again be threatened (a theme taken up in chapter 7). Study of expressive cultural practices like music and dance from different societies can help us achieve a balance between understanding cultural difference and recognizing our common humanity.

Anthropologist and scientist Gregory Bateson discusses the evolutionary potential of the arts from a different angle (1972a). He notes that the arts are a special form of communication that has an integrative function—integrating and uniting the members of social groups but also integrating individual selves, and selves with the world. Bateson argues that if normal language were all that was needed to communicate, then the arts would have withered and disappeared long ago. He suggests that artists communicate through the presentation of forms and patterns that serve as integrated maps of sensations, imagination, and experience and that it is through these patterns that we are most deeply connected to and part of the natural world.

Bateson posits that, like dreams, artistic creativity flows from the subconscious in what he calls *primary process*[3] and that through the manipulation of artistic materials—paint, stone, musical sounds, motion, words—this inner life is rendered in consciously perceivable forms. As we know from our dreams, primary process is *connective*; that is, it links images and ideas that 'rationally'[4] we might not think belong together. As in the strange combinations of images that sometimes come to us in dreams, the connections expressed through art flow from and create a deeper sense and a different type of understanding. Bateson's hypothesis is that artistic

2. William H. McNeill (1995) suggests the term "muscular bonding" for the sense of oneness derived from marching or dancing together in close synchrony; we might add the term "sonic bonding" when this occurs through music making.

3. Terms in the text that are marked with an asterisk are found in the glossary.

4. I use single quotation marks to denote terms that are to be understood in relation to specific discourses, e.g., 'rationally' in relation to modernist discourse, 'nation' and 'ethnicity' in relation to nationalist discourse.

patterns and forms are both the result of and articulate this integration of different parts of the self and thus facilitate wholeness. He concludes that the integrative wholeness of individuals developed through artistic experience—the balancing of connective inner life with 'reason,' sensitivity, and sense—is crucial to experiencing deep connections with others and with the environment, which is crucial for social and ecological survival.

Flow

Further illuminating Bateson's ideas about individuals' developing psychic wholeness through artistic experiences, psychologist Mihaly Csikszentmihalyi has created a theory of *optimal experience* or *flow* that helps explain how art and music aid individuals in reaching a fuller integration of the self (1988; 1990). *Flow* refers to a state of heightened concentration, when one is so intent on the activity at hand that all other thoughts, concerns, and distractions disappear and the actor is fully in the present. The experience actually leads to a feeling of timelessness, or being out of normal time, and to feelings of transcending one's normal self. Regardless of how intense the activity is—mountain climbing or kayaking a difficult river—Csikszentmihalyi's interview research suggests that people find flow experience restful and liberating, because the problems and aspects of ourselves that sometimes get in our way from reaching a clear, open state of mind disappear during intense concentration. Csikszentmihalyi claims further that this open state of mind is fundamental for psychic growth and integration.

Most people have probably had the experience of being so involved with a particular activity that an hour seemed like minutes. Coming out of this state of mind, one wonders, "Where did the time go?" Such experiences are examples of flow. While flow states are available to almost everyone and may be quite common for some people, Csikszentmihalyi's contribution has been to pinpoint the particular conditions within activities that enhance the potential for reaching flow states.

Perhaps the most important condition for flow is that the activity must include the proper balance between inherent challenges and the skill level of the actor. If the challenges are too low, the activity becomes boring and the mind wanders; if the challenges are too high, the activity leads to frustration and the actor cannot engage fully. When the balance is just right, it enhances concentration and that sense of being at one with the activity and perhaps the other people involved. Since flow is experienced as pleasurable, people tend to return again and again to activities that produce this state. As they do so their skill level grows, requiring the challenges to increase if the proper balance is to be maintained. A second condition for activities to readily produce flow states, then, is that they have a continually expanding ceiling for potential challenges. The third key condition for achieving flow is that the activity must contain the potential for immediate feedback on how one is doing, which, again, keeps the mind focused on the activity at hand. As the fourth condition for creating flow, activities should be clearly bounded by time and place so that participants can more fully concentrate on what they are doing and tune out 'the everyday.' The final feature that enhances the potential for intense concentration and flow is clear, well established goals that are reachable within the bounded time and place and in relation to the skills-challenge balance.

Csikszentmihalyi notes that with the right state of mind even the most mundane job can lead to flow if the worker continually sets her own challenges in balance with the task at hand—for example, continually increasing the number of items handled on an assembly line in the same amount of time. But certain activities seem specially designed to contain all the necessary conditions for reaching flow—sports, games, music, and dance primary among them—and this may be another hint as to why such activities remain universally valued in human societies. As I discuss further in subsequent chapters, certain types of music making contain the conditions for flow in unique and particularly pronounced ways.

Musical Signs and Meaning

Bateson's suggestion about the importance of the arts in human life can also be approached by considering how music and dance create and communicate emotion and meaning through signs. The American philosopher Charles Sanders Peirce (1839–1914) created a theory of signs known as *semiotics. Following Peirce, a *sign can be anything that is perceived by an observer which stands for or calls to mind something else and by doing so creates an effect in the observer. Thus, any sign situation has three aspects: (1) the sign or *sign vehicle, (2) the *object[5] or idea indicated by the sign, and (3) the *effect* or meaning of the sign-object relation in the perceiver. The actual effects generated by signs can range from a feeling to a physical

5. Peirce used the term *object* to refer to whatever the sign stands for, be it a person, a rock, a wind direction, or an abstract idea.

reaction to a thought or idea in the mind; from a Peircean perspective, all human feeling, action, and thought are initiated and mediated by signs. Most obviously, the words in language are signs, but Peirce's contribution to our understanding of musical meaning was that he provided theoretical tools for analyzing the nature of nonlinguistic signs and their potential effects. One way that he did this was by pinpointing three basic ways that people make the connection between a sign and what it stands for (its *object*). The manner in which a person connects a sign vehicle with its object determines the effects of the sign in important ways and distinguishes its semiotic function. Peirce's three most famous concepts—*icon, *index, and *symbol*—refer to the different manners by which a sign is related to its object. The vast majority of signs operating in music are icons and indices.

Icon

The first way that people make the connection between a sign and what it stands for is through resemblance, what Peirce called *icons* or iconic signs. A drawing of a horse is an iconic sign for the animal if, through resemblance, seeing the picture calls horses to mind. The most basic type of iconic process is the grouping of phenomena because of some type of resemblance. We group types of people because of similar clothing styles, speech accents, and other physical attributes; we recognize dogs as a *type* of animal because of some type of resemblance. We also recognize a new song as belonging to a particular style or genre because it *sounds like* other songs we have heard; the sound of steel guitar and a particular type of "twangy" vocal quality (*timbre) and ornamentation allow North Americans to immediately identify a new piece encountered as country music because it sounds like the country songs they have heard before. Iconic processes are fundamental to musical meaning in terms of style (token-type) recognition and are basic to our cultural classifications of most things, including people's identities. This kind of iconic process is usually so automatic and constant that it happens low in focal awareness until we encounter something that is not easily connected to a general type that is familiar to us—for example, a radically different kind of musical sound or a "scary noise." In daily life people habitually and continually group phenomena encountered through resemblances; a noise is usually scary only if we can't readily identify the type of thing that made the sound. As discussed in chapter 3, some electronic music composers purposefully choose sounds that are not easily iconic of sound sources that listeners would be familiar with, to the point that the music can create discomfort or anxiety.

Iconic processes are also basic to the recognition of patterns and *form* in music, art, and indeed all phenomena. Recognition of symmetry in the human body results from the resemblance of the two eyes, two ears, two arms, two nostrils, etc. When a composer repeats a musical figure (or **motive*), melodic passage, or section at different points in a piece, listeners perceive the repetition through the resemblance with what they have heard before and thus begin to perceive the 'shape' of the composition— as in a piece with two sections (A and B) organized as ABA or AABB or ABAB. The perception of musical form is thus similar to the way the iconicity of rhymed lines in songs and poetry allows us to perceive poetic form through the similar and contrasting sounds of words.

Perhaps most important for understanding the special potentials and effects of music, iconic signs create a special space for making imaginative connections. If the sounds of kettle drums in a piece of music make the listener think of thunder or cannons or the rumble of a subway (*objects* of the sign) because, for the listener, the drums *sound like* thunder or cannons or a subway, then the drum sounds function as *signs of resemblance,* or icons. Note that the composer may not have intended these particular connections and thus *communication*—the transference of intended meaning or information from composer to listener—was not involved.

As with maps or diagrams, iconic signs can be used to communicate intended meaning or information, but in other instances the resemblances perceived by observers may be a product of their personal history and experiences—what I call the *internal context* of the perceiver. Kettle drums will probably not suggest "the rumble of a subway" to a listener who has no experience with subways, but this connection may be the first thing that comes to mind for a daily subway commuter. The main issue for our purposes is that icons can spur imaginative connections of resemblance between the signs perceived and the objects stood for in light of the internal context of the perceiver. Inkblot tests used by psychologists operate on this principle; the patient is asked to use his imagination to see something in the randomly produced forms in order to draw out aspects of his past and perhaps his subconscious. When people see the shapes of animals or dragons in cloud formations, similar imaginative iconic processes are at work. In music and abstract visual art these same types of imaginative iconic connections are often made; whether intended by the artists or not, sounds in music may ignite the imagination by suggesting resemblances with other things outside the music. A slow, bittersweet melody or an upbeat tune can *sound like* what I happen to feel like at a particular time, the music being iconic of my mood.[6] One of the great functions of music and the other arts is to trigger people's imagination and feelings in this way. Musical icons offer the special potential of inspiring imaginative connections similar to the connections we experience in dreams.

Iconic signs can also be used purposefully by artists to render their imaginings in perceivable form and to push perceivers to make certain connections and consider new possibilities. For example, drawings of spaceships and robots in science fiction books predated the actual existence of these machines. Artists first imagined these possibilities and then rendered them perceivable in their art; the scientists and engineers took over from there. The Mbuti Pygmies of the central African rainforest iconically represent the "sound of the divine forest" by playing a trumpet to make animal sounds during their *molimo* ceremonies, thereby rendering the spiritual concept of the forest, as they imagine it, in perceivable form (Turnbull 1962).

Index

The second way that people connect a sign with what it stands for is by experiencing the sign and object together; Peirce called this type of sign an *index*. Smoke is an index of fire, lightning and thunder are indices of a storm, and a siren is an indexical sign for police cars and emergency vehicles. If a person often hears the same tune played as a bride and groom march to the altar, this tune might call weddings or marriage to mind even when heard outside a wedding situation. In advertisements, if a particular musical jingle is played every time the product is shown or discussed on TV, then the jingle can come to function as a *sign of cooccurrence* or *index* for the product. Because people commonly hear particular styles of music played by particular individuals or social groups or in particular regions, music typically serves as a powerful index for these types of identity (chapter 5). Music also commonly indexes the people and situations where we have heard the music; if you listened to a particular song with your first

---

6. Such sound-mood iconic relations are based in cultural musical conventions that attribute mood to certain sound features, such as minor keys with somberness or sadness or, in Peru, slow tempos with seriousness and fast tempos with happiness. Another musical feature such as a melodic line that rises in pitch and volume may be more directly iconic with feelings of excitement because it *sounds like* what happens in speakers' voices when they get excited.

love ("our song"), the piece might serve as an index for that person, or the feelings involved, when you hear it later in life.

We make the connection between indexical signs and their objects by experiencing them together in our actual lives. Consequently indices have a particularly direct impact; we typically do not reflect on the reality of the object that the sign calls forth, but we simply assume its reality as commonsense because it is part of our experience. We may go on to reflect about whatever it was that the index brought to mind, but the initial indexical sign-object connection is perceived as fact. Thus, just as icons open us to the realm of possibility and imagination, indices have a kind of reality function and are of the realm of direct connection. Certain indexical signs are interpreted as actually being affected by their objects; weathervane (index) and wind direction (object), facial expression (index) and inner mood (object), loud volume (index) and the high energy required for sound production (object) are examples of this causally related type that Peirce calls *dicent indices. As discussed in chapter 6, the much-debated issue of musical authenticity can be clarified by using the concept of dicent index.

Because indexical connections are created by experiencing sign and object together, and because we might experience the same sign vehicle at different times and in different contexts, indices potentially involve a kind of *semantic snowballing. Old indexical connections may linger as new ones are added, potentially condensing a variety of meanings and emotions within a highly economical and yet unpredictable sign. As discussed in chapter 7, members of the civil rights movement used preexisting tunes that indexed the church and progressive labor movements and set new lyrics about civil rights to these tunes. In effect what they were doing was combining the old associations of religious righteousness and progressive politics—directly felt through indexical connection—with their events and cause, thereby adding historical depth and emotional power. The emotional power of indexical signs is directly proportionate to the attachment, feelings, and significance of the experiences that they index, but since these signs operate to connect us to our own lives, they can be the most "personal" and tend to have the greatest emotional potential of all three sign types.

Like icons, indexical signs are somewhat unpredictable since they depend on the past experiences (internal contexts) of the perceivers and no two individuals' experiences are identical. Differences in experience are all the more pronounced when people hail from different social and cultural groups (chapter 4). Shared experiences, however, can lead common indexical associations among groups of people, and the mass media, especially advertising, is in the business of creating mass indices. Nowadays musical indices are commonly created and conventionally used in the mass media. Even very young children immediately recognize the musical sounds (indices) that communicate that a scary part is coming in a movie, because they have heard such sounds accompany scary parts before. No one has to tell them to shield their eyes: the reaction of timid young viewers will be direct, automatic. The effects of indexical signs are often like this.

Symbol

The third way that signs are connected to their objects is through linguistic definition. Words can be created and defined with other words, and we can assign a specific meaning to all sorts of signs ($=$, $+$, ♩) through linguistic definition. Peirce referred to such linguistically based signs as *symbols. To function for communication, symbols require not only specific linguistic definition but also social agreement; people have to agree on the definitions of words (documented in dictionaries) or the notational symbols of a musical score (documented in music instruction books) if a speaker's or composer's intentions are to be realized. The readers of this book will have to agree to understand *icon, index,* and *symbol* in the way that I am defining these terms (symbols) here if they are to understand my meaning in later chapters. Symbols, established through linguistic definition and agreement, have the greatest potential for relatively predictable communication.

Symbols are general signs. When operating symbolically, the word *cat* does not specify a particular animal but rather the concept of "cat" in general. If someone says "that cat" pointing to an animal in the room, then the words are operating with a strong indexical component of cooccurrence to establish meaning; many words in everyday speech have this strong indexical connection to their objects. Thus while symbolic sign-object connections typically involve language, linguistic signs (words) are not always operating as symbols. It is basic to symbolic operations that symbols are indexically linked most prominently to and cooccur with the other symbols (words) of their definition or linguistic discourse rather than to actual objects out there in the world. This is what Peirce meant when he stated that symbols are general signs about general objects. Symbols are signs that have other symbols as their objects. It is the strength of symbols that they do not require a resemblance to or cooccurrence with things out in the world to be meaningful; their meaning is linguistically based and socially agreed upon. Thus symbols can operate in a relatively context-free manner—for example, in lectures in a classroom about other things not present there. These qualities make symbols contextually flexible and the primary sign type for general description and relatively precise theoretical synthesis and analysis.[7]

Note that while indexical connections may be shared among people who have had common experiences, similar reactions to indexical signs are not formally agreed upon or remotely guaranteed; there are no dictionaries of indexical signs. Moreover, indices point to specific instances rather than generalities and thus do not serve well for theoretical discourse and analysis. We need symbols to generalize and theorize generalities, that is, to make sense of the vast array of specific phenomena that we encounter. Each sign type does a different type of semiotic work and has a propensity to create different types of effects.

Peirce outlined three basic types of effects created by sign-object relations: (1) a sense or a feeling; (2) a physical reaction or response; and (3) "a more developed sign in the mind" including sonic, tactile, olfactory, and visual images as well as word-based symbolic thought. So, for example, when hearing a song that one's mother used to sing around the kitchen, the listener might have a vague sense of longing, or bolt upright in his chair, or have an olfactory image (memory) of kitchen smells, a visual image of the kitchen, or the word-based thought "I'd better call Mom." In any of these hypothetical instances the song functioned as the sign; 'Mom,' 'home,' 'the kitchen,' 'childhood' were potential objects of the sign, creating the different effects described.

To provide a way to think about the dynamic nature of perception and thought, Peirce also outlined various types of *semiotic chaining processes*. Within one type, a given sign-object relation (*a*) creates an effect (*a*) which

7. Those interested in understanding Peirce more fully might begin by reading his articles "The Fixation of Belief," "How to Make Our Ideas Clear," "The Principles of Phenomenology," and "Logic as Semiotic: The Theory of Signs," all contained in Justus Buchler's edited volume *Philosophical Writings of Peirce* (Peirce 1955). Carl Hausman provides a useful discussion of writings about Peirce (Hausman 1993:xiii–xvii); his chapter "Classes of Signs" provides a good introduction to Peircean semiotics. Hausman's conception of the symbol, like that of many other writers, is broader than mine. I have written a longer article about the application of Peircean semiotics to music (Turino 1999). That paper falls short in not exploring the importance of indexicality in language, but it provides a fuller picture of the importance of both iconicity and indexicality, as well as other sign components, in music than I am able to provide here.

becomes the next sign in the chain (b), standing for a new object (b), creating a new effect (b), which becomes the next sign in the chain (c), with a
new object (c), and yet another effect (c), which becomes another sign (d),
etc., until this line of feeling/reaction/thought is interrupted.

Let me fill in the hypothetical example about Mom's kitchen with a true
story, the main action taking place in a matter of seconds. A middle-aged
man is relaxing in a chair, mind wandering, all well with the world. A
Mozart piece (sign a, object as yet unspecified) comes on the radio, initially creating a scarcely noticed sense of vague discomfort (effect a). This
feeling (sign b) is connected to a vague sense about his mother (object b),
making the man bolt upright (effect b); this physical reaction, complete
with rapid heartbeat, becomes the new sign (c), connected to a welling
feeling that something is wrong vis-à-vis Mom (object c), creating a sudden
burst of word-based thought exclaimed simultaneously out loud: "Damn!
Mom's birthday was two days ago. I forgot again!" (effect c). This sudden
remembrance (sign d) then inspires new chains of thought about how to
make excuses and amends to Mom, a lifelong Mozart fan (hence the musical index), as well as chains of self-incriminating feelings and a promise to
himself that he will write down everyone's birthday for next year (which,
to my knowledge, he never did).[8] Peirce's insight about the dynamic chaining of signs avoids strict body-mind and emotion-thought dichotomies by
providing a framework for analyzing the interactions of sense, physical
reaction, and "more developed signs in the mind"—a framework crucial
for understanding musical meaning.

Artistic Signs and Personal Integration

Armed with Peirce's semiotic tools, I want to return to Gregory Bateson's
idea that the arts are essential to human survival because they serve the
function of integrating different parts of the self and integrating individuals with each other and their environment.

As suggested above, each sign type has its own potentials for creating

8. This mundane description of semiotic chaining can be tested by studying
one's own processes of feeling/reaction/thought and determining the signs, objects,
and effects (dynamic interpretants) that made up the chain within a given instance.
It should be noted that Peirce was more interested in a different type of linking of
*interpretants, by which a community of observers would arrive at the final interpretant
for an object, which is the "norm or standard of the truth of all prior interpretants"
approaching the "truth" about the reality of the object.

different types of effects and doing specific types of semiotic work. Symbols are necessary for general thought and theoretical analysis. Because the objects of symbols are other symbols, the effects of this sign type will probably be symbolic thought. The strength of this sign type is also its weakness; while symbols can be used to generalize, their general, relatively context-free quality does not help us feel or experience what they are generalizing about. Indices connect us to our actual experiences, have a reality function, and can be emotionally potent in proportion to the emotional potency of the experiences called forth by the signs. The effects tend to be direct, automatic, "pre-interpreted," in relation to an actual object in the world and experienced sign-object relations.[9] Both feelings and physical responses are typical effects of indexical signs early in the chaining process, for example the anxiety felt and the hands automatically shooting up to cover the eyes when scary music is heard by a timid movie watcher. Signs of resemblance, icons, allow us to make *token-type* connections and to perceive form; they also allow for the play of the imagination. The initial effects of iconic signs tend to be at the level of sensual perception, sensation, and feeling. Iconic and indexical signs are signs *of* our perceptions, imagination, and experiences, whereas symbols are more abstract signs *about* things as generalities.

Different realms of social life tend to utilize certain sign types more than others. In academic and scientific writing and teaching as well as mathematics, symbols are prominent; academic work exercises the symbolic, analytical parts of the self. By contrast, the arts, even the linguistic arts, are distinguished by the preponderance of iconic and indexical signs with their propensity to fire the imagination and create sensory, emotional, and physical effects. Whereas linguistic signs in everyday speech may function iconically, indexically, and symbolically, the vast majority of signs operating in music and dance are icons and indices. It is possible for musical sounds to function as symbols, but not without the intervention of language. Symbolic instruction is not the way that most people make the connections between musical signs (sounds) and their objects, although music students and scholars, both professional and amateur, pro-

---

9. By "pre-interpreted," Hausman (1993:88) is pointing to the objective conditions in the world that influence semiotic processes, but the term might also be applied to the direct effects of signs when symbolic reflection is not involved. For example, when a sergeant yells "Attention!" and a well-trained soldier automatically snaps to, the direct physical effect of the sign is different from what we typically think of as interpretation.

vide special cases.[10] Rather, I would suggest that most people the world over connect the majority of musical signs to their objects either through resemblances or through cooccurrence.[11]

Different realms of social life are also *framed* in different ways so that we know how to interpret the signs operating. Bateson (1972b) discusses the concept of **frame* as a mental framework for interpreting a particular slice of experience. When someone winks and then says something insulting, the wink is meant to cue a frame of interpretation in which the words spoken are not be taken literally but rather should be interpreted as a joke ("joking frame").[12] Everything in daily interaction is framed in some way. When two acquaintances pass each other on their way to class and one says, "How are you?" the interchange is framed as "casual greeting," and the addressee knows that she is not expected to really explain how she is. This same question, however, might be framed differently when two friends make an effort to sit down to drink coffee and catch up. Here the situation plus indices of body language and tone of voice can cue a frame by which the addressee interprets the words as literal and sincere (she really wants to know how I am). The frame of academic classes, lectures, and books suggests that the signs should largely be interpreted as symbols and are intended as such, to be interpreted literally. Different genres of art, in themselves, cue particular frames of interpretation. A science-fiction movie or book cues us early on that the action to follow should be interpreted as fantasy; a historical novel invites us to wonder which parts of the story actually happened. The very genres of poetry and song cue us to

10. For example, if music students are instructed that the minor-major key change that occurs in the transition from the third to fourth movements in Beethoven's Fifth Symphony means 'triumph,' this passage may function as a symbol for 'triumph' if students make this connection based on the professor's linguistic definition.

11. Readers should assess this crucial proposition in light of their own experiences. They might choose a song or piece that is particularly powerful for them and then begin to isolate the sound features that make it so. Once this is accomplished, listeners can begin to analyze the prominent sound features (e.g., vocal or instrumental *timbre* or tone quality, tempo, nature of the melody, rhythm, lyrics, etc.) as signs, determine their objects, and think about their effects in relation to how the listener made the sign-object connections.

12. Of course the frames cued might not be accepted, and there are always frames within frames. For example, the insult leveled after the wink might still be interpreted as literal because this interaction is framed by both actors' knowledge of their broader relationship. If the addressee feels that the speaker did not actually mean what was said as a joke, protests such as "Hey, I was only kidding" will probably be of no avail.

expect and interpret metaphoric expression and other iconic and indexical language. The singer-songwriter genre is generally framed such that the signs in performance (the songs, body language, stage patter, etc.) are to be interpreted as dicent indices of the performer's actual self and experiences. The glam rock and opera genres are framed so that the artists are interpreted as playing a part; that is, their performances are interpreted as iconic representations of possible or imaginary people, and it is understood that they are not depicting themselves.[13]

Thus, not only is there a preponderance of iconic and indexical signs in music and the other arts, but these social fields of practice are framed to predispose us toward nonsymbolic interpretation and experience. Here is the key point: within the semiotic chains of effects produced by iconic and indexical signs in music and art, sensual perception, feeling, physical reaction, and symbolic thought may *all* eventually occur, thus involving and integrating different parts of the self which are sometimes conventionally referred to as 'emotional,' 'physical,' and 'rational.' This type of fuller integration is more likely to occur in response to phenomena like music and the other arts as opposed to fields where symbols predominate and primarily exercise the analytical parts of the self—hence Bateson's emphasis on the arts for developing wholeness.

Symbols tend to keep us in the realm of symbolic thought, reducing the interplay of feeling and physical reaction and, consequently, of these different parts of the self. This proposition can be easily tested by comparing your own reaction to a typical academic lecture with what occurs in you during a musical performance, movie, or play. Although a good professor will pepper her lecture with examples and stories that listeners can relate to (indices) and may even include controversial statements that elicit an emotional response, the main thrust in lectures and academic books is usually symbolic propositions about the subject matter, which critical students will assess at the symbolic level ("are these premises sound?" "are these propositions true?" "is this guy making sense?").

For many people, reactions to artistic performances strike a different balance because the main thrust is not symbolic but involves a different type of iconic richness and "indexical truth." Depending on the genre frame, performances likely may be judged on the degree to which the perceiver's imagination, physical reaction, and feelings drawn from past experiences were triggered by the art. The semiotic chains set in motion by

13. Erving Goffman has developed the concept of frame further in a book-length treatment (1974).

musical performance may well lead in and out of word-based thought, but many of the effects created will probably be at the levels of sense, feeling, and physical reaction, integrating all these aspects of the self. For those deeply engaged in listening, dancing, or playing music, symbolic word-based thought may be suspended *entirely* during those periods in which a flow state is achieved and the person is in the moment.

Iconic and especially indexical signs tie us to actual experiences, people, and aspects of the environment. Indices are *of* our lives and experiences and thus are potentially invested with greater feeling and senses of intimacy and reality. Indexical experience plus a perception of iconic similarity with other people and forms of life is the basis for feeling direct *empathic connection*. Spending time in artistic activities where such signs are emphasized enhances individual sensitivity and ability to connect—this was one of Bateson's main contentions about the evolutionary value of the arts. In contrast, since symbols are general signs about general objects, they are by nature more indirectly connected to actual phenomena in the world, so focusing on symbols makes it easier to lose touch with the actualities represented.

In a prominent symbolic discourse in the United States, trees, water, land, and even people are often referred to as 'economic resources.' Because this symbolic abstraction has been repeated again and again in the public media, it has begun to take on an indexical reality of its own. That is, the redundant indexical connection between the words *trees, water, land, people, economic resources* has naturalized a synonymous quality among the objects of these signs. This ideological transformation helps create public acceptance for corporations and governments' treating trees, water, land, and people accordingly—as *things* to be harvested, or primarily exploited for economic purposes—without taking into account the much larger circuits of life of which they are part. Bateson argues that the continuing recognition of these circuits of life is necessary for the survival of life as we know it. His argument, and mine, is that the psychic wholeness enhanced by engagement with music and the other arts supports such empathy and recognition.

The Possible and the Actual

A final hint as to music's importance in social life is that, like the other arts, musical experiences foreground the crucial interplay between the Possible and the Actual, an idea suggested by my friend and colleague James Lea

(2001). The Possible includes all those things that we might be able to do, hope, think, know, and experience, and the Actual comprises those things that we have already thought and experienced. The interplay between the Possible and the Actual is, in fact, basic to all experience, and yet it often goes unnoticed. Even the act of taking the next breath is only a possibility until we actually do so, yet we live with the faith that the next breath is assured until we no longer live. Belief in the next breath is founded on the similarity of all actual breaths taken in moments past. We usually do not focus on our breath or our belief in the next one until some dramatic event occurs, like being forcefully submerged in water or having the wind knocked out of us. Dramatic events like these, or a fantastic vacation, or an interesting visitor, or a tragedy like the destruction of the World Trade Center, awaken us from our habitual routines, remind us that each breath is precious, make us sit up and evaluate our lives anew.

Most of us live firmly in the day-to-day, the Actual. We have our routines and act out of habit. We make routine decisions circumscribed by a repertoire of choices available within the societies and social groups of which we are part: I get up in the morning and decide whether I should wear blue jeans or slacks that day, whether I should eat cereal or eggs for breakfast or only have coffee. Some societies and positions of social status provide a larger repertoire of choices than others, but the vast majority of our habits and actions are learned from and similar to those of the people around us. As discussed in chapter 4, these shared habits of thought and action and our repertoires of choices are what anthropologists generally refer to as *culture*. Without these cultural frameworks for living we would not be able to get through a single day. Imagine, for example, that upon waking every morning we had to invent a totally new mode of dress or new meals for breakfast without established models; we would never get out of the house!

Much in our Actual lives is habit based and needs to be, but a strictly habitual life leads to stagnation and boredom. We also need the Possible — dreams, hopes, desires, ideals: these are the elements of life that add dynamism and challenge and that make us want to keep living. If we apply Csikszentmihalyi's model for flow to all of life, we might say that a good life is one that has the right balance between the Possible and the Actual. If there are too many possibilities, it is difficult to act; if there are not enough, life becomes dreary indeed.

The arts are founded on the interplay of the Possible and the Actual and can awaken us from habit. The arts — music, dance, rituals, plays, movies, paintings, poems, stories — are a type of *framed* activity where it is expected that the imagination and new possibilities will be given special license. As a result, the arts are a realm where the impossible or nonexistent or the ideal is imagined and made possible, and new possibilities leading to new lived realities are brought into existence in perceivable forms. Art is not really an "imitation of life"; it would be more accurate to say that artistic processes crystallize the very essence of a good life by dramatically emphasizing the interplay of future possibilities with experiences and things we already know from the past—all within in a specially framed and engrossing present. As with the next breath taken, the crucial interplay of the Possible and the Actual often goes unnoticed in daily life. Successful artistic experiences and performances draw special attention to this interplay, wake us from habit, and thus provide that temporary sense of a life more deeply lived.

This description is, itself, a rather abstract rendering of the possibilities of artistic experience—an ideal that is realizable and yet sometimes difficult to achieve. Let me offer a personal example to explain what I mean. I have been playing music with friends and in bands in the United States for thirty years and, as part of my ethnomusicological activities, have had the delight and privilege of performing music with community groups in Peru and Zimbabwe. Although I practice music alone and often play at home for my own pleasure, I greatly prefer to play with others. One of the main things I seek through musical performance is a particular feeling of being deeply bound to the people I am playing with. This sense is created when my partners and I feel the rhythm in precisely the same way, are totally in sync, and can fashion the sounds we are making so that they interlock seamlessly together. The musical sound provides direct, immediate, and constant feedback on how we are doing; when a performance is good, I get a deep sense of oneness with the people I am playing with. I think that what happens during a good performance is that the multiple differences among us are forgotten and we are fully focused on an activity that emphasizes our *sameness*—of time sense, of musical sensibility, of musical habits and knowledge, of patterns of thought and action, of spirit, of common goals—as well as our direct interaction. Within the bounded and concentrated frame of musical performance *that sameness* is all that matters, and for those moments when the performance is focused and in sync, that deep identification is *felt* as total. This experience is akin to what anthropologist Victor Turner (1969) calls *communitas*, a possible collective state achieved through rituals where all personal differences of class, status, age, gender, and other personal distinctions are stripped away allowing people to temporarily merge through their basic humanity.

For me, good music making or dancing is a realization of ideal—*Possible*—human relationships where the identification with others is so direct and so intense that we feel, for those best moments, as if our selves had merged. It is the sounds we are making, our art, that continually let us know that we have done so or that we are failing to achieve this ideal. Being in seamless synchrony with others feels wonderful, and it is one of the main experiences that attracts me to musical performance again and again. I have this feeling often when playing with my son because our musical habits are so similar. The ability to sync is common among family groups but also in communities I have visited in Peru, Zimbabwe, Cajun country in Louisiana, and Texas-Mexican communities where people grow up participating in their local music and dance styles together frequently from an early age. Growing up participating in the same styles allows people to form similar habits of style that facilitate musical synchrony and thus the deep feelings of identification that musical-dance performance can create.

The mass media are often celebrated for the array of musical choices they provide; by now we can buy recordings, enjoy, and even learn to play styles from most places in the world and from any time during the twentieth and twenty-first centuries. The eclecticism fostered by the music industry is positive in some ways, but it also has its drawbacks. Few cosmopolitan North Americans now grow up participating in the same community-bound music and dance styles from infancy. With the array of musical choices available, there is larger variety in habitual time sense and musical sensibility, and this often makes finding people to sync with more difficult.

In addition to playing with my son, I have had the experience of musical merging in particular bands, with particular music partners, and even when playing with people I didn't know in, say, an old-time music jam session. But in many performances I have been part of, this ideal was not fully reached with everyone in the group. It is the desire for this feeling—sometimes actually achieved in the past, but only a future possibility—that keeps me playing music. Yet my desire for this ideal also leads to frustration when it doesn't happen and makes me particularly finicky to play with. Because of my attention to sonic syncing, when people aren't locked in together it feels particularly uncomfortable, awful.

To compound difficulties, the sense of musical sync is a subjective experience that varies among performers and among performers and listeners. One person in a band might feel that everything is clicking along nicely while others feel that she is off. I have had the experience of audience members telling me that my band was sounding particularly good on a night that I felt was particularly problematic. Conversely, I have genuinely commended friends on their performance only to find that it felt terrible to them. This lack of shared awareness of how things are going only makes me feel worse, since my goal is an identity of sense and sensibility, expressed through musical sound but also recognized collectively during and afterward. Like the good human relationships they index, good musical relationships are difficult to achieve and require continual work to sustain. Ideal human relationships emerge only in those special moments—of music making and dance, of lovemaking, of sports teamwork and timing, of seamless conversation, of comprehended silences, of ritual *communitas*—and then they are gone.

Often when bands break up there is emotional fallout like that following a romantic breakup. Reasons for this include the experiences of intimacy achieved and then lost, as well as the desire for an ideal of Possible musical/social relationships left unrequited. But just as a desire for the Possible gets most people dating again after a breakup, it always inspires me to search for a new band, to seek those musical situations where I have experienced merging or near merging before, and to maintain those musical relationships that have been the source of so much joy.

———

This description of what I look for in musical experience is just one personal account. Other people may approach the Possible in music by listening to recordings and letting their imagination or feelings hold sway. Others may use computers to fashion sonic images, new sounds that have never been heard before and were only initially possibilities in the composer's imagination. Others may turn to a musical performing and recording career in the hope of possible fame and fortune. One of the central themes of this book is that music is not a single art form—that musical goals, values, practices, experiences, effects, and social functions are extremely varied.

In order to make sense of this diversity, in chapter 4 I outline a series of models for thinking about individual subjectivity, identity, and the dynamics of cultural difference as these intersect with musical practices. The concept of *habits* serves as the fulcrum for this discussion, and I develop a distinction between *cultural formations* and *cultural cohorts*, the latter being more specific interest/identity groups existing within broader cultural formations. In chapters 2 and 3 I suggest another way of breaking up the notion of 'music' as a unitary art form by outlining four distinct *fields* of music making. In chapter 2 I discuss two fields that pertain to real-time performance—*participatory* and *presentational* music making. In chapter 3 I suggest two distinct fields that pertain to the making of recorded music— *high fidelity music* and *studio audio art*. Within the four-fields framework, each field is differentiated by its own frame of interpretation, values, responsibilities, practices, sound features, and distinct conceptions of what music is.

Through selected case studies (chapters 5–7), I suggest that different types of societies and cultural cohorts value certain musical fields over others due to broader systems of value and social goals. Chapter 5 describes participatory performance in Zimbabwe. It also traces the rise of a new cultural formation in that country during the twentieth century and with it the emergence of presentational and high fidelity music making in a place where formerly only participatory performance existed. Chapter 6 is a description of old-time music and dance in the United States and investigates a cohort-specific participatory tradition that provides an alternative to major trends in the broader capitalist cultural formation. Chapter 7 looks at the semiotics of musical signs within two political movements: Nazi Germany and the civil rights movement in the United States.

Intent listening to a presentational performance or to recordings can create flow experiences. Listening can create imaginative experience as well as draw one deeply into one's own life and history through indexical musical signs. Without diminishing the importance of music listening, I would suggest that music making and dancing provide a special type of activity for directly connecting with other participants, for the intense concentration that leads to flow, and for an even deeper involvement with the sonic signs that create effects of feeling and physical reaction and thus personal integration. Building on these thoughts, in chapter 8 I make a series of suggestions about the potentials of new cohort creation and about participatory music making as an experiential model for fashioning alternative social futures and richer individual lives.

Ultimately, this book is meant to provide a series of basic conceptual tools and ethnographic examples for thinking about music and dance socially and for thinking about individual subjectivities, social groups, and social movements musically. I draw on ethnomusicological fieldwork and musical experiences over a period of thirty years in Peru, Zimbabwe, and the United States. I also draw on the ideas of many scholars, but I have attempted to integrate and present them in a way that will be useful and accessible for anyone—hopefully with a beginner's mind. Armed now with ideas from Bateson, Csikszentmihalyi, and Peirce, let the arguments that I make symbolically in the following chapters be tested through each reader's own indexical experiences. I will be satisfied if something here triggers new ways to think about those experiences.

2 Participatory and Presentational Performance

CD = 1&2, 3&4, 6&8

Because we have the one word—*music*—it is a trick of the English language that we tend to think of music making as a single art form. Certainly we know that there are different kinds of music. We have a lot of words, ranging from rather broad ones—*folk, popular, classical, world music*—which are meant to encompass everything, to ever more specific labels—*(rock) roots, psychedelic, alternative, grunge, glam, punk, (metal) heavy metal, speed metal, death metal*. Musical categories are created by musicians, critics, fans, the music industry, and academics alike. These labels are used to distinguish styles and products, but they tell us little about how and why people make the particular music they do and the values that underpin the ways they make it.

Regardless of the category in question, when North Americans download a song or go out to buy a CD they believe that they are purchasing music. This belief points to a culturally specific conception of what music is. When people buy a photograph of a person, they understand that it is only a representation of that person, not the real thing. Older indigenous Aymara musicians with whom I worked in Peru during the 1980s treated the recordings that they made of their festival music as we might use photographs. After a festival was over, they often listened together to the recordings that they had made on their boom boxes, largely to remember and replay what had been happening in the festival at that point. That is, they used the recordings much as North Americans might use snapshots of a recent vacation—to show friends and remember the special times that were experienced. The recordings were a representation of a celebration and of social interactions realized in a special way through playing music and dancing together. For them a recording is to 'music' what, for us, a photograph is to the person in the snapshot: a representation of something else, not the real thing. My Peruvian friends tended to think of music as being as much about the event and the people as about the sound itself. As often as not, when the next festival came they would record over the previous sonic snapshot, its use value—reminiscing with friends during the weeks following the fiesta—fulfilled.

In English the word *music* is a noun, and cosmopolitans more generally tend to think of music as a thing—an identifiable art object that can owned by its creators through copyrights and purchased by consumers. The strength and pervasiveness of the music industry and its mass-mediated products during the past century have helped to create this habit of thought. If we briefly consider the products of the music industry over time, we can glimpse cosmopolitans' gradual shift in thinking of *music making* as a social activity to *music* as an object. In the nineteenth and early twentieth centuries, the major forms of popular-music-industry product were sheet music (the 'software') and musical instruments such as pianos, guitars, banjos, accordions, and mandolins (the 'hardware'), often sold through catalogs to be played in the home after dinner or during times of leisure. These products required and were the basis of active participation in music making among average people. Recordings and the radio began to change people's conceptions, but not entirely. Radio broadcasts began by airing live performances, largely to be replaced by recordings later. By the mid-twentieth century the phrase *high fidelity* was used by the industry to refer to recordings. At that time the understanding of music as an activity involving live people performing with or for other live people was still predominant, and recordings were marketed as a faithful (high fidelity) *representation* of such performances. Even in the late twentieth century there was a commercial to sell cassette tapes that used the slogan "Is it live or is it Memorex?" suggesting that the sound recording was not the whole ball of wax but rather was capturing, representing, something else (e.g., see Mowitt 1987).

North Americans still attend live performances in the early twenty-first century, but in the popular music realm at least, such performances are often closely linked to recordings and other merchandise. Either we attend a concert because we have heard an artist's recordings, or once we are there the band wants to sell us their CDs. Many clubs in North America no longer even bother with live acts that sing or play musical instruments and instead hire DJs who use recordings and playback devices as their instruments for performance. One of the most popular nightclubs in my town would sometimes feature live bands before the DJ, but the musicians, regardless of their international stature, had to vacate the stage promptly at 10:00 so the main entertainment—playing and manipulating recordings—could begin on time! For the club manager in question, no disrespect to the bands was intended. It was simply an economic reality that in 2006 more young people came for the scene DJs created than for live bands. Yet this illustrates a strange reversal among these young people in their very conception of what music is as compared to an era when recordings were considered a *representation* of live music and would have been considered a poor substitute to a live band.

The cultural conception of music has shifted toward recordings—the form in which most cosmopolitans experience music—as the 'real thing,' not as a representation of something else. In capitalist societies, 'real' or at least successful musicians and music are largely conceptualized in relation to professional presentations, recordings (both video and audio), or (usually) some combination of the two. Even for local bar bands it has become requisite to make CDs for promo and sale at gigs if they are to be taken, and are to take themselves, seriously.

Yet in the United States, as throughout the rest of the world, there are a multitude of music-dance activities that do not involve formal presentations, the star system, or recording and concert ticket sales. These other activities are more about *the doing* and social interaction than about creating an artistic product or commodity. Singing in church and playing music at home with friends "just for fun" are common examples of the latter type in North America, but there are many other pockets of participatory music making and dance ranging from contra, salsa, hip hop, and swing dancing to drum circles, garage rock bands, bluegrass or old-time jams, and community singing that take place in bars, coffeehouses, community centers, and private homes on a weekly basis. Regardless of how important these activities are to the participants, I have frequently heard such people say, "But I am not *really* a musician," because of the broader system of value that holds professionalism as the standard. In what follows I want to argue that these situations of participatory music making are not just informal or amateur, that is, *lesser* versions of the 'real music' made by the pros but that, in fact, they are something else—a different form of art and activity entirely—and that they should be conceptualized and valued as such.

Thus, rather than thinking about music as a single art form subdivided into various style and status categories, I have found it useful to conceptualize music making in relation to different realms or *fields* of artistic practice. Pierre Bourdieu's idea of *social field* (e.g., 1984; 1985) refers to a specific domain of activity defined by the purpose and goals of the activity as well as the values, power relations, and types of *capital* (e.g., money, academic degrees, a hit song, athletic prowess, the ability to play a guitar) determining the role relationships, social positioning, and status of actors and activities within the field. Over the next two chapters I describe four musical fields in turn. In this chapter I discuss fields involving real time musical performance—*participatory* and *presentational* music making. In the following chapter I introduce the *high fidelity* field and *studio audio art*, both of which involve the making of recorded music.[1]

Briefly defined, *participatory performance* is a special type of artistic practice in which there are no artist-audience distinctions, only participants and potential participants performing different roles, and the primary goal is to involve the maximum number of people in some performance role. *Presentational performance*, in contrast, refers to situations where one group of people, the artists, prepare and provide music for another group, the audience, who do not participate in making the music or dancing. *High fidelity* refers to the making of recordings that are intended to index or be iconic of live performance. While high fidelity recordings are connected to live performance in a variety of ways, special recording techniques and practices are necessary to make this connection evident in the sound of the recording, and additional artistic roles—including the recordist, producers, and engineers—also help delineate high fidelity as

---

1. Although I believe I coined the term *studio audio art*, the symbols I have chosen for the other three fields are not new in scholarly literature. Most famously, ethnomusicologist Charles Keil developed a theory of "participatory discrepancies" in a body of work that was inspirational for the framework I am developing here (1987; 1995; also Progler 1995). Keil identified a series of textural, timbral, and timing features in music that enhance participation. His work was the point of departure for my thinking about participatory performance as a separate artistic field, which, in turn, led to conceptualizing the other three fields. James Bau Graves juxtaposed the concepts of participatory and presentational music in his discussion of 'folk' festivals and 'folk arts' organizations (2005). I took the term *high fidelity* from the music industry, but it is used much as I do here by Edward Kealy in his discussion of the changing practices of recording engineers (1990). I briefly outlined the four fields in my book on Zimbabwean popular music (2000:47–51), and by now some of my students have begun to use these concepts as set forth below (e.g., Scales 2004; Livingston and Caracas Garcia 2005). Sparked by Keil, the development of this framework is the result of various collaborative efforts in classes and seminars at the University of Illinois since the mid-1990s and from comparing my own musical experiences in Peru, Zimbabwe, and at home with the work of other scholars and students.

a separate field of practice. *Studio audio art* involves the creation and manipulation of sounds in a studio or on a computer to create a recorded art
object (a "sound sculpture") that is not intended to represent real-time
performance. Whereas in high fidelity recordings studio techniques are
masked or downplayed, in studio audio art processes of electronic sound
generation and manipulation are often celebrated and are overtly represented in the ultimate recording or sound files.

Because this framework requires shifts in the very conception of what
'music' is, it is worth emphasizing that the four fields do not refer to musical genres or style categories such as jazz, rock, or classical, although
issues of style will come into it. Rather, the four fields of practice and
conceptualization often crosscut our received genre categories and even
the work of single artists and bands. In their live performances, one jazz
ensemble might largely pertain to the participatory field by emphasizing
its role as a dance band (e.g., Duke Ellington during the swing era, Big
Voodoo Daddy), while other jazz artists might primarily be geared toward
formal concerts and club presentations (e.g., Coltrane, Monk). The same
band might switch fields from one performance situation to another or
at different points in its career. Ellington's orchestra played for dancing
and gave concerts. The Beatles began as a participatory club dance band
in their Hamburg days, changed to a presentational and high fidelity approach in their early days of fame, and created studio audio art in their
later period—their musical style, modes of practice, and conceptualization of themselves as artists changing as they shifted fields.

The focus here is on the types of activity, artistic roles, values, goals,
and people involved in specific instances of music making and dance. Yet
the goals, values, practices, and styles of actors within a given field are
shaped by their conceptions of the *ideologies and contexts of reception* and
the purposes of music within that field. Thus, the manner of preparing
for and playing music or dancing in participatory events will vary in a
number of predictable ways from presentational preparation and performance. When the goal is a high fidelity recording, new artistic roles in
making the music are added (recordist, or producer and engineers), as are
new sound-shaping processes such as microphone placement, mixing, and
editing. The basic manner of performing is often distinct for high fidelity
recordings made in a studio, and new concerns about reception, for example how the recording will sound on different types of playback equipment and how it will work for repeated hearings, shape the music-making
processes in fundamental ways.

The recorded music produced by one artist on a computer in a studio will also differ in predictable ways if it is intended to be used in a disco or club dance scene as opposed to being heard at an electro-acoustic composers' forum or conference. In the first instance, the sound is shaped for its intended use for participatory dancing and thus represents a mixing of fields; the second instance is a "textbook case" of studio audio art. If the sounds produced on the computer for participatory dancing are intended to iconically represent what performers do live, then it is a mix of high fidelity + participatory; if the recording is not intended to represent a 'live music sound,' then it is a mix of studio audio art + participatory; if the recording combines a presentational style of singing with electronic sounds for participatory dancing, then it may be intended as a combination of high fidelity + studio audio art + participatory. In all these instances, the requirements for participatory club dance music (e.g., long, consistent, compelling musical grooves) will be evident as sonic signs. As these examples suggest, there are a variety of traditions such as karaoke, raves, disco, and DJing that combine aspects of the different fields. But these combinations, as well as historical shifts in the social emphasis on different fields, can be more clearly understood after the fields are delineated as separate types.

Participatory Performance as a Separate Art

There are many forms of musical participation. Sitting in silent contemplation of sounds emanating from a concert stage is certainly a type of musical participation, as is walking in the woods or down a city street to the soundtrack of music coming through the headphones of an iPod. Here, however, I am using the idea of participation in the restricted sense of actively contributing to the sound and motion of a musical event through dancing, singing, clapping, and playing musical instruments when each of these activities is considered integral to the performance. In fully participatory occasions there are no artist-audience distinctions, only participants and potential participants. Attention is on the sonic and kinesic interaction among participants. Participatory performance is a particular field of activity in which stylized sound and motion are conceptualized most importantly as heightened social interaction. In participatory music making one's primary attention is on the activity, on *the doing,* and on the other participants, rather than on an end product that results from the activity.

Although the quality of sound and motion is very important for the success of a participatory performance, it is important because it inspires greater participation among those present, and the quality of the performance is ultimately judged on the level of participation achieved. Quality is also gauged by how participants *feel* during the activity, with little thought to how the music and dance might sound or look apart from the act of doing and those involved. That is, the focus is primarily inward, among participants in the moment, in contrast to the presentational and recorded fields, where artists' attention involves varying degrees of concern with listeners not involved in the actual doing. The result is that participatory music making leads to a special kind of concentration on the other people one is interacting with through sound and motion and on the activity in itself and for itself. This heightened concentration on the other participants is one reason that participatory music-dance is such a strong force for social bonding. It also leads to diminished self-consciousness, because (ideally) everyone present is similarly engaged.

The Participatory Frame

you go there to participate, usually knowing you should have to participate

A primary distinguishing feature of participatory performance is that there are no artist-audience distinctions. Deeply participatory events are founded on an ethos that holds that everyone present can, and in fact should, participate in the sound and motion of the performance. Such events are framed as interactive social occasions; people attending know in advance that music and dance will be central activities and that they will be expected to join in if they attend. Most people go to participatory events because they want to make music and/or dance. This is like attending a party in the United States where people know in advance that conversation will be the central social activity and that if they attend they will be expected to chat. Most people go to parties because they want to socialize. In some societies, and in certain cultural cohorts within North American society, music making and dancing are the central activities during social gatherings, and in such places people grow up making music and dancing as a normal part of social life. For people in the capitalist-cosmopolitan formation where music and dance have become more specialized activities, it might be hard to imagine that music making and dancing are as basic to being social as the ability to take part in friendly conversation, but such is the case in places I have visited such as Zimbabwe and Peru.

During participatory music and dance occasions there is a subtle and sometimes not so subtle pressure to participate. While not everyone has to be playing or dancing all the time, a general sense is created that people who do not participate at all are somehow shirking their social responsibility by not being sociable. Imagine attending a small party among close friends where everyone is playing charades with the exception of one friend who refuses to play and sits alone in the corner. A similar range of reactions to such a person might be experienced in a participatory music setting—everything from direct invitations to join in, to teasing and cajoling, to ignoring him, to worrying that something might be wrong. Typically people do not want to stand out in this way and so might join in, even if with token gestures, even when they don't really feel like taking part. As with any party, people attend participatory music occasions for a variety of reasons, and in a variety of moods, and engage with what is going on as suits them.

Performance Roles in Participatory Performance

Typically, the members of ensembles specializing in presentational performance will be relatively similar in their level of musical competence. The responsibility of providing a good performance for an audience inspires presentational performers to seek out the best possible ensemble mates. Musical-dance skill is primary; other aspects such as personality, the ability to work together, and, depending on the tradition, features such as appearance and stage presence also become key criteria for selecting individuals for the ensemble. Participatory traditions differ fundamentally in that anyone and everyone is welcomed to perform. The inclusion of people with a wide range of musical investment and abilities within the same performance creates a unique dynamic as well as a series of constraints on what can or should be done musically.

There is a common idea in the United States that participatory music must be uniformly simple so that everyone can join in, as, for example, with the singing of campfire songs. In places where participatory music making is the mainstay this is not the case. If there were only simple roles, people who are deeply engaged with music and dance would likely become bored and not want to participate. If everyone is to be attracted, a participatory tradition will have a variety of roles that differ in difficulty and degrees of specialization required. This can be understood in relation to Csikszentmihalyi's flow theory, discussed in chapter 1. As was suggested, the most important condition for flow is that the activity must include the proper balance between inherent challenges and the skill level of the actor. If the challenges are too low, the activity becomes boring and the mind wanders elsewhere; if the challenges are too high, the activity leads to frustration and the actor cannot engage fully. When the balance is just right, it enhances concentration and a sense of being "in the groove," at one with the activity and the other people involved. Participatory traditions usually include a variety of roles demanding different degrees of specialization, so that people can join in at a level that offers the right balance of challenge and acquired skills. Csikszentmihalyi has observed that because flow experiences are pleasurable, people return to the activities that provide them again and again. As they do so, their skills for the activity increase, requiring ever higher challenges. In places where participatory music and dance are at the center of social occasions, opportunities to improve one's skills are common.

The inclusion of people with a wide range of abilities within the same performance is important for inspiring participation. The presence of other people with similar abilities as oneself makes joining in comfortable. If only virtuosic performers were present, the gap between them and neophytes would be too great, and inexperienced performers would be discouraged. When rank beginners, people with some limited skill, intermediates, and experts all perform together, however, people at each level can realistically aspire to and practically follow the example of people at the next level above them. In participatory contexts, the full range of the learning curve is audibly and visually present and provides reachable goals for people at all skill levels.

To keep everyone engaged, participatory musical and dance roles must have an ever expanding ceiling of challenges, or a range of activities that can provide continuing challenges, while, at the same time, there must be an easy place for young people to begin and for others who, for whatever reason, do not become dedicated to performing but still want to participate at some level. Thus some roles are quite simple, such as clapping the basic beat or singing a chorus melody, while others may require a good deal of practice and specialization, such as playing core instrumental parts or improvising a lead vocal in relation to a chorus response. Some roles, such as dancing, singing, or playing elaboration percussion parts, may allow for a wide range of expertise where beginners and highly advanced performers alike can take part at their own level of ability.

· I use the terms _core_ and _elaboration_ to refer to different musical roles in relation to their relative necessity to the overall event. In a rock 'n' roll dance, for instance, the rock band's rhythm section (drums, bass, rhythm guitar) provides core parts that allow the lead guitarist and singer to provide elaboration and that allow everyone else to dance. The rhythm section is _core_ relative to the singer and lead guitarist, and the entire band has a *core* role in relation to the dancers. Core and elaboration roles may or may not correspond with levels of expertise. While crucial core parts are typically taken or guided by experts, they may include less skilled performers (as in the singing of a basic chorus melody); elaboration parts typically encompass the full range of skill levels, e.g., from the most basic to the most advanced singers and dancers. There is more room in elaboration parts for the different skill levels because while skillful elaboration certainly enhances the spirit of a performance, the people who take these parts are not responsible for keeping the entire performance going, as is true for core players.

Some performance roles inherently offer an expanding ceiling of challenges (you can always become a better dancer, lead singer, or lead guitarist), whereas others are more restricted regarding what is appropriate to play in support of other roles and activities. For example, the core *hosho* (gourd shaker) part in Shona *mbira*[2] music (chapter 5; also figure 2.1) must be played in a straightforward and relatively simple manner if the rhythmic groove required for dancing and the other musical parts is to remain intact, and the same is true for a rhythm guitarist, bassist, or drummer in a rock, zydeco, or reggae band. Artistic freedom and experimentation in these core roles are restricted by the responsibility of providing the musical foundation that allows others to participate comfortably.

Within participatory traditions, however, there are a range of roles available to individuals in any given event. Sometimes people simply prefer one type of activity over others, such as playing a given instrument, singing, or dancing, much as individuals might prefer, and be better at, playing different positions on a softball team. But the range of roles also offers variety and the possibility for new challenges. The participatory contra- or square-dancing tradition in the United States is a case in point. Experts in this tradition might participate as musicians, dancers, and dance callers (a person who verbally teaches and directs each dance) within a given dance weekend (chapter 6). Often people enter this scene as beginning dancers, but those who master dancing might go on to take up an instrument used in contra dance bands or might learn dance calling so that they can participate in other ways and find new challenges that keep them engaged with the activity.

2. *Mbira* refers to an instrument with twenty-two metal keys attached to a sound board and usually played within a calabash resonator. The keys are played with the left thumb and right thumb and index finger. It is the type of instrument sometimes referred to as "thumb piano" in the United States.

Participatory Musical Values

One key feature that differentiates participatory and presentational traditions involves issues of *value*. Participatory values are distinctive in that the success of a performance is more importantly judged by the degree and intensity of participation than by some abstracted assessment of the musical sound quality. My Zimbabwean mbira teacher, Chris Mhlanga, once told me that the best mbira players could offer their best performance at a ceremony but if no one joined in singing, clapping, and dancing, the performance would be considered a failure. Shona ceremonies for the ancestors are deeply participatory, and the quality of the ceremony is judged by the intensity of participation that inspires spirit possession. Although the drummers or mbira players perform the most specialized core musical roles in ceremonies, they are not considered the stars of the event with other contributions being secondary. Rather, they, along with *hosho* (shaker) players, are more like workmen with the special responsibility to provide a firm musical foundation that allows and in fact inspires others to participate.

This issue of responsibility will come up again later in regard to shaping the sound of participatory performance. Here I would simply say that regardless of core players' ability and desire to play flashy improvisations or to play faster than people find comfortable for dancing, they have the responsibility of performing their parts in a way that will not exclude others. Participatory values place a priority on performing in ways that invite participation, even if this might limit a given performer's desire for personal expression or experimentation. Each field has its own positive potentials and constraints. In presentational music there is much more room for personal innovation, and in fact innovation is often highly valued for the interest it provides for the audience. The distinctive values and responsibilities that underpin participatory and presentational music making are fundamental to understanding major differences between them.

In participatory events everyone's contribution to the performance is valued and in fact is considered essential for a performance to be deemed successful. But this doesn't mean that everyone in the event is necessarily happy about some people's inept or clumsy contributions to the music and dance. In a typical contra dance, newcomers and experienced dancers alike are encouraged to join in dancing. Newcomers are encouraged, partly because people in a local scene want it to grow and remain vibrant; they need "new blood." More generally, contra dance scenes operate with a participatory ethos, and it is simply considered a Good—in the spirit of the scene—to be welcoming and helpful to newcomers. Nonetheless, new dancers interrupt the flow of the dance when they become confused about what they should be doing, and it is the feeling of 'flow' (a word contra dancers use themselves) that draws many experienced dancers. If there are too many new dancers in a given event or scene, some experienced dancers may become inwardly exasperated, comment about this among themselves, or even, sometimes, show their impatience on the dance floor. Shows of impatience, however, are generally considered bad manners, because they conflict with the welcoming, communal ethos that contra dancers usually value about the scene and themselves.

Among indigenous Aymara people of Conima, Peru, music making is highly participatory.[3] Any male community member is welcome to perform panpipes or flutes with his community's ensemble, and any man or woman is welcome to dance. The values guiding musical performance are part of a more fundamental social style in which egalitarian relations and conflict avoidance are typical (Turino 1993). At one fiesta I participated in, two men showed up to perform with our ensemble with flutes tuned at a different pitch level from the instruments we were using. Nonetheless, they joined in and performed with us throughout the two-day fiesta. The result was that the overall sound was extremely out of tune. This drove me crazy, and I tried to stand as far away from these individuals as I could in my attempt to ignore the sounds they were making. I was surprised by the fact that none of the other players gave any indication that anything was wrong or suggested to these men that they might try to find flutes that were better in tune with the ensemble. No sign of any kind that might have discouraged their participation was given during the public performance. I returned home with Feliberto, a deeply dedicated musician and the friend I was staying with. Once we were alone, he began to complain bitterly about how terrible the sound was. He had felt the same way I had about these musicians' contributions to the performance. But even he, an older and well-respected musician in the community, felt that he couldn't say anything to these men during the fiesta.

These stories point to a subtle but crucial point about the participatory ethos. It is not that people do not make qualitative judgments about

3. The term *Aymara* refers to a major native American language spoken in parts of southern Peru and Bolivia in the Andes Mountains. Conima is a rural Aymara-speaking district in the state of Puno in southern Peru. I conducted research with Aymara musicians from 1984 to 1986.

other participants' performance inwardly or that everyone is happy about problematic contributions to a performance—overall, people have a better time when the music and dance are going well. It is simply that in participatory traditions a priority is placed on encouraging people to join in regardless of the quality of their contributions. In highly participatory traditions, the etiquette and quality of *sociality* is granted priority over the quality of the sound per se. Put another way, participatory music and dance is more about the social relations being realized through the performance than about producing art that can somehow be abstracted from those social relations.

For those of us who hail from a society where presentational and recorded musics are the most valued forms and where music is conceptualized as Art, participatory values may be hard to grasp and accept in relation to music making. It might be helpful to think of participatory performance as being similar a pick-up softball game. When a group of good friends come together to play, even the guy or gal known to be a lousy player will be included. Like the core musicians in participatory performance, the better softball players keep the game going and make it fun for everyone. If no one can hit, catch, or pitch, the game goes nowhere and becomes boring, just as if no one can create a compelling rhythmic groove, no one will want to dance. Competitive or deeply invested softball players may groan inwardly when an inept teammate flubs an easy fly ball, but if they have any class, they will shout encouragement, make a joke of it, or say nothing. After all, it is only a game, for fun and to bring friends together. Participatory performance is like this—it is about the opportunity of connecting in special ways with others and experiencing flow.

What is important to understand is that for certain social groups throughout the world, participatory music, dance, games, sports, and festivals are not merely the informal sidelines to the "real" event—professional athletics, music, and entertainment—but rather they are at the center of social life. The values and practices that underpin participatory arts, sports, festivals, and other activities are important because they inspire more people to be involved with, and to develop skills in, these life-enriching activities. As compared with the other musical fields, participatory music making/dancing is the most democratic, the least formally competitive, and the least hierarchical. As such, participatory performance does not fit well with the broader cultural values of the capitalist-cosmopolitan formation, where competition and hierarchy are prominent and profit making is often a primary goal (who would buy tickets to watch a pick-up softball game or a square dance?). For this reason, in places like the United States participatory traditions tend to be relegated to special cultural cohorts that stand in opposition to the broader cultural formation. Participatory activities exist beneath the radar of mainstream official and popular attention in staunchly capitalist societies, and yet they still exist—some people seek them out or create them because they offer special resources for individual and social integration and experience, flow, and fun.

Sounds and Practices of Participatory Performance

It is not surprising that on the surface, indigenous Shona music of Zimbabwe, Peruvian Aymara music, and Midwestern contra dance music sound nothing alike. These three traditions are geographically distant and have not been directly influenced by common diffusion. What *is* surprising is that below the surface, these three types of music making share a variety of sound features, basic principles of organization, and performance practices. When I first started studying village music in Zimabawe after having worked in Peru for many years, I was struck by the number of similarities and was at a loss to explain them. Moreover, I found that the list of sound features Charles Kiel discussed as participatory discrepancies correlated with the parallel features I found in the cases I knew. This inspired my students and me to undertake comparative research of the sounds and performance practices of traditions meant to inspire participation in different parts of the world.

As the result of this work, we compiled a list of sound features and performance practices that turned up more often than not in participatory traditions—the features summarized and discussed below. Our main conclusions were that these sound features (1) functioned to inspire or support participation; (2) functioned to enhance social bonding, a goal that often underlies participatory traditions; and/or (3) dialectically grew out of or were the result of participatory values and practices. I am not asserting that all of these sound features will always be present in traditions guided by participatory goals, but rather that many likely will be present in some form or other because they *work* to inspire and enhance participation. In his 1964 landmark study *The Anthropology of Music*, Alan P. Merriam suggested one of the most widely accepted ideas in ethnomusicology, that music is best understood in relation to its systemic components of *sound, behavior,* and *concept.* Given this premise, it should not be surprising that different musical traditions that are founded on similar values and social goals (concepts) should exhibit similar practices (behavior) and style features (sound). This conclusion seems warranted for participatory music making.

FORM AND REPETITION. The forms of European classical music and most contemporary popular songs are fixed so that they typically begin, progress, and end in the same way every time the piece is played and are balanced in terms of repeated and contrasting sections.[4] For classical music, most aspects of the composition are notated in the score; dynamics, shifting emphasis on different instruments, key modulations, tempo, and meter changes among many other features are built into the piece to provide contrast between different sections and to provide interest for listeners. The details of a popular song may be fixed similarly in a score or by a recording. The majority of presentational music is in this type of *closed form* with predetermined formal contrasts and a set beginning, middle, and end. Since high fidelity music and pieces of studio audio art are, by definition, defined by the recording, they are the most markedly set musical items.

Participatory music differs fundamentally from the other three fields in that it tends to be in *open form;* further, since what happens musically depends on individual contributions and interactions in the moment, many of the sonic details of a performance are not, and cannot be, preplanned. *Open form* refers to music that is open ended and can be repeated for as long as the participants and situation requires. The forms used in participatory music are typically short (i.e., a single rendition of the entire piece may last a minute or less), but the entire form is repeated over and over. Cyclical (*ostinato*) forms, in which the same short repeated melodic-harmonic-rhythmic unit constitutes the basic piece, are common in participatory music, as are short sectional forms (e.g., AABB, AAB-

---

4. In music jargon, *form* refers to the overall 'architecture' or design of a piece of music as it unfolds through time. The three aspects that help us recognize musical form are *repetition, variation, and contrast.* The repetition of small melodic or rhythmic units (*motives*), a *musical phrase,* or a whole *section* (a larger, relatively complete unit) unifies a piece and makes it coherent through iconic relations; we recognize motives, phrases, or sections *as units* because we have heard them before in the piece. The opening four notes of Beethoven's Fifth Symphony is a famous example of a motive that is repeated and structurally important elsewhere in the work. Units must also be distinguished from each other by some type of contrast or difference. *Variations* represent a midpoint between stark contrasts and exact repetition.

[margin handwriting: Don't want to feel awkward → enhance audience & participation]

BCC), and strophic form.[5] One of the most common stylistic features of participatory music is the emphasis on the heightened repetition of musical material—at the levels of motives, phrases, sections, and the entire form—which is then repeated over and over again for a relatively long time.

In participatory performance, pieces often have what I call "feathered" beginnings and endings. That is, the start and conclusion of the piece are not sharply delineated. One or two people may begin pieces and others join in gradually as they recognize it and find their place. Likewise, endings may be cued, but frequently people do not strictly conclude together but rather "fall out" at the end; this creates a "feathered" quality even when, as in old-time string band or Aymara wind music, there are habitual opening and concluding formulas (e.g., "four-potatoes" and "shave-and-a-haircut" as opening and concluding formulas in old-time music; CD track 1).

Although the creators of presentational, high fidelity, and studio audio art frequently utilize dramatic contrasts to create interest in the music (there are, of course, exceptions such as "minimalism" and "New Age" music), preplanned dramatic contrasts are largely absent from participatory music. Constant repetition of the core musical parts is important so that newcomers and people who have not carefully prepared or rehearsed the music won't be caught off guard and be made to feel awkward. Variation is used in participatory music, but it tends to be *intensive variation*—that is, subtle variations added within, or on top of, the basic musical material. In the other three fields *extensive variation*—variations or extensions of the overall form—are more possible (Chester 1990).

There is often a heightened degree of repetition of melodic material in participatory traditions. The use of genre-specific *formulas*[6] and motivic repetition in predicable places within a given piece make it easier to learn and join in a performance quickly. These characteristics are particularly

5. *Strophic* refers to a song form in which the music stays the same, verse after verse, while the lyrics change with each stanza. The verse-chorus and verse-chorus-bridge structures so common in popular songs are variations of strophic form; the choruses (or *refrains*) usually have music that contrasts with the music of the verses, and the same music and text are repeated for each chorus, which is alternated with the verses. *Bridges* are a third contrasting music-text section, which often occurs only once in the song.

6. By melodic *formula* I mean a set melodic motive or phrase that turns up in different pieces, usually in the same places or with the same function, as in *cadence formula* or *introductory formula*.

FIGURE 2.1 Aymara sikuri (panpipe) musicians in Conima, southern Peru.

pronounced in the Aymara panpipe and flute music played in the Conima region of southern Peru (figure 2.1). Although there are many different Aymara musical genres, the form is extremely predictable; pieces in all genres are almost always in AABBCC form (CD track 3). Among the great majority of genres, each has its own stock introductory and concluding formulas and formulas that come at section cadences (endings; see/hear

Turino 2008).[7] For each fiesta, a group of core musicians will compose new pieces for their ensemble to be premiered on the opening festival day. Many community members who come to participate in the fiesta, however, do not attend the rehearsal where the new pieces are composed and practiced. When trying to pick up the tune quickly during a performance, these newcomers first join in on the formulaic parts they have played in other pieces before, and since there is so much motivic repetition across the sections of a given piece, they are able to quickly learn and participate. In short, there is relatively little new melodic material to learn from one piece to another within a given Aymara genre; this, in combination with the fact that the same short piece will be played for a long time, allows most people to master a new tune on the spot during performance. The use of a stock form, formulas, and a good deal of motivic repetition across sections also allows the core musicians to compose two or three new pieces relatively rapidly in a single night.

Like most Shona music, the mbira (figure 2.2) music of Zimbabwe also has a predictable form and a good deal of internal melodic repetition. The vast majority of pieces played on this instrument have four phrases of twelve quick beats (12/8 meter) within an overall forty-eight-beat cyclical form that is repeated for extended periods. Commonly, half of a prior phrase is carried over into the next phrase (CD track 5). Similar observations can be made about the stock form, formulas, and motivic repetition of old-time stringband music (CD track 1; chapter 5).

The heightened repetition of forms and melodic material in participatory music provides *security in constancy*. Participants in Shona villages grow up with mbira music and know its form; they know that it will continue to cycle for a long period and that once a piece is going they can join in at any point without fear of radical shifts or contrasts that would trick them up. Likewise, the underlying rhythmic groove of the hosho (gourd rattles) part never varies, is repeated for as long as a piece lasts, and is the same for the great majority of mbira pieces. Thus at a ceremony using mbira music, the same rhythmic pattern will be played all night, providing another kind of constancy that makes dancing comfortable and easy. This constancy of

7. This feature of Conimeño music is clearly demonstrated through discussion, charts, and the accompanying sound recording in the first chapter of the book *Music in the Andes: Experiencing Music, Expressing Culture* (Turino 2008). The issue of heightened motivic and melodic repetition in Andean music more generally is explored in the second and third chapters of that book and demonstrated with the accompanying CD.

FIGURE 2.2 Shona mbira, Chris Mhlanga and Bernard Matafi.

rhythmic motion is also true for Aymara music in Conima, where one or two genres and rhythmic grooves will be played repeatedly throughout festivals that can last up to seven days. Rather than leading to boredom, as it might for a seated audience, highly repetitive forms and rhythms actually add to the intensity of participatory performance because more people can join in and interact—through synchronized, interlocked sound and motion—and it is this stylized social interaction that is the basis of artistic and spiritual pleasure and experience. The redundant underlying rhythmic feels of mbira music, Aymara wind music, contra dance tunes, and the vast majority of dance musics allow participants to get into the groove and stay there—both individually and with each other—creating what anthropologist Edward Hall would call *social synchrony.*

RHYTHMIC REPETITION AND SOCIAL SYNCHRONY. In his book *Beyond Culture,* Hall emphasizes that in everyday life all harmonious social interaction is grounded on synchrony of movement and body language. He has observed that when locked in conversation, people will often imitate each other's stance and hand positions (in pockets, folded across the chest, etc.), or gesture in an interlocking fashion that mirrors

the alternated interlocking of their words. Such 'choreography' of similar body positioning and motion leads to comfort in congenial social interactions. Through studying films, Hall has also documented the fact that when walking down a crowded street or airport hallway, people will move together in a culturally appropriate pace and rhythm—*in sync*. This idea becomes apparent in the awkwardness one feels when moving with others in an unfamiliar city or country, an experience I have had countless times. In daily interaction, the synchrony of body language and movement remain fairly low in focal awareness. In addition to what is said or done overtly, people often feel comfortable or uncomfortable with others without really pinpointing why. I, for one, never noticed the signs of social synchrony until I read Hall, but afterward I began to observe how often my own physical stance and movement mirrored those of the people I was with, and I began to pay attention to the whole range of body signs that color social interactions.

The fact that the signs of social synchrony are typically low in focal awareness doesn't mean that they are not registering. The subtle feelings of comfort or discomfort we experience in given social interactions are typically based in these signs, which we often only vaguely feel rather than directly attend to. When people are in sync, the signs of social synchrony function as icons insofar as similarities of gesture and motion lead to a tacit identification and thus comfort; a lack of iconicity conversely leads to discomfort. More important, 'body language' and movement styles are often interpreted as *dicent indices* in that they are perceived, however vaguely, as being directly affected by the inner moods and the nature of the person in question. It is precisely because such signs are icons and dicent indices that they can operate directly and do not require symbolic assessment; thus they can remain lower in focal awareness and function as "natural" or authentic signs of the people and situation in question. Being in or out of sync with others results more in what we *feel* than in what we can verbalize about a given situation—what we *know* about it with a different part of ourselves because of the types of signs involved.

Now if issues of synchrony and body language are a constant in and important to daily interactions, they have an even more crucial importance in music and dance events, where issues of rhythm and synchrony are the very basis of the activity and focal attention. Our responses to presentational musicians are influenced by the dicent indices of their facial and physical expressions and movements during performances. One of the special burdens of recorded forms in many genres is that they must affectively project the persona of the performer without a physical presence, that is, through the sound alone. This is one reason that the human voice—an index, *the sonic body*—is heavily emphasized in popular music recordings. Yet our responses to presentational and recorded musical sounds still involve shared codes about movement and rhythm, such that listening to certain recordings may make us want to dance, alone, while cooking in the kitchen.

It is in participatory settings, however, that focal attention to synchrony becomes the most pronounced and important. Because the music and dance of participatory performances are not scripted in advance, participants have to pay special attention to the sounds and motions of others on a moment-to-moment basis. In contra dancing, for example, people change partners rapidly and continually throughout the dance. Each new (momentary) partner moves differently, swings differently, and dancers have to continually adjust. In a Shona ceremony, singers and dancers try to interlock their parts with the parts of those around them. As people introduce new formulaic or improvised melodies or dance movements, which are then repeated for some time, others may change their sung, hand-clapped, or dance parts to fit with these new contributions on an ongoing basis. Thus special attention to what is going on in the moment is required. This enhances the potential for *flow* and a special awareness of other participants as realized through their sounds and motions. This need to pay attention results in a kind of heightened, immediate social intercourse; when the performance is going well, differences among participants melt away as attention is focused on the seamlessness of sound and motion. At such moments, moving together and sounding together in a group creates a direct sense of *being* together and of deeply felt similarity, and hence identity, among participants.

Knowing and hence being able to perform appropriately in the style is itself a dicent index of belonging and social identity, because performance competence *is both a sign and simultaneously a product of* shared musical knowledge and experience—shared habits. In music and dance performance a higher level of attention is placed on rhythm and synchrony; participants are acutely aware of the groove and their relation to it and through it their relation to the other participants. In participatory performances, feelings of social synchrony are at a higher level of focal awareness but still involve iconic and indexical signs which typically create effects of feeling and direct experience rather than symbolic assessment. When a performance is going great I doubt many people stop to symbolically reflect, "Gee, we are really moving as one," although this is what is *felt* during the performance and remembered afterward.

Repetition of the rhythmic groove and predictable musical forms are essential to getting and staying in sync with others. Social synchrony is a crucial underpinning of feelings of social comfort, belonging, and identity. In participatory performance, these aspects of being human come to the fore. When things are going well they are experienced directly in a heightened way, and the performance as a whole becomes a dicent index—a direct effect of social unity and belonging. This is one reason that group music making and dance so often form the center of rituals, ceremonies, and activities intended to strengthen and articulate social bonds—ranging from the chanting of military cadences by recruits while jogging, to singing in churches, to Shona ceremonies and Aymara festivals, to the Nazis' use of collective singing. It is *in the doing* that the feelings and direct experience of being in sync with others is most pronounced, and this is one reason that participatory music is so valuable in societies throughout the world. It is also why politicians, fascists, and nationalists use this same potential (chapters 5 and 7).

The very musical features of repetition and formal predictability that help create social bonding in participatory music lead to boredom in presentational contexts. It is not that one type of music making is better or more valuable than the other; it is simply that they are different, with different social functions, responsibilities, and thus sound features that make them work. It is for these reasons that participatory musical styles do not transfer well to presentational stage situations, in spite of nationalists', folklorists', and academics' attempts to bring them into presentational settings. It is also for these reasons that it is a mistake to judge music making in one field on the terms of the other.

MUSICAL TEXTURE, TIMBRE, TUNING, AND DENSITY. Dense *textures* and *timbres* are among the most common traits of participatory music, and they have an important role in inspiring participation.[8] Mu-

---

8. In music jargon, *texture* refers to the relationships among, or the arrangement of, voices and instruments as they are sounding simultaneously. There are a variety of standard musical terms that refer to different types of texture. A single melody, even if a number of people are singing it together, is referred to as *monophonic texture*. A solo melody accompanied by chords played on a guitar or piano or sung by other voices is called *homophonic texture*. When two or more melodic lines compete for attention, this is *contrapuntal texture*. When a number of people play or sing slight variations on a single melody simultaneously so that their pitches and rhythmic articulation do not match up precisely, this is called *heterophonic texture*. Within a single performance,

sical textures and timbres can be described in relation to their relative density or transparency. *Transparent texture* refers to music in which each instrumental or vocal part that is sounding simultaneously can be heard clearly and distinctly; *dense texture* refers to music in which the different parts overlap and merge so they cannot be distinguished clearly (compare CD tracks 1 and 2; 3 and 4; 6 and 8).

The density of participatory music is produced in a variety of ways. Often a constantly shifting heterophonic approach to the performance of specific melodies—which may be arranged overall in homophonic or contrapuntal texture—leads to overlapping and a lack of clarity. This is a sound ethnomusicologist Steven Feld calls *in-sync-out-of-phase* since, collectively, the different variations will be in sync with the underlying groove but as they are not in strict unison, the different voices or instruments playing a given part are slightly out of phase with each other (Feld 1988). In addition, the entrance and arrangement of different parts may be staggered to create overlapping. For example, in central African Pygmy singing, groups of men and women may each sing their own heterophonically rendered ostinatos that begin in different places and seem to cycle on top of each other, one beginning somewhere in the middle of the other cycle.

In addition to issues of texture, the characteristic density of participatory music is created through timbre and related issues of tuning. A typical feature of participatory traditions is that the tuning of instruments and voices on any given pitch tend to be purposely 'wider' than in standard cosmopolitan music. For example, Shona instrument makers tune unison and octave pitches on an mbira slightly apart, and the overtones that each key produces will also be slightly different, creating a tremolo effect known as beats when the two keys are sounded together. The tuning of accordions, Indonesian gamelan orchestras, and Peruvian panpipes and flutes, among many other examples, follows this same procedure. The wide tuning of fundamental pitches and the resulting richly staggered overtones help produce dense timbres. I speculate that a preference for wide tunings actually comes from being socialized in a community where participatory traditions are the mainstay. Because of the range of musical skill included, people's tuning precision will vary somewhat, and wide tuning will become the norm. Musical values and senses of intonation are the result of the sounds people grow up with. Thus there is probably a dialectical relationship between participatory traditions and a preference for wide tuning (CD track 3).

---

different textures can come into play. The term *timbre* refers to the tone quality of voices and instruments.

Dense timbres are created in participatory music in a variety of other ways. Mbiras, for example, are constructed with bottle caps attached to the soundboard; these function as rattles, creating a buzzy aura around the instrument's basic sound. Such devices are found on instruments throughout the sub-Saharan region of Africa. The gourd shakers or rattles that accompany much African and African-derived music and Amazonian music create a buzzy aura around the entire ensemble. Snare drums and certain kinds of cymbals in a standard drum set create the same type of effect. The heavy-handed bow technique of old-time American fiddlers helps create the fat or buzzy violin timbre that is characteristic and preferred in this tradition.

Densely overlapping textures, wide tunings, consistently loud volume, and buzzy timbres are extremely common sound features of participatory music throughout the world. Taken together, these aspects provide a crucial *cloaking function* that helps inspire musical participation. Imagine this: You are a neophyte flute player and are asked to go out onstage and join in with another solo flautist performing before a large, silent, attentive audience. Now imagine that you are a neophyte flute player and you have the option of joining in with thirty other Aymara flute players performing in a dense, loud heterophony, accompanied by loud buzzy snare drums, in a situation in which almost everyone else is dancing, drinking, or standing around talking. Given the volume and density of the Aymara ensemble's sound, any mistakes you might make would not stand out much, and no one would really be paying attention to the musical sound *in that way* in the first place.

In light of these two scenarios, it is understandable why some people would habitually experience stage fright and stress in relation to musical performance if they grow up in societies where highly specialized presentational music is the most prominent and valued field. Some individuals, however, relish the challenges inherent in presentational performance and the opportunity to have their accomplishments stand out to please an attentive audience. The pressures of presentational performance, however, limit the number of people who go on to become musical specialists in societies where presentational music is the norm. Conversely, people growing up in societies where participatory music is the mainstay rarely feel stress in relation to musical/dance performance. Rather in such places music making and dance, like conversation, are simply enjoyed as a normal part of social life. Participatory music making constrains individual creative freedom to a greater extent than the other fields do, while it provides more individuals the opportunity to develop their musical/dance skills over a lifetime. Something is lost and something is gained with each field.

VIRTUOSITY AND SOLOING. The overall effect of participatory music is a fairly undifferentiated wall of sound—different instruments and voices merging together. Certain voices or instruments may move in and out of relative prominence within the sonic mesh, but such dynamic shifts are not preplanned or arranged as much as they are the result of particular individuals' waxing and waning enthusiasm and dynamism in particular moments of performance. In keeping with the overall dense, communal, unplanned quality of participatory music, arranged sections for virtuosic solos are not common. Virtuosity, while present, tends to be intensive, like variation itself, and is usually subtly merged with the overall collective sound. Too much emphasis on virtuosic soloing would be counterproductive within participatory traditions, because it would overvalue experts at the expense of others' contributions and thus prove detrimental to inspiring general participation. Call-and-response singing is one common format in participatory traditions where there are spaces for highlighted solos, but the solo spaces tend to be relatively brief and 'song-leader' roles usually rotate among core participants, for example, people who remember and begin particular songs. Moving to the center of a dance circle to "show your stuff" is also common in participatory situations like Brazilian samba de roda and Zimbabwean jerusarema (chapter 5). In these examples, *simultaneous* and *sequential* participation are combined, as discussed below.

In Aymara panpipe performance in Conima, Peru, musicians play in pairs; each musician's panpipe has only every other pitch of the series, and so he has to fit his notes into those of his partner's part to render a complete melody—a technique called *interlocking or hocketing (Turino 1993; 2008). Each musician typically lays out when his partner is blowing his melody notes. To keep themselves interested and challenged when playing the highly repetitive formulaic melodies, however, advanced panpipe players have developed a technique called *requinteando;* they play formulaic or improvised harmonic pitch sequences to accompany their partners' melody pitches. An important musical value among Aymara musicians in Conima is that one's contributions should merge with, and not stand out from, the overall sound of the flute or panpipe ensemble. Thus, when performing requinteando, musicians play the accompanying harmonic pitch formulas so that they add to the overall rich density of sound without standing out. Here is a case where "soloing" appears to have the sole function of providing a space for *play* and for challenge so that advanced musicians can stay interested in the activity and experience flow, rather than as an overt display of individual virtuosity. While this may be a particularly pronounced example, the blending of intensive variation and improvisation within a dense mesh of sound is common for participatory traditions.

The style characteristics of participatory music create *security in constancy* and a *cloaking* of individual contributions which, in turn, create comfort for participants. These sound features have evolved dialectically in relation to the particular goals and value of inclusion. Participatory sound style actually functions to inspire people to join in, and this type of music making serves a deeper function of creating a special sense of social synchrony, bonding, and identity. Finally, in societies where participatory music is the most valued form, almost everyone will grow up taking part in music and dance and develop some competence; music and dance will be available to everyone as normal human activities.

Simultaneous and Sequential Participation

The type of participatory music that I have been discussing thus far involves situations in which everyone potentially performs together simultaneously. There is, however, a second major subtype that we might call *sequential participatory music* in which everyone takes a turn alone or smaller groups perform for the other people in the event; in a sense, then, sequential participatory traditions begin to include features of presentational music making. In her wonderful book *Engendering Song*, Jane Sugarman describes the singing at Prespa Albanian weddings. The participatory frame is very much in place, and she suggests that social pressure to participate is strong. "As an important means of asserting one family's respect for another, singing is regarded as a moral act. What this means, practically speaking, is that each guest at a wedding who attends an evening gathering, or who participates in any ritual activity, is expected to lead, or 'sing,' at least one song on each occasion" (1997:59).

Men and women sing separately. The song leader is accompanied by a second singer of the same gender who performs a supporting polyphonic part adjusted to the lead singer's. In addition, Sugarman notes, "at any social occasion, every person in the room of the same gender is expected to join in on the drone [part]" (1997:73). Although any number of women might join in droning with someone's song, giving the appearance of simultaneous participation, there is the idea that each song leader is taking a turn and performing for others present. At an intimate, somewhat informal in-family gathering that was part of one wedding, the men did not feel obligated to sing; rather the women kept the music going. Sugarman writes, "As each song ended, the older women conferred among themselves as to who should sing next and gently encouraged each woman in turn. Slowly the order of singers progressed, roughly from oldest to youngest, so that it followed the seating order fairly closely" (49). This turn taking, in which group attention is trained on a given individual, represents a different, sequential, type of participatory tradition where a component of presentation starts to be mixed in.

Because everyone is expected to perform in Prespa weddings and people have different levels of musical expertise, there are customary ways that more experienced singers help the less experienced, thus making successful participation possible. The main singer of a song certainly renders the core part, but if she is not an experienced singer, women with more expertise will serve as accompanists and help her through her performance. This practice, along with the fact that everyone in the room of the same gender will have to sing at least one song, encourages participation. If only the most skilled people sang, it might be embarrassing for a neophyte to offer a song, but since a range of singing skill will be heard over the course of the evening and each person is encouraged regardless of skill level, the prospect is less daunting.

As noted, Prespa wedding singing blends aspects of simultaneous and sequential participation. Karaoke provides a well-known example of a participatory tradition that is more strictly sequential. Karaoke is also interesting in relation to the four-fields framework because it blends aspects from other fields. Most obviously, high fidelity recordings are used as accompaniment. In bars where karaoke is performed, aspects that cue a presentational frame are present, such as a stage, a microphone, an MC (the KJ or karaoke jockey), and applause (or at least audience reaction) after a performance. The style of performance is presentational; one or several singers use a microphone to sing for everyone else in the bar. Yet the key feature that makes karaoke participatory is the underlying ethos that others present will eventually do a song. Describing karaoke in Japan, Rebecca Hale notes that "the nightclub is still the main location for Japanese karaoke. Whether advertised or not, most possess equipment, and attendance requires that you will sing at some point during the night" (1997:21). This fact makes everyone's participation more comfortable, and in a sense possible. The fact that everyone should perform eventually during the evening creates a camaraderie and an empathy for people with different levels of skill.

In the United States things are somewhat different, because karaoke is a less established tradition and because public music making is so strongly associated with professional presentational performance—that is, North Americans will typically gauge themselves against the stars. Karaoke actually encourages such comparison, since the songs people sing have been made popular by professional performers and the accompaniment back-up tracks index the original hit recordings. So in the United States extra effort is sometimes required to get people to participate, and the karaoke jockey (KJ), serving as master of ceremonies, often plays a key role. Hale writes:

> Unlike in Japan, the choice for Americans whether or not to sing is left to the individual. Many don't hesitate to participate, and still others remain dedicated to the audience. But for some, a trip to the stage represents a long dilemma and conquering of stage fright. Before, during, and after the song, the KJ offers encouraging remarks, and demands a corresponding response from the audience. As performers leave the stage, they are rewarded with either canned or real applause, and sometimes both. Alcohol is served throughout the night, and often bars offer drink specials aimed at tables of singers (e.g. pitchers of margaritas), or lowered appetizer prices. In American marketing and advertising, karaoke is portrayed as play—something to be done for fun. The Japanese are also aware of karaoke's playful attributes, but within the realm of fun, there is still a decorum (native to Japanese culture) to be adhered to. (Hale 1997:25–26)

In Champaign-Urbana, Illinois, if a person frequently attends the same karaoke sessions (e.g., ones held weekly at the same bar), after a few sessions the regulars will begin to recognize the individual and, via encouragement and cajoling, may put pressure on her to do a song. The power of the participatory frame is important here. Describing the late 1990s, Hale notes that "in Champaign-Urbana, six different bars offer a 'karaoke night' each week. These nights are widely advertised at campus locations and in the papers, and thus few people arrive at the club merely by chance: most have come specifically for the opportunity to sing, to be seen, hear others, and participate" (1997:31). Some participants who judge themselves to be good singers, and who have received audience approval in the past, take karaoke performance quite seriously and might even practice at home. Others use comedy and parody to make their performances entertaining. While a few might hope that karaoke performance could serve as a stepping stone to performing professionally, most simply do it for fun and to experience the Possible—what it would feel like to be a singing star. As in all participatory traditions, the fact that people with different levels of musical skill perform for each other helps bolster confidence among the less secure.

In the United States, where the presentational and recorded fields are most highly valued and where commercial popular music is the type most widely known, karaoke provides a rather telling participatory space. It allows people to imagine and project themselves as presentational per-formers, against the backdrop of prerecorded music, but for most, this is possible only because of the participatory frame and the frame of karaoke itself, which indicates 'this is only play.' In a society where participatory traditions are not particularly developed, people need extra encourage-ment and direct guidance, and thus the importance of the KJ for karaoke, whose role parallels the role of the caller for square and contra dancing (chapter 6). Karaoke is particularly interesting because it is a sequential participatory tradition stripped down to the barest essential—the par-ticipatory frame itself—which paradoxically allows participants to play at being presentational performers with high fidelity backup.

In chapter 1 I suggested that the different sign types (icons, indices, and symbols) have different human functions and pertain to different parts of the self (feeling, physical reaction, symbolic thought). I also suggested that it is important for individuals to include activities in their lives in which the different sign types are emphasized in order to develop, exercise, and integrate the different parts of the self. People need the arts because of the limits of symbolic thought, just as they need the symbolic because of the limits of iconic and indexical experiences. While participatory traditions tend to constrain individual creative freedom, the fact that they allow more people to take part in the artistic realm over a lifetime has important benefits for individual and social health. Since each musical field offers its own benefits for different types of individuals, it would be optimal if all fields were equally valued in every society so that any individual could engage in music making as best fit her personal dispositions and habits. Issues of social conception and value are crucial here, and we will return to this topic in the final chapter.

Presentational Music

Presentational music is a field involving one group of people (the artists) providing music for another (the audience) in which there is pronounced artist-audience separation within face-to-face situations. Obviously the musicians in any type of ensemble participate with each other making music, and so they will experience many of the social and musical aspects such as syncing described for participatory music. But the goals of presentational musicians go beyond this to fashioning music for nonparticipating audiences, and this goal generates a variety of different values, practices, and style features that distinguish the participatory and presentational fields. Participatory music is *not for listening apart from doing;* presentational music is prepared by musicians for others to listen to, and this simple distinction has many ramifications.

European classical music concerts are perhaps the most pronounced form of presentational performance, where the audience sits still in silent contemplation while the music is being played, only to comment on it through applause after a piece has been completed. Bebop or country music concerts are also typical presentational events, although the conventions of audience reaction (e.g., applauding after each bebop solo) may differ. Indian classical music concerts are likewise presentational events. Knowledgeable Indian audience members often quietly clap the metric cycle (*tala*) in stylized ways during a performance, but clapping tala and the clapping in a participatory Shona mbira performance differ; in the Zimbabwean case the clapping is considered an essential part of the musical sound, whereas keeping tala is not—it is mainly a guide for skillful listening. The *frame* for presentational performance is typically cued by devices like a stage, microphones, and stage lights that clearly distinguish artists and audience. A swing, zydeco, contra, or rock dance band may also play on a stage and so use some of the trappings of presentational performance, but if the main goal and effect of the music are to get everyone dancing, it is a participatory performance that simply involves different functional roles—instrumentalists, singers, and dancers.

The values and goals of presentational performance lead to different criteria for creating and judging good music. Moreover, in this field, performers' social responsibility is of a different kind from that of performers in participatory events; musicians must provide a performance that sustains the interest of an audience that is not participating in making the sound or dancing, and the audience has its own responsibility of granting more or less attention to the performance *depending on the genre frame.* Contemporary classical concerts and singer-songwriter performances typically cue interpretive frames in which the audience is expected to pay close attention to the musicians and music, the frame for a presentational rock band playing in a bar is often more relaxed. Although varying somewhat with the genre frame of reception, the requirements of presentational music lead to different practices in preparing and presenting the music as well as to a different set of style features that contrast with participatory performance.

Preparation for Presentations

The core musicians involved in participatory performance may get together to prepare for an upcoming festival or ceremony, but the dynamics of preparation typically mirror participatory performance itself. Aymara musicians of Conima just play through a number of pieces from past years as a warm-up and then spend most of the 'rehearsal' time composing new tunes (Turino 1993; 2008). To my knowledge, most Shona village musicians do not rehearse at all before a ceremony, although they play together over time both informally and in community events. Participatory performances usually do not have fixed programs or set lists; any number of pieces might be introduced in any order during the performance as participants desire or the event requires. Moreover, the dynamics and shape any piece takes will depend on the individual contributions of participants during performance, and these cannot be planned or predicted in advance. Since this is generally understood, it would not occur to participatory musicians to attempt preplanned detailed arrangements of who should do what when or where a particular rhythmic or dynamic shift should occur; indeed this would be counterproductive, since it would confound participants who did not attend the rehearsal. The process of getting ready for a participatory performance, then, is of a looser, more general nature, without all the care and angst of preparing for audience scrutiny.

In rehearsing for a presentational performance, musicians expect that the audience will be attentive to the details of what they play. They also know that if their performance is to be successful they have to make the music interesting and varied for the audience. In the presentational field, then, rehearsals tend to be much more goal directed and detail oriented. Often the complete program to be presented will be planned and rehearsed in advance so that there are smooth, quick transitions from one piece to the next and so that the program as a whole offers both coherence and internal contrasts to keep the audience interested and attentive.

For symphonic music, the conductor rehearses the details and his or her interpretation of the score and will stop the orchestra, as they are playing, to work out problem areas by repeating or talking through them. Even for music that is not scored, pieces will be arranged as *closed forms*. The determination of the form, the order and length of people's solos, and set beginnings and endings will be planned, among other details, with the expectation that the piece will be performed in the manner planned and rehearsed. This mode of preparation indicates the conception of a musical piece as a set item, an art object, whereas in participatory music a piece is more like a set of resources, like the rules and stock moves of a game, refashioned anew during each performance.

At a more specific level, the processes of rehearsal will vary widely according to the personalities of particular conductors or the leadership structures and social relations within particular ensembles, as well as the nature of the tradition itself, and these cannot be generalized. For example, preplanning and attention to detail will be more pronounced in symphony and big-band jazz rehearsals than in those of smaller jazz or rock groups, where more dynamism and spontaneity on stage are possible. Nonetheless, amidst all this variation, there is a major difference between the processes and feel of rehearsals for a participatory event and those for a presentational concert. In rehearsals for presentational performance, a greater amount of attention to detail and arrangements is possible because personnel is typically fixed and it is known in advance that the members of the ensemble will control the performance. Unlike musicians and dancers in participatory contexts, the members of presentational ensembles tend to be approximately at the same level of expertise, and members are often selected to a large degree on their musical/performance abilities. This parity of skill enhances the potential for predictability and control during presentations, whereas unpredictability is a basic feature of participatory performance.

Presentational versus Participatory Values: Issues of Responsibility and Constraint

There are fundamental differences in the goals and types of responsibility, and hence in the preparation and sound, of participatory and presentational performance. More to the point, there is a different "head" or mindset among musicians who habitually operate in one or the other of these two fields. It would not occur to Aymara musicians in Conima or Shona people in Zimbabwean ceremonies to arrange anything within individual pieces in advance or to adhere to a preplanned script for the performance instead of going with the flow of participants' contributions in the moment. The members of presentational rock bands think about and prepare what they are doing in a different way. Their songs are conceptualized and rehearsed as scripted pieces with set beginnings, contrasts, development, and endings, and the musicians tend to perform according to the script regardless of what else is happening in the performance space. If they are a cover band, the script is often predetermined by the model of the recording. Moreover, whole performances are scripted—the order of songs is arranged in advance to produce variety and dramatic progression—in the form of set lists (e.g., see Bennett 1990).

Rock musicians who conceptualize themselves as presentational performers may arrange pieces with dramatic shifts in rhythm and tempo to make the music artful and interesting for listening audiences. I have had the experience of trying to dance to such bands due to my own indexical associations of rock with dance music. On one occasion I invited a partner out onto the floor because a song began with a rhythm that was attractive for dancing, only to be left standing there feeling awkward when the song shifted in the middle to something that wasn't danceable. This was my mistake; I misjudged the nature of the band. But an ensemble that unpredictably changes its rhythms and tempos will not be trusted by dancers; I certainly did not ask anyone else to dance that evening. Again, more to the point, musicians with a participatory mindset would not have altered the rhythm and tempo of the piece, even if the changes had been preplanned, once they saw dancers move onto the dance floor; they would have shifted their performance for the sake of the dancers. Highly scripted presentational performers simply think about what they are doing in a different way. Depending on the musical tradition, there are probably many ensembles that combine presentational and participatory attitudes, although my guess is that one or the other orientation will ultimately emerge as more fundamental for decision making and practice. Let me offer a personal example to explain what I mean.

I lead a zydeco band that exemplifies a kind of compromise between the requirements of a presentational ensemble and a participatory one, and our mode of preparation and performance reflects this. We play in clubs where some people just sit and listen, but our primary goal is to get and keep people dancing. For listeners we include certain types of contrasts, such as sections led by the fiddle, accordion, or guitar alternated with vocals, but for dancers we try not to alter tempo or groove. We rehearse set beginnings and endings so that we appear tight onstage, but the length of time we play a particular song and the number and placement of sung verses and instrumental solos cannot be scripted and rehearsed because such decisions depend on what is going on in the room. If we have a room full of enthusiastic dancers, we keep playing long and hard, cuing additional fiddle, guitar, or accordion choruses as we need them. If dancers start to look tired, we conclude. If a third couple has just gotten up to waltz on a sparsely populated dance floor after I have cued the ending, I recue the group and we go a little longer so that they will not be embarrassed. If no one is dancing, I try to string together some of the hottest tunes that usually get people up. If this fails (and we consider it a failure), I start choosing songs that are better for just listening—and so on.

In rehearsals we select and learn pieces, organize the beginnings and endings, and just play through tunes as Aymara musicians would do. We preplan some basic things that *could* happen in performance—e.g., the guitarist accepts or declines a solo spot for a particular song—without predetermining in what order or how many of these preplanned features will actually happen when we play; I just cue things as we go. We do not plan set lists, because I cannot predict what we will need or what will feel right at particular points in the evening. Thus while we include some aspects of presentational performance, we operate most fundamentally from a participatory orientation. We have had some turnover of personnel and have found that this style of operating is not for everyone. But those who are or become accustomed to the flexible open form approach seem to find it challenging and fun; when it is working, it leads to a special type of trust and communication among us.

Since presentational performers do not feel the responsibility to make music that will provide a comfortable basis for others to join in, they have greater artistic freedom to use creative contrasts of many types. All sorts of repetition and predictability are extremely helpful for inviting and inspiring the participation of people at a variety of skill levels, but this tends to constrain advanced musicians' freedom to play with dramatic contrasts, new innovations, and *extensive variation*. For example, since people often show up to participate in Aymara festivals in Conima without prior rehearsal, preplanning and scripting performances is impossible, and this also constrains musical innovation more generally.

One year the core musicians of a Conimeño Aymara community ensemble created a particularly novel flute (*tarka*) piece for carnival that did not use the standard formulas and melodic shape. They were quite excited

FIGURE 2.3 Carnival in Conima, Peru: participatory music and dance.

about the piece and thought that its novelty would draw attention and acclaim to their community for their originality. As they waited to make their entrance into the town plaza on the opening day of carnival, a number of men who had not attended the previous night's rehearsal showed up at the last minute and joined the ensemble. The core musicians ran through the novel composition, hoping that those who had just arrived would pick it up so that they could play it for their entrance. But the newcomers were not able to learn the tune fast enough, and so the composition was dropped and not played again. This event was mildly frustrating for some of the core musicians, but they did not express their disappointment publicly and soon got over it as they fell into the swing of carnival. After all, participatory performance is really about something else. Figure 2.3 provides a glimpse of musicians in one Conima carnival.

Presentational Style Features

The primary style features common to presentational music are in direct contrast to those of participatory music. The textures and timbres of presentational music tend to be more transparent so that audiences can attend to the details of what is being performed. The cloaking function that is so important to participatory music making is counterproductive in presentational music, where musicians want their individual contributions to stand out clearly for both their own and the audience's edification. Presentational music tends to be in closed prearranged forms, pointing to a conception of musical pieces and even entire programs as set artistic items. Because the preparation process is more detailed, and especially if scores are involved, the forms themselves can be longer and more varied—thus creative possibilities for the composer and/or arranger are more abundant. In the presentational field, the variation of musical material can be *extensive* (extending the form itself) because of preplanning and rehearsal. The use of longer, more varied forms is important for sustaining the interest of an attentive listening audience.

Planned contrasts of all types—rhythmic, metric, melodic, harmonic, dynamic, a shifting emphasis on different instrumental timbres—are built into performances to sustain audience interest. Whereas dramatic contrasts and shifts in the basic musical elements are counterproductive in participatory settings, they are crucial to the goals of presentational music. In presentational performance, dramatic contrasts and interesting shifts in the basic musical elements of a piece function as *indexical nows* that draw listeners' attention back to the moment of performance.[9] Moreover, once they are first introduced, dramatic sonic events promise future events and so help to keep listeners tuned in and attentive; *security in constancy* is counterproductive in this regard. Depending on how they are arranged, contrasting sonic events are necessary to create a sense of progression or musical development, which also helps keep listeners tuned in. The indexical moments are set against a basic backdrop of sonic iconicity—the overall ensemble/instrumental sound, the metric, rhythmic, melodic, harmonic framework established as the piece. Presentational musicians have the primary responsibility of creating interest for others through sound as well as through other performative aspects such as gesture and choreography. Thus, the iconic-indexical balance must be different from that of participatory performance, where iconicity reigns.

The style features that characterize presentational music can be charted as they contrast with participatory music in the following way:

9. Cornelia Fales explains the idea of *indexical nows* in terms of "the cognitive economy of the nervous system [which] often functions by attending to events only when they offer new information" (2005:165). That is, we tend to tune out redundant sensory input, e.g., white noise, although I think the effect is different when actors are involved in *doing* redundant activities.

Participatory music	Presentational music
Short, open, redundantly repeated forms	Closed, scripted forms, longer forms and shorter performances of the form available
"Feathered" beginnings and endings	Organized beginnings and endings
Intensive variation	Extensive variation available
Individual virtuosity downplayed	Individual virtuosity emphasized
Highly repetitive	Repetition balanced with contrast
Few dramatic contrasts	Contrasts of many types as design
Constancy of rhythm/meter/groove	Variability of rhythms/meter possible
Dense textures	Transparent textures/clarity emphasized; varied textures and density for contrast
Piece as a collection of resources refashioned anew in each performance like the form, rules, and practiced moves of a game	Piece as set item (although exceptions such as small ensemble jazz and Indian classical music exist)

The differences between participatory and presentational styles can be understood by considering the transformation of a participatory tradition into a presentational one. The usefulness of these fields is suggested by the fact that very similar transformations occur regardless of the society in question. In the United States, for example, as old-time string bands (a participatory dance and player's music) evolved into bluegrass (a presentational stage and high fidelity tradition), dense group unison or heterophonic textures gave way to transparent, more fully homophonic textures. Repetitive open forms with little contrast gave way to shorter, closed, arranged forms with solo/ensemble and vocal/instrumental contrasts planned into arrangements for variety. There is virtually no soloing in old-time string band performance; everyone just plays the tune over and over again with heterophonic variations. The main interest in bluegrass performance is in the virtuosic solos. In between sung verses and choruses, the various instrumentalists—banjo, fiddle, mandolin, guitar—take turns playing hot solos. While the solos appear improvised, they are typically prepared in advance or are at least formulaic—comprised of motives and passages, 'licks,' the musician has played before. The different necessities of participatory and presentational performance also help us understand the shift from the denser, more rhythmically driving claw-hammer banjo style in old-time to the clearer, more virtuosic three-finger, or Scrugg's, banjo style of bluegrass. Likewise bluegrass fiddlers typically use a clearer violin timbre whereas old-time fiddlers tend to bear down harder on the strings with the bow to create a denser timbre and louder volume (chapter 5; compare CD tracks 1 and 2).

These same stylistic transformations have occurred in various parts of the world when participatory traditions are adapted for presentational performance. The highly participatory indigenous Andean panpipe and flute music was the roots style for an urban-folkloric tradition of music performed in nightclubs and 'folk' clubs in Paris, Buenos Aires, and La Paz, Bolivia, among other places (see Turino 2008, chap. 5). In the presentational Andean style, textures became homophonic, the texture and timbres became more transparent, solo/ensemble contrasts were added, timbral contrasts within the ensemble and timbral clarity of each instrument were emphasized, virtuosic solos were highlighted, and forms became tightly arranged and closed. Paralleling the old-time to bluegrass shift, indigenous Andean music is used for community dancing in festivals whereas the folkloric nightclub style is typically not a dance music but is played in presentations for seated audiences (CD tracks 3 and 4).

Some of the same style changes occurred in ceremonial Shona mbira music when it was adapted for guitar-band performance in Zimbabwean nightclubs and for high fidelity recording. Guitar band renditions of mbira music involve more planned, set arrangements, and pieces are conceptualized as set musical items. Thus Thomas Mapfumo's band, the Blacks Unlimited, performed pieces in the 1990s identically to the way they had been recorded in the early 1980s (see discography). As with the other examples just described, the ensemble textures become clearer, as do the vocal and instrumental timbres. Set contrasts—between vocal sections and instrumental breaks, and between solo and backup vocalists—are also preplanned to create sonic interest. Unlike the bluegrass and Andean nightclub styles, however, Zimbabwean guitar bands play for dancing and thus have a participatory function; performances of the same piece remain long and, because of the structure of the indigenous models, cyclical. As an artist, Mapfumo has been oriented toward high fidelity recording as well as live performance since the 1970s, and as mentioned, his recordings and live renditions of a particular piece tend to be very similar, the recordings serving as a set model or script for live performance. In this case, attention to detail in the recording process itself may help explain the stylistic transformations of participatory mbira music in his live shows. In Zimbabwean music, the contrasts between participatory and presentational styles are most clearly heard when one compares the singing that accompanies indigenous dance drumming (CD tracks 6 and 10) with the presentational traditions favored by the African middle class (CD tracks 8 and 9; see chapter 5).

Contextual Features of Presentational Performance

In addition to, and sometimes even more important than, the music, there are other aspects of musical events that add to audience interest and excitement and constitute reasons for going to live presentational performances as opposed to simply staying home and listening to recordings. Perhaps the most common element for all musical genres is the social aspect. People go out to concerts and clubs because they like to be with other like-minded people, to see and be seen, to socialize, and to meet new people. This is even more obvious for scenes based around recordings, like DJ club performance, where fashion display and meeting new partners seems to be uppermost in many people's minds. The presentation of a given musical style creates a fulcrum around which given identity groups can form or be maintained. Musicologist Christopher Small argues that contemporary classical music concerts in the United States are ritual occasions celebrating upper-middle-class and elite values and heritage and, for some concertgoers, are as much about the ritual occasion as about the music being performed (1987). Cultural cohorts often form around particular presentational music styles such as jazz or bluegrass. People who frequent jazz clubs can at least assume an aesthetic like-mindedness among the patrons, but, depending on the club, often other nodes of identity such as upper-middle- or elite class standing, urban residence, and social sophistication can also be assumed.

Like participatory music occasions, presentational events can thus connect individuals and identity groups, although the two fields differ in the type of engagement and the level of intimacy and scale. I would suggest that participatory music making connects people more intimately and powerfully because of shared interactive engagement among all participants in *the actual doing* of the activities with each other. This tends to be most effective on a relatively small scale—mass rallies involving collective singing and chanting perhaps represent the outside boundary (see chapters 5 and 7). Presentational performers and styles can provide fulcrums for identity cohort formation hinging on a shared fan dedication to, and the modeling of oneself on, the style presented, and this can work on a broader geographical scale through wide-ranging artist tours and mass media exposure. Here, however, group bonds are partially channeled through the presentational performers rather than each member of the group's focusing on each other directly through dancing and making musical sound together. Fans do interact directly in other ways such as listening together, sharing information and ideas about the music and performers, and attending events together.

People also go to live shows to *see* the artists they have heard on the radio and recordings for a whole host of reasons ranging from wanting to be in the presence of greatness or fame to wanting to make personal contact with someone who has moved them through recorded music. Even now when many people's main experience with music is via recordings—the sound alone—I think many still harbor the old idea that music has something to do with people, communication, and direct connection and there is a desire for a human aura, the physical, visual dicent signs of an authentic being. When my son Matt was little, the first thing he would do when I put on a new album was to pick up the jacket cover to look at the picture of the performers, as if seeking a fuller sense of the people who had made the sounds. Presentational performance is attractive because it fulfills, to different degrees, this desire of connecting with the artists—whether or not we get a real sense of the people we admire or only the groomed public personas they wish to present. John Corbett has suggested that the popular music industry actually trades on this desire for an authentic and human connection by producing music products (including live shows) that suggest but do not consummate the connection, always leaving consumers wanting more (1990). Mark Rubel, who has worked in the music business for some time, suggests that people want heroes. In the contemporary United States, the sports, movie, and music industries are in the business of supplying heroes—celebrities—who can be shared by, and hence unite through common reference points, masses of people. People in New York and L.A. can gossip on their coffee breaks about Brad Pitt's recent love interest, as if gossiping about someone in their community. Young guitar players of a certain generation across America could emulate Eddie Van Halen as Shona youth might look up to the best mbira players in their village. Part of the lure of live concerts, especially by well-known performers, is to make contact with, or at least be in the presence of, heroes whom we may hold in esteem because of what their music has meant to us or because of their industry-produced image and fame, or some combination of the two.

Some concertgoers want to hear their favorite pieces performed live very much as they were recorded. Others are curious to see what new songs or variations on familiar pieces might be presented in concert. These alternative desires will of course depend on the dispositions of given fans, but they also correlate with particular *genre frames* and sets of shared values among the fans of a given genre. Jazz fans expect creativity and innovation onstage and might judge a performance harshly if it mainly involved pieces and solos that they had heard before; Britney Spears fans might hope to hear a performance that closely mirrors the recordings they have come to love.

A few years back I attended a Bob Dylan concert. I went partially because I have listened to his recordings for most of my life and wanted to *see* him, to be in the presence of a legend, but also to get a sense of what he could and would do outside a recording studio—formerly my only window to his work. He performed many of his well-known pieces, but each one was done in a way that contrasted with the recorded version in terms of phrasing, vocal style, and instrumentation, thus balancing familiarity and innovation. I would have been disappointed if he had done only familiar tunes "just like the record," but I was also pleased to hear songs that I knew.

Dylan stood relatively still while performing his songs, there was minimal talking between numbers, and only he and his back-up musicians, with their guitars, fiddle, and electric bass, were onstage. The message was that this concert was *about* the songs and the musical performance. In the stage presentations of other artists, and in other genres, many different types of performance elements are combined. In contrast to Dylan, singer-songwriters often talk a good deal about their songs and their own experiences between numbers. This genre is typically framed by ideologies of personal authenticity; it is expected that the songs are the result of the writer's own experiences (are *dicent*), and fans expect to get a sense of the genuine person in performance. Although earlier in his career Dylan was involved with ideologies of 'folk' authenticity, by the time I heard him perform he seemed to ignore this aspect of the singer-songwriter frame.

In other genres, such as contemporary R&B, soul music of the 1960s, and African popular music, dance and choreographed movement onstage play a key role in generating excitement during concerts. James Brown's acrobatic movements and dance prowess are legendary. Dance was perhaps as important as the musical sound in Michael Jackson's performances, and this remains true for a host of young contemporary R&B and pop performers who follow in this tradition. Performance artist Laurie Anderson combines music, dance, spoken dialogue, costume, and electronically projected visuals to form unified pieces in her live presentations. Mexican wrestling masks, witty, understated choreography, and the dry humor of their stage patter make the surf rock band Los Straight Jackets a delight to witness. While they are technically excellent musicians, it might be difficult to sustain audience interest for a two-hour show with only their string of instrumental surf rock tunes, as they perhaps realized.

Sexual/romantic appeal and fantasy are one of the great draws for music audiences. While it is often considered impolite to stare at attractive members of the opposite sex, there is special license to do so when they are on stage. Performers of many types—from Elvis to classical music divas—have benefited from their sexual appeal, some purposefully accentuating it onstage through movement and dress. In a related phenomenon, some performers attract audiences through special personal qualities often referred to as *charisma*. Charismatic individuals have the ability to make the people they interact with feel special about themselves and feel an intimate connection—through body language, tone of voice, and other physical signs as much as by what is overtly said and done. Some people can project charisma when interacting with groups and even crowds of people; the careers of politicians, salespeople, and performers are greatly enhanced by this ability.

The list of elements that are variably combined to make presentational performances attractive could go on indefinitely. For the purposes of general description and analysis, however, it is important to identify the frame for a given type of music—the ideology, imagery, and expectations that guide interpretation. For example, I suggested that the singer-songwriter genre is framed by an ideology that the songs are dicent signs of the composer's own experiences, and consequently performers in this genre tend to cultivate an image of personal sincerity, directness, and simplicity onstage. The ideology and imagery underpinning country music involve working-class attitudes about masculinity and femininity, rural residence and work, Christian religion and 'family values,' and patriotism which are projected through the lyrics of songs, the stoic body language of male performers on stage, and the dress 'work clothes'—cowboy hats, boots, and denim—worn onstage and for album cover photos. The frame for interpreting country involves issues of dicent authenticity of rural working-class experience. Likewise, the frame for rap involves dicents of African American inner-city experience, signaled through the lyrics, clothing and movement styles, and tough stage personas that index black urban youth. In contrast, the frame for interpreting glam rock eschews, and in fact often parodies, ideologies of authenticity; this genre is framed in such a way that artifice is celebrated. Antoine Hennion has suggested that the making of a successful popular song involves the fitting of the image of a performer to the style and content of the music he or she performs (1990). This matrix, however, varies with the specifics of the frame of expectations for particular types of music, and these are open to analysis and understanding on a case-by-case basis.

Because of recent technology, the fit between the sound of live performances and studio recordings has become more intertwined. Musician, record producer, and sound engineer Mark Rubel explains that now there are computer programs commonly used in recording studios that 'correct' or standardize the pitches recorded by vocalists so that they will be 'perfectly in tune' on the finished recording. As use of such programs became more common, CD-buying and radio audiences came to expect this type of intonation. Now there is also an electronic device that standardizes the tuning of vocalists onstage. Presentational performers' microphones are plugged into this device so that the pitches that emanate from the PA speakers are corrected electronically en route and will match the 'perfect' vocal tuning heard on recordings. It has also become common in popular and academic music to use prerecorded tracks as part of the mix in combination with the playing of instruments during stage performances. Lip-syncing, karaoke, and DJ performances simply represent further extensions of this type of practice, which blurs the lines between the recorded fields and presentational performance. In any event, presentational performance and high fidelity recordings are integrally connected and, taken together, provide the greatest contrasts with participatory music, on the one hand, and studio audio art, on the other. This suggestion will become clearer in the following chapter after we explore the two fields pertaining to the making of recordings: high fidelity and studio audio art.

3 The Recording Fields
High Fidelity and Studio Audio Art

At the beginning of the twentieth century a musical revolution was taking place. In 1877 Thomas A. Edison invented a machine that could both record and play back sound, but for over a decade he could not figure out the uses his recording machines might best be marketed for. In 1890 a dealer of the machines invented a prototype of the jukebox: coins inserted into a slot played cylinder recordings of music and comic monologues (Thompson 1995:137). Thus it was discovered that people would pay good money to hear recordings of music! And with this novel idea, the seeds of a new industry were planted. Around the same time a similar machine was developed; known as the gramophone, it used flat discs instead of Edison cylinders. The advantage was that discs could be mass-produced from a master disc; the industry was on its way, and a new musical field came into being.

Describing the early twentieth century, musicologist Emily Thompson notes that

> as phonographic technologies provided a means to mass-produce identical *recordings of musical performances*, people increasingly experienced music not by attending unique live performances or by producing music themselves in their homes but instead by purchasing recordings, carrying them home, and reproducing the music on machines in their parlors, whenever and as often as they desired. Cultural critics as diverse as John Philip Sousa and Theodor Adorno

have examined the significance of this transformation. (1995:132, my emphasis)[1]

By the turn of the twenty-first century, cosmopolitans' most common experiences with musical sound were through audio and video recordings. Since at least the midtwentieth century many scholars have studied the processes and social effects of recording technologies from different vantage points and have decried and celebrated recorded music from a variety of ideological positions.

My point of departure for this chapter is simply that music recordings are a ubiquitous fact of contemporary social life and that production processes, uses, and the significance of recordings are as varied as for the sounds and activities of live performance. To help make sense of the diversity, I propose two distinct fields of making music recordings—*high fidelity* and *studio audio art*. What is important from my perspective is that we place these fields, *as musical fields,* on par with participatory and presentational performance. That is, I propose that we conceptualize the making of high fidelity recordings and studio audio art simply as other distinct modes of musical activity, each with its own advantages and constraints.

High Fidelity Music

High fidelity music refers to musical sounds heard on recordings that index or are iconic of live performance. High fidelity recordings (both audio and video) involve an ideology of dicent representation of live performance at some level—*dicent* in that live performance is believed to have affected the signs of liveness in the recording in some way. The ideal form of high fidelity music involves the actual recording of live performances in a ceremony or concert to be heard/seen at a later time as a representation of that event. 'Live concert' albums and videos and 'ethnographic' field recordings and films released by institutions like the Smithsonian are of this type. In addition, studio recordings that are meant to represent what an ensemble actually does, or could ideally do, on stage or in a ceremony are included in the high fidelity field. There is typically a dialectic between live perfor-

---

1. Sousa (1854–1932) was a prominent band leader and composer for marching band. Adorno (1903–1969) was a cultural critic who wrote about music and was often critical of mass-produced popular music.

mance and the recording process for ensembles that work in these two fields. That is, what is worked out for live performance influences what is recorded; pieces and particular features of pieces that receive approval or generate enthusiasm among live audiences will influence what is recorded. But the details and parts worked out with care in the recording process may also influence what is done on stage. If there is a close relationship between an ensemble's recordings and live performances, I consider the recorded versions high fidelity. A clear example of high fidelity recordings for a mass audience were the Atlantic and Stax-Volt soul music records made during the 1960s (e.g., Sam and Dave, Aretha Franklin, Solomon Burke), where people in the studio would actually make audience sounds as icons of live performance. While musicians can make high fidelity recordings for their own private purposes and bands make them to distribute among their local audience base, commercially released high fidelity recordings mediate between artists and audiences that are usually not in face-to-face contact.

Ethnographic Field Recordings as High Fidelity

Like photographs, ethnographic field recordings and live concert albums have a strong dicent indexical quality; the microphones and tape recorder, like the camera, are assumed to simply capture what is in their presence — a live music event. Thus the object of the sign (the live performance) is assumed to actually affect the sign (the recorded sound) in a direct 'natural' way. Unlike studio audio art, high fidelity recording in a studio aims to make the recording process 'invisible' or at least to downplay production processes so that the recording will be received as a faithful representation of lifelike musical performance.

A number of students and colleagues have questioned the validity of high fidelity as a separate field comparable to participatory and presentational performance, because they see the recording process as parasitic on, and secondary to, the 'actual' music making. Especially for ethnographic recordings they feel that the musical performance would go on in much the same way regardless of the presence of the documenter. The importance of emphasizing the high fidelity field is precisely to unmask the 'naturalness,' 'invisibility,' and secondary nature of the recording, mixing, and editing processes and to suggest that the people directing these processes have a crucial role in shaping high fidelity music. Note, for example, that even though orchestra conductors do not make a sound, people easily conceptualize them as integral to presentational performances; we have to make a similar leap for recordists, studio producers, and engineers, who play equally integral roles in shaping the sound of high fidelity recordings.

In fact, the sound of documentary field recordings can be, and usually is, manipulated through microphone placement and sound equalization (reducing or augmenting certain frequencies) to *create,* not merely capture, the sound that the documenter wants to hear and present to others on a recording. In normal Shona mbira performance the sound of the hosho rattles is so loud that the details of the mbira parts are obscured. This is fine in situations where people are dancing, since the hosho provide much of the rhythmic drive of the music. If this live sound were reproduced literally on a recording, however, largely what listeners would hear, piece after piece, would be the same loud, repetitive shaker pattern. This would make for a very boring recording (not enough indexical nows) and would not help listeners understand the details of mbira playing. Ethnomusicologists, myself included, who have published recordings of mbira music to introduce it to non-Shona audiences have placed the microphones very close to the mbiras and as far from the hosho player as possible so that the details of the mbira parts can be heard clearly. In addition, ethnographic field recording sometimes involves specially arranged or staged performances so that optimal microphone placement, sound separation, and balance can be achieved. As a radical case, ethnomusicologist George List reports that he recorded rural Colombian musicians by placing and miking the members of an ensemble in different rooms of a small house so that they could still play together but he could get maximum separation between the parts for later analysis (1980). This emphasis on clarity of parts, also true for mbira and other field recording, is a common stylistic goal in the high fidelity field both in and out of the studio.

As with studio recordings, field recordings that are commercially released typically involve an editing and selection process whereby the recordist/documenter chooses the 'best' or 'most representative' performances based on her understanding of the tradition and what she wants to get across with the recordings. The long repetitive performances, so important to participatory events, are shortened with fade-outs so that the recording doesn't become boring (CD track 3). Awkward or insecure moments, which on a recording might sound like mistakes, are edited out, as are parts of recordings with too much background talking or noise. Pieces are typically chosen and arranged on the recording so that there will be variety and one track will contrast with the next—similar to the way presentational performances are planned. Genres that are not even played in the same events or times of year are placed side by side on ethnographic recordings. Thus, even for ethnographic field recordings, supposedly the purest form of high fidelity music, the documenter purposefully shapes the sound in the recording and editing processes.

The requirements for a good high fidelity recording are simply different from the requirements for a good live performance, because the recording is directed to an audience not present and participating in the face-to-face event and because the frame for listening to recordings, even field recordings, is radically different from that for live performance. Continuing developments in recording and playback technologies have led consumers to expect higher quality and clarity of sound.[2] Even more than in presentational performances, on recordings sound alone carries the burden of sustaining attention and interest. Moreover, the sound presented has to stand up to repeated listenings; this fact requires a different type of detailed attention to the sound presented and influences the selection, mixing, and editing processes, as well as the processes of playing music in a studio, in fundamental ways.

The Studio Production of Liveness

Sound manipulation is all the more pronounced in high fidelity music created in a studio. While the presentation of ethnographic field recordings often involves editing out some of the 'liveness' (overly loud instruments, talking, awkward moments, long performances), studio sound manipulation often involves effort to create signs of liveness.[3] The ideology underpinning high fidelity recordings is that what you hear on records has been or could be performed live. In the early days of recording this was important because all 'real' music was still tied to the idea of live performance. Even today, certain artists and genres rely on notions of authenticity involving live performance (e.g., rockers like Bruce Springsteen, 'African music') and thus operate with a close relationship between the presentational and

2. For example, earlier in my career, field recordings made on a Sony Professional Walkman cassette recorder were accepted as good enough for publication. This was no longer the case after the emergence of digital technology and CDs; at that point recording companies began to require greater clarity and less sound-to-noise ratios than cassette recorders could produce.

3. A number of articles in the book *Wired for Sound* (Green and Porcello 2005) provide excellent detail of the processes and meanings of producing signs of liveness in studio recordings.

high fidelity fields. In her detailed study of the making of a Zulu *mbaqanga* music recording in South Africa, Louise Meintjes comments that "liveness is an illusion of sounding live that is constructed through technological intervention in the studio and mediated symbolically [in Peirce's sense] through discourses about the natural and the artistic. To sound authentically African is to sound live. This is an ideological position sustained by the promotional engine of the music industry, and it is kept alive by African and non-African South Africans in the studio" (2003:112).

Achieving what is perceived as a live sound in the studio involves a good deal of technological intervention. It also involves other musical roles, especially those of the record producer, who orchestrates, arranges, and designs the sounds of the recording, and the engineer, who manipulates the technology to the producer's specifications. Meintjes writes,

> West [the producer] says he wants a sequenced synth or clavi bass riff. He sings the riff. Peter [the engineer] programs the basic sound on the studio's DX7 keyboard. But West wants a warmer version of it. So while West chats to the singers, Peter alters the coordinates on the keyboard and EQs [equalizes] the sound a little at the recording console.
>
> "Okay, let's try one more time," Peter instructs Makhosini, who is playing the riff on the Yamaha DX7 keyboard. Peter starts the click track [a recorded track providing the basic beat of the song] and counts the keyboard entry for Makhosini, who then plays along with the rhythm tracks. (2003:109)

So in the process of creating this high fidelity album, the musicians do not even play with each other simultaneously. Rather, Makhosini plays along with prerecorded rhythm tracks.

Recording in a studio is a different field of music making from live performance; good recordings, even those intended to represent the live feel of presentational music, have different requirements from those of stage performance. The lack of visuals and aura of the musicians' presence, which create excitement and interest onstage, must be made up for through sound quality alone to end up with a satisfying product. Recording the different instrumental and vocal parts on separate tracks is important so that each can be manipulated independently to create the desired result.

A South African recording engineer, John Lindemann, explained, "The black producers we mix with want everything right up there. They want to hear the works. They want to hear every guitar line, they want to hear every vocal line, they want to hear everything else that's going on—not like a white approach to music where there are a lot of holes, a lot of different levels—they want it all there. It used to be quite difficult to get all of this lot to mesh, and to get it in there all at one level, and be able to hear everything without losing the drive of it" (Meintjes 2003:114). So the aesthetics and conceptions about what live music is among different cultural groups affect the recording and mixing processes. Lindemann points out that black producers want to create the sonic effect of density ("get it in there all at one level") while still being able to hear each part clearly, whereas white producers want more "space" and part separation in the recording. In either case, however, the same emphasis on the clarity of parts that characterizes presentational music is of even greater concern in high fidelity music.

There is another consideration for high fidelity music that doesn't pertain to live performance. Not only do engineers and producers have to worry about what the recording will sound like in the studio, they have to shape a sound product so that it will be effective on all types of playback machines. Again Meintjes quotes Lindemann:

> I think what it's got to do with is that I think that the average black person [in South Africa] is listening through a cassette player through lousy little speakers. And I think the bottom line is that it's all very well if it sounds great on big hi-fi speakers, but you've got to somehow get some drive into that thing so that when that person listens through their little ghetto blaster or whatever it is, it's got to work. . . . They get their music brought to them on radios, and through tiny little speakers. . . .
>
> The heavier your bass is the more it swings. That means grooves [the actual grooves of a record] used to cut into each other. So in the old days those portable record players they used to use, by doing this the record would suddenly jump—that's from the bass cutting into each other.
>
> So [as a sound engineer] I used to cut that bottom out to create that clicky mid-type sound on the bass. Also they used to play a lot of cymbals. Everything was high-pitched. I removed that. Because that also created a lot of sibilance, which those record players didn't like. Eventually what I created was a loudness on the record, by using about around 4.8 [Hz], which used to give me a lot of mids [mid-range frequencies]. And somehow it worked.

Meintjes concludes, "The consumption practice—dancing, listening to the radio—is imagined right at the moment of production. The necessary technological intervention is used to boost, not only to accommodate, the bass aesthetic [of South Africans]" (2003:115–16). Similarly, record producers I knew in Zimbabwe, and one I worked with in the United States, would *mix* (manipulate the recorded sound by altering the balance, equalization, and compression) a recording and then listen to it on various types and qualities of playback machines. These tests were then the basis of remixing the recording in a way that would make it work on a variety of playback machines.

Electronic manipulation—specific uses of reverb, echo, sonic spacing (panning), equalization, and compression—is required to create a live sound in a studio, and certain studios are known for having the facilities to work toward a high fidelity sound. Drums and loud instruments that bleed into other tracks might require their own sound booths, or techniques such as sound barricades around a drummer, if the band wants to record together with the drummer in the room. Bands and producers operate differently depending on their conceptions of what they want for the finished product. Let me offer several more examples.

In 1992–93 I performed single-row button accordion with the Zimbabwean guitar band Shangara. We recorded an LP at Shed Studios in Harare, capital city of Zimbabwe. In the making of this high fidelity recording, the drum tracks were laid down first against a click track. Then the guitarist and bassist played their parts together—instruments plugged directly into the console—while listening to the drum part through their headphones. The producer then wanted to record the lead vocal, which Josh Hlomayi Dube, the leader of the group, sang in a sound booth with the instrumental tracks coming through his headphones. In the next phase, I was put in a sound booth, and with the rest of the band, the producer, and the engineer watching me through the glass, I played my accordion parts, which were designed to interlock with the lead vocal and lead guitar parts.

We recorded in the studio on weekdays. On some weekends during the same period I had the opportunity to attend and sometimes play mbira in participatory spirit possession ceremonies. In the ceremonies, as I will describe in a later chapter, people are packed closely together making music and dancing inside a small space. Physical proximity, even feeling the body heat of those around you, heightens the feeling of social intimacy. In the studio I sat and played alone in the sound booth, as if in a fishbowl or a clinical observation booth. Instead of concentrating on and interacting musically with the *people* around me, in the sound booth I focused on the isolated *sound* of my instrument in relation to the *sound* coming through the headphones. At the time I was struck by the radically contrasting nature of the recording process and participatory music making; it occurred to me then that 'music' itself was not the same phenomenon in these two types of situations.

The final recording stage with Shangara involved the addition of the background female vocals. The two singers recorded their parts together on the same microphone with the other tracks coming through their individual headphones. The producer frequently stopped them for retakes because he felt that they were singing out of tune. Ultimately, still unsatisfied with the results, the producer asked Josh to sing along with the women to strengthen the background vocals. In the final mix, he would be singing background vocals that overlapped with his own lead parts, not something that he could do onstage.

Once all the basic tracks were recorded, the producer and the engineer took several days to mix the sound; more sessions would be devoted to this phase for a higher-budget recording. While the musicians were present in the studio for the mixing, there was little for them to do. The producer would listen to the rough mix and then instruct the engineer to alter any number of things. For example, they would equalize different parts to change the timbre and presence of a given instrument for a variety of reasons; in one case, the sound of a drum was altered because it merged too much with the frequencies of the bass and muddied the sound. While the producer would consult with Josh about certain decisions, the musicians were largely left out of the mixing process. With the exception of volume balance, they did not have the expertise to even know what the technological options were.

As in the example reported by Meintjes, the producer and engineer of Shed Studios were not mere technicians neutrally capturing what the musicians played more or less as they would on stage. Rather, they were partners, albeit with distinct roles, in the high fidelity music–making process. They made aesthetic judgements about the manipulation of the recorded sound, but the producer also made aesthetic judgements about the intonation of the background vocalists and altered the way the group normally performed so that it would work *as a recording*. The musicians also played in a very different manner from the way they did on stage— alone or in pairs, and doing vocal and instrumental parts separately. The songs had been composed for and tested in live performances, the bread and butter of the group, but making a successful recording of those songs required additional personnel and different technologies and performance processes. High fidelity sound is distinguished by an even greater concern for textural clarity and part separation than in the presentational field, a concern that determines many facets of the music-making process.

I recorded with my group, the Squeezetones Dance Band, in Pogo Studios in Champaign, Illinois, in 1996. This was quite different from my experience with Shangara at Shed Studios. In the first place we were paying for the studio time and controlled the process as 'self-producers' with Mark Rubel serving as engineer and gentle guide. We were doing the recording mainly for ourselves, as a record of our music at that time, and we never released anything. Our idea was to perform pieces together in the studio much as we did at home and in performances. We were primarily a live participatory music ensemble, and we were used to feeding off each other when we played; we wanted to try to capture that type of energy and spontaneity on the recording. Pogo Studios was perfect for this approach in that it has a large living room–like space, but this manner of recording had its own drawbacks. The drums were too loud and bled into other people's microphones. Mark placed sound barriers around the drums to reduce the problem. My Cajun accordion bled into my vocal mike, and Randy Cordle's bass also bled into other microphones. The number of microphones used overall was not extensive. We overdubbed a few percussion parts, and I overdubbed a rhythm guitar part on one of my accordion compositions, but mainly what we recorded were first or second takes of songs played together as we always did.

This manner of recording reduced the possibilities at the mixing stage. Without full separation on the different tracks, we could not equalize or change the balance of individual parts very much, and what we ended up with was largely what we did at home or onstage. I still listen to this recording and enjoy it much as I enjoy looking at photos of old friends, but lacking clarity and separation it does not sound like the vast majority of commercial recordings, and it would probably not be considered successful according to the values of the high fidelity field.

Our recording process contrasted in many ways with the approaches described by Meintjes for recording Zulu popular music in South Africa and by me for Shangara's Shed studio sessions in Harare, where, for the most part, musicians recorded their parts individually. Thus even within the high fidelity field, the ideological importance of, and approaches to, representing liveness will vary according to different genre frames, social contexts, and bands. Live participatory performance for dancing was central to the Squeezetones' identity as a band, and we emphasized this in our manner of recording. Tom Porcello describes a similar ideology and approach to recording by bands in Austin, Texas. On signs in the airport and in tourist brochures, Austin bills itself as the "Live Music Capital of the World," "which pointedly marks a musical identity based in performance that Nashville's 'Music City, U.S.A.' does not. Out of this basic dichotomy has evolved an ideology that, as expressed in Austin, ties liveness to musical authenticity (which is fundamentally linked to sincerity and personal expression) and recording to alienated, calculated corporate profiteering schemes" (Porcello 2005:111).

Porcello describes the recording of bands in Austin, whose methods prove somewhat similar to those of our Pogo sessions: "Rarely, in my experience, did members of the rhythm sections of Austin bands record individually; the common approach was for the ensemble to perform and record live with the intent of keeping all of the live rhythm tracks (bass, drums, possibly keyboards and rhythm guitar) for the final mix. In effect, then, the rhythm tracks were generated in live performance, and significant overdubbing was reserved for lead and solo instruments and voice" (2005:107). Note that the *core* parts were performed together in the studio to create a live feel while overdubbing was reserved for *elaboration* parts (chapter 2).

Porcello goes on in great detail to discuss how the drum kit is miked in the studio, because "in most contemporary popular music, drum sounds are the single most important source of information [signs] about roominess, and they therefore have a dramatic impact on the degree of liveness evoked in a recording" (2005:107). Each drum and cymbal in the kit is "close miked" with one or more microphones and

> often its own track on the multitrack tape. A composite kit sound is then mixed by the sound engineer, who manipulates the balance among the individual elements at the recording console. The goal of this process is to achieve maximum isolation on the tape for each piece of the drum kit. . . .
>
> In order to record live-sounding, ambience-rich ("roomy") drums, one can technologically induce liveness simply by running the close-miked drum tracks through a reverb machine (a signal processor that creates or simulates reverberation). But in my studio work in Austin, such technologically facilitated solutions were often viewed with skepticism. (2005:108–9)

Instead, and so as not to sacrifice the control achieved through close miking, additional ambient mikes were placed a further distance from the drums so that the real room sound could later be mixed with the close-miked drum tracks.

The point of this somewhat lengthy technical account is to illustrate the complexity of achieving a 'live' music sound on recordings. Even in situations where commitment to simulating live performance is at its highest, primary attention remains on shaping the artistic product. Great efforts are made to separate and control the different sounds (even the different cymbals of the drum set) so they can be manipulated later in the mixing process.

The uniqueness of the high fidelity field is defined by ideologies of authenticity connected to live performance on the one hand and the special demands of making recorded music that can represent people, live performance, and be captivating through sound alone on the other. Of course the desire to achieve a high fidelity sound depends on particular frames of interpretation and reception which are rooted, more fundamentally still, in broader systems of social value, identity, and basic conceptions about what music is. As Porcello remarks, in the Austin scene live performance is still linked to ideas about sincerity and personal expression—to people making music with 'real' instruments in 'real time' for people. Although these Austinites may be somewhat more traditionalist than cosmopolitans elsewhere, I would suggest that this basic attitude is still quite widespread. It is this conception of music as essentially a 'live' phenomenon, coupled with the valuing of professionalism, specialization, and artistic control, that explains why the presentational and high fidelity fields are the most highly favored—the most mainstream—in modernist-capitalist societies.

For the three fields discussed so far, live performance and the representation of live performance are still central to the conceptualization of the art and activity. The participatory field is radical within the capitalist cosmopolitan formation in that it is *not for listening apart from doing*—and we still tend to think of music as something meant for listening. Participatory performance is also radical in that it hinders professionalism, control, and the creation of commodity forms. The fourth field, studio audio art, is radical in a different way in that it has been freed from ideologies of authenticity involving people making music together in real-time performance. Studio audio art is the realm of electronically manipulated sound for the creation of an art object that is purposefully disassociated from live performance. Historically, the emergence of this field during the midtwentieth century is a logical extension of people's acceptance of recordings as the actual music rather than as high fidelity representations of 'real' (i.e., live) music; the birth of studio audio art indexes this shift in cultural conception.

Studio Audio Art

Studio audio art is recorded music that is patently a studio form with no suggestion or expectation that it should or even could be performed live in real time. Being freed from ideologies of authenticity involving live performance, studio audio art has extremely different dynamics, goals, and potentials from those of the other three fields. This field involves the manipulation of taped sounds, synthesized sounds, or digital technology for the creation of sonic art objects that exist only in electronically reproducible form (recordings, sound files) and in which the goal is the creation of the recorded piece itself—to be listened to after it is completed, much as a painting is to be viewed once it is finished. While the recordings of computer music or other studio audio art pieces can be played by a reproduction device for an audience in a concert hall or other presentational settings, this is more akin to viewing sculpture or paintings in a gallery than it is to listening to a live ensemble performing.

The most developed examples of studio audio art are the electronic and computer pieces produced in cosmopolitan cultural institutions and universities and known under the general category of *electroacoustic* music. Around 1948, French composer Pierre Schaeffer began working in *musique concrète,* a term that refers to pieces made with prerecorded sounds and with techniques for manipulating the taped materials: tape loops, cutting and splicing, speed changes, direction changes. Other composers such as Varése, Messiaen, Berio, Stockhausen, Cage, and Boulez also worked in this genre. In the 1950s electronic music studios were created; in Europe they were often connected to state-run radio stations, and in the United States they were typically connected to universities. These studios contained advanced tape recorders, oscillator banks, mixing boards, reverberation chambers, sound filters, and other devices for manipulating sound. Sound-generating synthesizers were developed in the 1950s and became more available after the mid-1960s, superseding the need to manipulate taped materials. The use of computers for musical composition developed after the late 1950s; computers have become the most important, flexible tool for studio audio art composers.

It should be emphasized that the use of a synthesizer or a computer, in and of itself, does not define studio audio art; these instruments are also used to create high fidelity music, for example to create a string-orchestra sound on a pop record. Moreover, electronically produced and recorded portions of a piece have been composed to be combined with acoustic instruments specifically for presentational performance, a purposeful mixing of fields that is ultimately presentational in the overall goal. Unlike high fidelity, studio audio art does not mask the processes of electronically creating and manipulating sound; rather, these are usually transparent and even celebrated through the sound quality of the music itself. Sound collage and tape manipulation techniques (e.g., playing a taped guitar line backward) foreground the processes of electronically fashioning sound. Again, the distinguishing feature of studio audio art is that it is presented through recordings that are not intended to index or be used in real-time musical performance.

In many cases a single studio audio artist will create all the tracks or parts necessary for a piece and then assemble and sonically shape them, initially with tape, then synthesizers, and now computers. Forming something like the first draft of a poem or the roughing out of a sculpture, the artist can then go back to the original material assembled and add, subtract, and change sounds and tracks to come up with the finished piece. Repeated listening to early drafts of the piece can spawn new ideas, additions, extensions, and deletions, and the artist or artists can keep working with the taped, synthesized, or digital materials until they are completely satisfied with the result.

Thus, one attraction to working in this field is that an individual artist can have maximum control over the finished piece. The creator does not need to depend on, or collaborate with, the ideas and abilities of performers. Moreover, musical complexity is no longer limited to what performers can play. Initially, maximum artistic control seems to have been a major impetus for composers working in this field—it is a space for working out one's own musical ideas and imaginings in the most direct way possible with the help of machines and without the encumbrances of humans. Edgard Varése, "the father of electronic music," is quoted as saying, "I no longer believe in concerts, *the sweat of conductors* and *the flying storms of virtuosos' dandruff*, and am only interested in recorded music" (quoted in Mattis 1992:557, my emphasis). A more telling remark about this composer's view of the human equation in musical performance is hard to imagine. A more distanced position from the values of participatory musicians is also hard to imagine.

Another attraction of the studio audio art field is that synthesizers and computers can provide an almost infinite pallet of sounds to work with and thus have potential for expanding the limits of 'musical sound' beyond what previously existed. Cornelia Fales, an ethnomusicologist who studies music perception, argues that the very processes of perceiving and processing certain electronic music sounds are different from those for acoustic music because of habitual perceptual processes relating to sound that are hardwired in humans: "Human interpretation of complex sound stimuli has been shown to be precisely geared to source identification. Lower-level processing, in particular, is based on what appears to be hardwired information about sound sources" (2005:163). Since auditory information is often incomplete and unfolds through time, Fales suggests that the mind fills in the blanks and makes "after-the-fact" corrections about sound sources. It is easy to understand how this basic mechanism of perceiving sounds in relation to their sources in the objective world has a survival function in evolutionary terms, but certain electronically created sounds create a problem because they have no correlates in our "canonical" *types* of sound producers.

Fales outlines four basic kinds of electronic musical sounds on a continuum. The first kind is iconic of real world sounds, "derived perhaps from unaltered sampled sounds. These might be acoustic instruments, environmental noises, or other sounds that demonstrate" an iconic reference to some sound source that we already know and can identify. The second class of iconic sounds diverges from known sound sources but is close enough to suggest a *possible* relation to such a source. She explains, "While not pointing to a specific referent, that is, these sounds indicate sources that follow the rules of the acoustic world, and they conform to our canonical sense of how sound works in the world; these are not shocking sounds, they are simply ones we have never heard before" (2005:169–70). Sounds in her third category, those used in electronic music, work through the infraction of acknowledged rules of the acoustic world: "these are sounds that are impossible, that could never exist in the perceptual world in which we believe so wholeheartedly" (2005:170). And sounds in the fourth category provide no iconicity whatsoever in relation to our understanding of the world. "Sounds in this category exist in total autonomy from any canon of sounds we might favor. A deluge of these sounds makes us anxious for a foothold, for something familiar to direct our auditory efforts" (ibid.). Thus, according to this account, studio audio art not only reduces the human equation in relation to performance but also can be used to confound and reorient our basic human perceptual apparatus in relation to sound (CD track 7).

The goal of pushing the very borders of musical conception has led to another trend in studio audio art. Composers have begun to write computer programs that generate pieces on their own. Since human musical conception is largely bounded by what is known, it is difficult to radically push the limits of the possible—humans are limited by the limits of their own imaginations. By writing computer programs that generate sounds based on theories involving indeterminacy, chaos theory, or some other system, these composers make the machine able to generate music that goes beyond human imagination and the known. Composers who work in this way seem as interested in the conceptual process of creating music as they are in the finished product. As with participatory music, but in contrast to the presentational and high fidelity fields, process rather than product comes to the fore or is at least of equal importance for composers working in this way. Unlike participatory music, however, interactive relationships for studio audio artists are usually between the composer and her instruments (sound generating and recording devices) and between the finished recorded piece and listeners.

Academic Composers and Studio Audio Art

Many pieces in the electroacoustic repertory are purposefully devoid of sounds that iconically suggest conventional music; indeed when I play John Cage's electronic piece "Cartridge Music" in my general music appreciation classes, students often reject the idea that it belongs to the category *music* at all. Contemporary academic composers who create studio audio art are primarily concerned with the original fashioning of art objects through the organization and manipulation of a variety of sound sources in new ways. The pieces are often intended to be unique, self-contained systems of arrangement and logic that are stylistically connected to this specific musical tradition by the very goals of formal and sonic autonomy and difference. This makes for difficult listening. Let me try to explain what I mean.

When we view 'realistic' paintings of a person or a landscape, the iconic representation of things we know from indexical experience gives us an easy point of entry into the artwork. Even people who do not know much about visual art can relate to such works through their knowledge of the subjects being presented. In abstract paintings, however, viewers are challenged to attend to the forms, colors, and textures presented in the painting—to the artwork itself—without intended outside references. Uninitiated viewers might still relate to abstract paintings much as they do to an inkblot test. That is, they might imagine *possible* subjects that are being presented through some type of iconicity, but this is usually not what is intended by the artist. Abstract art is about the art itself and about the piece as an object that is autonomous from daily life. Highly abstract studio audio art is also like this.

In most popular music and in the classical repertories of the eighteenth and nineteenth centuries, the use of known musical instruments, closed, recognizable forms, the tonal harmonic system, and a wide variety of musical conventions (shared indices) give us points of reference to interpret a newly encountered piece. At the most general level, a newly discovered piece in these repertories is immediately recognized as *music,* and as a certain *type* of music (classical symphony, pop, country, R&B), with all the indexical associations that these conventions and genres carry. Against the genre-specific frame of interpretation, a listener then may attend to, or be affected by, the specific features of the piece. By the early twentieth century, elite European and American composers increasingly sought to free music from the tonal harmonic system and traditional musical conventions. They created new systems for organizing sounds. For example, composers began creating harmonic and melodic relations in a given piece in terms of a predetermined order of twelve pitches, known as twelve-tone music. In effect, each piece had its own self-contained harmonic-melodic system based on an original twelve-tone row.[4] Composers also began to extend the types of sounds included in musical compositions, at first through experimentation with new timbres available on conventional instruments and new combinations of conventional instruments. Computers, and recording studio techniques more generally, provide advanced possibilities for creating new types of sounds or using 'found' sounds and organizing them into finished recorded pieces, each with its own form and logic. In their efforts to extend the boundaries of what constitutes music, composers often avoid sounds and musical structures that provide easy iconic and indexical references to things and music that listeners already know; thus

---

4. For twelve-tone music the composer chooses and orders twelve pitches; the *row* is used as a unique scale. In the standard tonal music system of earlier classical music and most contemporary popular music, the same scales are used as a unifying feature to create melodies and harmonies across different pieces. In twelve-tone music each piece is like its own melodic-harmonic system.

such studio audio art often sounds abstract and even nonmusical to the uninitiated. As with abstract painting, one intent is to draw attention to the piece in and of itself as an autonomous art object.

In a second related trend, for centuries composers in the European classical music tradition sought to gain fuller control over the way their pieces were performed. In earlier centuries scores provided a general sketch of how a piece should be rendered, but performers had a good deal of leeway for interpretation. By the eighteenth and especially the nineteenth centuries, composers increasingly included more specific instructions in their scores regarding how all features of their pieces were to be realized in performance (tempo and dynamic markings, markings to indicate instrumental timbres, specific orchestration), although performers always have the option of interpreting things differently. Studio audio art can be seen as the most advanced stage of this trend, whereby the composer can eliminate the performer altogether and create an art object all by herself in a finished recorded form in the studio. Computers and other tools in the sound studio provide the most advanced possibilities for full artistic control over audio art and in a sense allow for the fullest play of individual artistic imagination.

The desire for maximum individual artistic control and autonomy is understandable from a certain cultural perspective, but it is hardly universal. For example, participatory Aymara musicians prefer to compose collectively, in spite of all the compromises that such a process requires, and their compositions will not even be played unless they remain highly formulaic (chapter 2). Like the desire to create abstract art with its assertion of autonomy from daily life, the valuing of individual artistic control is specific to a particular cultural value system that has developed over a long period in Europe, the Americas, and, by now, modernist-cosmopolitan circles more broadly.

Socially and artistically studio audio art is the most autonomous field, and, like the other fields, it has its own positive aspects and drawbacks. On the positive side there is artistic control and a broad sound pallette; on the negative side there is less human interaction to guide the artistic process (e.g., direct audience response), or to be enjoyed as a basic part of music making. These drawbacks are somewhat mitigated by a major context where new studio audio art is exhibited: composer conferences, forums, and workshops where criticism and feedback from colleagues are possible. These contexts, however, fortify the connection between this field of music making and a particular cultural cohort comprising the composers themselves, and thus reinforce the values of the cohort. There is no inherent problem with this—many types of music are cohort specific—unless a composer would like his music to be enjoyed in the society more broadly. If the music is to appeal to people outside the cohort, compromises would have to be made between the goal of pushing the boundaries of musical sound and conception and including musical conventions that would provide footholds for the uninitiated.

Studio Audio Art and Rock

Following the lead of academic composers, commercially successful rock artists began to work with studio audio art in the 1960s, and for similar reasons—to expand the possibilities of musical sound and conception. With *Revolver* (e.g., "Tomorrow Never Knows") and more explicitly with *Sgt. Pepper's Lonely Hearts Club Band* (e.g., "A Day in the Life") and *The White Album* (John and Yoko's "Revolution 9"), the Beatles shifted from their earlier high fidelity recordings to the studio audio art mode. "Tomorrow Never Knows" includes tape loops and recorded guitar lines played backward, following techniques established in *musique concrète,* and electronically altered vocals. These sounds are integrated with conventional rock instrumentation and song form.

On the piece "Sgt. Pepper's Lonely Hearts Club Band (Reprise)" applause and audience sounds are included. In the context of the album, however, these sounds form *part of* the piece and suggest a parody of high fidelity recordings, and suggest further that this is precisely *not* what this album is about. The final applause on this track fades into "A Day in the Life," which begins with quiet acoustic guitar and piano accompanying a vocal that could easily be performed in a presentational setting. But a variety of dramatic and at times surreal orchestral and other electronically manipulated sounds are soon added to the mix to comment on the authenticity and mundane quality of what is being presented both musically and in the text, as are dramatic tempo and rhythmic shifts. This is not a high fidelity recording to which other sounds are added, as might be argued for "Tomorrow Never Knows." Rather, it is a unified art object fashioned through the juxtaposition of different types of sounds and studio manipulation. This piece could be likened to a sonic portrait "of a day in the life" to which surrealistic tints were added precisely to comment on the bizarre character of daily life.

With "Revolution 9," Lennon and Ono leave the pop-song format altogether to create an abstract sound collage of different 'musical' and 'nonmusical' sounds around the repeatedly spoken words "number nine."

While this is a far cry from "She Loves You" and "Long Tall Sally," the frequent use of orchestral and other conventional musical sounds in the collage at least iconically suggest *music* (albeit 'experimental music') as it is generally understood in the United States and Europe. The context of the album as a whole, which contains conventional songs, likewise creates an indexical frame for such an interpretation. "Revolution 9" is an excellent example of studio audio art; it is a radical extension in this field as compared to other work by the Beatles, but it remains a conservative example as compared to compositions in the electroacoustic art music tradition since the midtwentieth century and the techno style complex more recently. That is, all the sounds on the Beatles' albums fall in Fales's first category of easy iconically recognizable sounds.

Following the Beatles, Pink Floyd and other rock groups experimented in the studio audio art field, but as with "Revolution 9," the more radical experiments represent a minority in the overall recorded output. As synthesizers and computers became more readily available, electronically manipulated and recorded sounds have become standard in presentational performances and thus in high fidelity recordings. These technologies have also spawned new popular mixtures of studio audio art and participatory music in genres such as techno, house, and electronica. Although ignoring proto-examples such as the Beatles, Fales notes that "early techno was a synthesis of latter day disco, hip-hop, and *the first attempts* by European groups to use the electronic techniques of the classical avant-garde in popular music" (2005:160, my emphasis). She goes on to mention the techno subgenre drill'n'bass, as developed by Squarepusher, that leaves out the component of participatory dancing altogether, thus moving toward a purer form of studio audio art; drill'n'bass "is characterized by a driving bassline that is so rapid and irregularly syncopated that it prohibits dancing" (161).

Given the pallette of sounds electronically available to studio audio artists—by Fales's account ranging from the 'easily-iconic' to the impossible to the anxiety producing—a variety of reactions to the more radical (anti-iconic) pieces produced within this field are to be expected. I have experienced intense feelings of anxiety when listening to certain recordings. As I suggested earlier, some of my music appreciation students rejected the idea that even Cage's rather old-school electronic piece "Cartridge Music" could be considered music at all. For traditionalists who strongly associate the sounds of acoustic instruments and human voices with the concept 'music,' the very electronic timbres of studio audio art can index machines and mechanization and be experienced negatively for their 'inhuman' quality.[5] In other, sometimes surprising, social contexts, however, this same dicent-indexical relationship between electronic sounds and advanced electronic technology can have a positive connotation. As Paul Greene notes:

> Technology and its sonic traces can embody for listeners the hopes and dreams of modernity, of western technology and freedom from hardship and want. This desire for a technological utopia, a perhaps unrealizable vision of the "technological sublime" (Penley and Ross 1991:xii–xiii), is evident in certain dance clubs, among specific (often underground) groups, in particular age brackets, in certain geographic locales, and in particular venues where one longs for the self-consciously digitized music product.
>
> A longing for technology is particularly evident in the ways in which people talk about it in Asia and elsewhere in the non-western world. (2005:10–11)

People in antimodernist cohorts, and I count myself among them, are advised to remember that while we tend to celebrate the participatory activities of indigenous communities in places like Peru and Zimbabwe, there are people in those same countries who relish new technologies and their "sonic traces." During the 1980s in Peru, for example, there was a style of music known as *chicha* that was extremely popular among the teenage children of lower-class highland migrants in the coastal capital of Lima. This style combined the melodic features of the most ubiquitous highland genre (*wayno* or *huayno*) with the rhythm of Colombian *cumbia* and was performed with electric guitars, bass, keyboards, and Cuban *timbales* (drums) and percussion. Chicha was basically a participatory dance music and a high fidelity form in which indices of the teens' highland family background (wayno features), urban residence (cumbia is associated with city life), youth, and modernity (electronic 'rock' instrumentation) were combined into a single coherent model for their own complex identities, as fans themselves recognized (see Turino 1990; 2008, chap. 4, with accompanying listening examples). What is striking about chicha recordings by major groups like Los Shapis is that they prominently included 'non-

5. This indexical association itself has been used artistically. A good example is Laurie Anderson's piece "Big Science," which juxtaposes an obviously synthesized organ sound with 'primitive' drums to parallel the 'nature versus technology' theme of the piece (from the album *Big Science*).

musical' electronic sounds (akin to the sliding sounds that video games used to make) that were not part of their live performances. These modest studio audio art features seem to have been included, precisely as Greene suggests, as indices of electronic technology and modernity itself.

There are many other phenomena to explore that again suggest combined aspects of the different fields or perhaps new fields. For example, there are ongoing openly collective projects in which people can go online and electronically manipulate sound files in interactive music Web sites. Such practices create new ambiguities for the very definition of recordings as objects or artifacts and suggest new possibilities for collective musical participation. With the crucial components of face-to-face interaction and real-time performance left out of the equation, however, I do not think that interactive Web sites can simply be considered a new form of participatory music making; with a completed art object left out of the equation they likewise cannot merely be considered studio audio art with fluid participatory aspects mixed in. Rather, there seems to be something fundamentally new and different here. Just as the advent of recording and then of electronically generated sonic art objects required the conceptualization of new fields in addition to those of real-time performance, novel musical technologies and practices like interactive Web sites will require the conceptualization of additional musical fields in the future. The *four-fields* framework sketched here has to be considered open ended and will have to be creatively augmented if it is to remain analytically viable as new musical fields emerge.

Conclusion: The Four Fields as Continua and Compared

Participatory performance is more about an activity and a special type of direct social intercourse than it is about creating a finished artistic product. In this field, music is often thought of more as a *social* process and interaction, like a game, a ritual, or a conversation, than as an item or object. Given the number of human variables and the ethos of inclusion in participatory traditions, artistic control and preplanning tend to be at a minimum; surprises and things unfolding in the moment according to the abilities, needs, and desires of participants tend to be at a maximum. Studio audio art falls at the opposite end of the spectrum, where primary attention and value is placed on the *artistic* processes and product and artistic processes may involve only limited direct social interaction or none at all. Human variables are increasingly reduced to a minimum (no more sweat, no more dandruff), and artistic control is maximized. There can certainly be surprises in the making of studio audio art, but they won't be surprises by the time the piece is finished. If we use these two fields as the poles, the four fields may be understood along a series of continua, as shown in the "Live Performance / Recording Music" table.

As should be obvious by now, the four fields described here are not meant to be airtight rubrics for neatly categorizing styles of music. Rather, they are meant to point to the distinctive nature of different types of musical goals, values, musical roles, processes, practices, and styles. Ultimately the four fields point to fundamentally different conceptions of what music is and what it can do for people. While certain types of music consistently correlate with given fields, others do not. Common practice European symphonic music will almost always be presentational in live performance and high fidelity in terms of recording. Note, however, that string quartet music of the same period might be participatory when played by a family after dinner and presentational when played in the concert hall. Aymara panpipe music of Peru will almost always be participatory in live situations and high fidelity in recorded form when involving village musicians. But because of nationalist and folkloric projects, sometimes these groups have been put on stage in presentational situations, often with odd results.

In certain musical traditions aspects of different fields are combined. One of the best examples of this mixing is karaoke that uses high fidelity recordings as accompaniment for sequential participatory performances that imitate presentational performance. Technological advances have made it possible to combine electronic 'studio audio art–like' sounds with live performance through the use of recorded and sampled tracks onstage. This practice expands the sonic resources for presentational music and consequently the conception of what high fidelity recordings can sound like. Art music composers have been combining *studio* tape pieces with acoustic instruments in presentational performances for some time, and popular musicians in many genres have now followed suit. Around the turn of the twenty-first century, house and techno followed their disco predecessor as popular traditions that used studio audio art technique for recordings that were specifically designed for participatory dance scenes. This music sometimes strongly indexes studio audio art with its electronic timbres and sounds, yet it is also designed with the *security in constancy* principle of participatory music to inspire dancing. The pieces are long with unwavering, powerful rhythmic grooves, repetitive minimalist melodies and harmonies, dense textures, and flat, loud dynamics. It is music produced in a studio by one or more artists with machines and is experienced through recordings, yet the participatory goals are clear through the very style of the music as well as its uses. There are many other examples of combining aspects of different fields. Yet such fusions do not negate the validity of the four fields; rather, I find that having a clear conception of the nature of each field helps me analyze the combinations.

This framework is meant to challenge people to suspend their habitual conceptualizations of what music is and to actually think of the four fields as separate art forms with different potentials for human life. Based on the continua shown in the chart I would suggest, for example, that studio audio art has more in common with sculpture, painting, and other studio art forms than it does with participatory performance. In spite of the use of sound as the artistic medium uniting the four fields, I would also suggest that participatory music has more in common with a neighborhood baseball game or a good conversation than it does with presentational music and the recorded forms. Participatory music *is not simply for listening;* studio audio art is *not for doing with other people.* This is not just a mental exercise in slicing reality pie along different lines. The four fields provide tools for thinking about the processes, quality, value, and potentials of different types of music making, each in its own terms.

As illustrated throughout the rest of the book, different societies tend to value certain fields over others for particular reasons in given historical moments. In the United States presentational and recorded music tend to be valued more highly than participatory music, whereas in indigenous Peruvian and Zimbabwean communities participatory music is at the center of social life. Because of their experiences and processes of habit formation, people in indigenous Aymara or Shona villages will tend to think of music as a social activity more in line with the way North Americans might think of a neighborhood softball game; by contrast, cosmopolitans in the United States will tend to think of music as an art object to be listened to in presentations and on recordings. These are major tendencies of thought that inform the value or prestige of the other fields within these societies.

As I have tried to indicate, each field has its own positive potentials and limitations for artistic activity and human interaction and experience. Music making in one field should not be mistaken for or judged using the evaluative criteria of another field. All four should be equally valued, and hence made available and legitimate, for what they can offer to different types of people and in different types of situations. Studio audio art offers the potential to expand the borders of musical sound itself and to realize the creative products of individual imagination through heighte̶

	Live Performance	
	Participatory	**Presentational**
Goal	Maximum sonic, kinesic participation of all present	Preparation of music for maximum interest for others
Conception	Music making as social intercourse and activity among face-to-face participants; emphasis on *the doing* among all present	Music as an activity and object created/presented by one group (musicians) for another group (audience) in face-to-face situations; emphasis on *the doing* (artists) and listening (audience)
Roles/ Mediation	Little or no artist-audience distinction, only participants and potential participants; few or no physical barriers or markers distinguishing participants although activities (singing, dancing, playing instruments) can vary among participants	Clear artist-audience distinctions; artists and audience mediated by physical markers such as stages, lights, mics, video cameras and screens (e.g., in stadium concerts) within face-to-face situation
Time and Attention	Focus is inward among participants, is on the act of doing, and is in the moment; sound-motion exists only in the moment	Focus for musicians is on themselves, the audience, and the sound; for the audience is on the musicians and the sound, attention is in the moment, sound-motion exists only in the moment
Continua	less physical/semiotic separation among actors less planning/control of musical sound more attention to music as social activity less attention to music as art object quality of social interaction is central to the conception of 'music' and 'good music' sound-motion in the moment, immediate feedback as to how one is doing; sound is ephemeral social focus inward among participants	

Recording Music

High Fidelity	Studio Audio Art
Recorded to represent live performance	Maximum attention to shaping the sonic object
Music as an object to be recorded by one group for consumption by another group not present in face-to-face situations but referencing such situations; emphasis on the art object and the representation of live performance	Music as an art object to be created by one group for consumption by another group not present in face-to-face situations and with no reference to live performance; emphasis on the composition process and final product

Artists not necessarily in each other's presence in studio; artists mediated by electronic devices, sound booths, etc.; artist-audience relations mediated by recordings

Musicians'/producers' focus is on sound for a record-buying audience; for the audience focus is on recorded sound; unspecified time delay between production and reception; sound has a semi-permanent existence	Focus is largely inward within studio audio art cohort; artist focus on compositional process and product; audience focus on compositional process and product; unspecified time delay between production and reception; sound has semi-permanent existence
	more physical/semiotic separation among actors (artists + audience)
	greater planning and control of sound
	less attention to music as social activity
	more attention to music as art object
	quality of sound is central to the conception of 'music' and 'good music'
	indefinite time delay between music making and listening; feedback delayed; sound is semi-permanent
	social focus is outward for musicians/ producers toward an audience and for the audience toward sound alone

control and autonomy. The price of control and autonomy, however, is often a reduction of social collaboration and interaction. Participatory music has the potential to make artists of us all, even the shyest of individuals, and for social synchrony and bonding and fun. But participatory traditions place constraints on individual creativity and experimentation. Presentational music offers the challenge of demonstrating the heightened abilities one has developed for others without the safety net of high fidelity editing, and to provide inspiration and enjoyment for others with those abilities. Presentational performance, however, generates anxiety—stage fright—in certain types of individuals and thus alters the performing experience and limits the number of people who choose to perform. High fidelity recordings provide the possibility of diffusing music to greater numbers of people across space and time than ever would be possible through live performance. Through editing and mixing, high fidelity recording also provides the potential for more 'ideal' presentations of the music. Recordings are used and are important in myriad ways in people's personal lives, and they have become the basis of a huge capitalist industry with all the pluses and minuses entailed.

In chapter 1 I suggested that practicing music, dance, and other arts is important for integrating the self and human communities. If at times I seem to emphasize participatory music more than the other fields it is because participatory music is both the "most democratic"—potentially involving the most people—and the least understood and valued within the capitalist-cosmopolitan formation. One goal for creating the four-fields framework is to redress this imbalance but also to suggest how and why music making and dancing can be available to everyone in a number of different, equally important, ways.

4 Habits of the Self, Identity, and Culture

As we drove to town my children began to squabble. "It's my turn!" my twelve-year-old daughter cried. "It's my turn; you got to decide last time," my son, fifteen, answered. "I want to listen to *my music*," she insisted. "We always listen to *your music*," he responded, forcefully blocking her move to control the radio dial. And so the battle continued, voices escalating as if lives were at stake.

When my children were younger, the phrase *my music* echoed around our house. When I used this phrase, I meant the music I composed or at least played on instruments. My daughter meant the music she liked to listen to, but there was more to it than this. The ongoing battles in our house or car for control over the radio or CD player were more than just a question of musical preferences. My children, like many people, identified themselves through musical style—sounds heard outside that represented how they felt and who they felt they were inside.

Controlling the sonic space was a way to assert this individual identity and sense of self within the family—an identity, in our case, that is both gender and age specific. Controlling the sonic space was literally one way to project oneself throughout the house. During middle school, my children learned what "their music" was largely from friends and from listening to the radio. While musical style was used to distinguish sister, brother, and father as separate identities at home, it was also used to establish common identities among friends and along gender lines outside the home. In our case the two radio stations struggled over were a college 'alternative rock' station and a pop/dance/R&B station; the music played on each was age and gender targeted just as the "oldies" or "classic rock" station was directed at me. The sounds and imagery piped in over the radio and Internet and on videos shape adolescent senses of gendered selves as well as generational and more specific cohort identities (e.g., alternative versus metal versus techno), but the tastes among and styles created by young people also influence what the music industry will produce and send out over the airwaves. This is simply one example of the ongoing dialectics through which individual dispositions are shaped by the social environment while broader cultural patterns are in turn shaped by the practices, values, and ideas of individuals who are active, creative members of the social world.

Coming to know oneself and grappling with personal and social identities are central activities of life that are especially intense during young adulthood. Simon Frith has remarked that the artists and styles one forms attachments to during these formative years often remain affectively powerful throughout one's lifetime (classic rock as "*my* music"), precisely because the music of one's youth indexes this tumultuous period of *becoming* (1987). As I mentioned at the beginning of chapter 1, ethnomusicologists have emphasized the importance of music for expressing and creating social identities in many societies around the world. Indeed, the relationship between musical performance and identity formation has been a prominent theme in ethnomusicology over the past two decades, just as ethnomusicology itself was defined as the study of "music *in* culture" and later "music *as* culture" by scholars such as Alan P. Merriam in earlier decades (e.g., 1977). Since the concepts *identity* and *culture* have been foundational to the study of music as social life, they merit some detailed consideration here.

In the United States we use the words *self, identity,* and *culture,* in common everyday conversations without necessarily thinking about what they mean. The culture concept has been thoroughly discussed from a variety of vantage points by anthropologists (e.g., Tylor 1973 [1871]; Kroeber 1963 [1923]; Benedict 1934; Geertz 1973; E. Hall 1977; Harris 1979:46–47; Rosaldo 1989), whereas, with a few exceptions (e.g., S. Hall 1996), the meaning of the term *identity* has often been assumed and even used as a synonym for 'self' or 'subjectivity.' In this chapter I suggest operational definitions for these key terms and propose a unitary framework for thinking about the concepts *self, identity,* and *culture* in relation to each other — a framework based on the focal concept of *habits.*

One of the oldest debates in social theory revolves around the question of whether society is the predominant force shaping individuals or whether exceptional individuals prominently shape society ('great man' theories of history). In the model of the self, identity, and culture sketched here this is not an either-or question; rather, what is suggested is ongoing dialectical interactions between individuals and their social and physical surroundings realized through observable practices. In terms of the practicalities of doing ethnomusicological field research and social analysis, however, I begin and end with individuals. I suggest that any general theories about artistic processes and expressive cultural practices would do well to begin with a conception of the self and individual identity, because it is in living, breathing individuals that 'culture' and musical meaning ultimately reside. In what follows I conceptualize the *self* as comprising a body plus the *total* sets of habits specific to an individual that develop through the ongoing interchanges of the individual with her physical and social surroundings. *Identity* involves the *partial* selection of habits and attributes used to represent oneself to oneself and to others by oneself and by others; the emphasis on certain habits and traits is relative to specific situations. Finally, what is usually referred to as *culture* is defined here as the habits of thought and practice that are shared among individuals. Of particular importance, I discuss different ways that shared habits bind people into social groups according to specific aspects of the self (gender, class, age, occupation, interests, etc.), what I call *cultural cohorts*, as well as the broader more pervasive patterns of shared habits that give rise to *cultural formations.*

Following C. S. Peirce, by *habit* I mean a tendency toward the repetition of any particular behavior, thought, or reaction in similar circumstances or in reaction to similar stimuli in the present and future based on such repetitions in the past. The value of thinking about the self, identity, and culture in relation to *habits* is that habits are both relatively stable and also dynamic and changeable; thus this model explains the consistent yet dynamic nature of individuals and cultural formations. The use of *habit* as a focal concept also helps us understand how the dynamics of individual lives are fused with social life through the processes of *socialization:* the attainment of habits that is realized through active learning from, as well as through the imitation of, those around us at different levels of focal awareness. Finally, habits influence practices and are therefore real forces in individual lives and in the social world.

Nature, Nurture, and the Self

The relationship between nature and nurture is another well-worn problem in social theory. Are we the way we are because of our genes, the way we were hardwired at birth (nature), or are we largely the product of our social environment and learning (nurture, socialization)? The many variables that influence a person's development make this question hard to answer. Perhaps the best way to begin thinking about this problem is with the premise that both nature and nurture are involved and that they interact over lifetimes in complex ways. Most people are born with the ability to eventually speak, walk upright, run, make and distinguish musical pitches, and think symbolically. At a more individual level, some people are born with bodies that make running quickly, or singing loudly, or making synthetic connections easier than it is for others.

The 'nature' side of the equation provides capacities and propensities for the species as a whole, as well as for individuals; the results of these natural capacities and propensities, however, often depend on the social environment. Although most humans are born with the capability to speak, the first language and styles of speaking we learn depend on the imitation of people around us. Social groups define what is beautiful—in a singing voice or a body—and people often develop their capabilities to match that which is socially valued as much as they can. In a society where thin bodies are considered beautiful, people can shape eating and exercise habits to be thin (nurture), although staying thin is easier for people with certain types of metabolisms (nature). We are born with a female or male body, each with its own potentials—giving birth, breastfeeding, having a higher voice, or typically having greater size, more muscle mass, and a lower voice. But definitions of masculinity and femininity, and the ways of acting accordingly, are defined and learned socially and differ from one society to another just as languages do.

Systems of values that define what is desirable or good in the artistic and affective realms of life also involve the nature-nurture dialectic. Indigenous Quechua people in Peru, for example, have a general preference for high-pitched music; thus women, particularly young women, are the preferred singers because of their natural capability to sing higher than men. In this example, as in so many others, inborn capabilities combine with cultural factors to define specific roles and practices. Guided by their musical values, Andean men compensate for their physical vocal limitations by tuning and playing their wind instruments in high-pitched ranges. Like other tools developed by human groups, these wind instruments are what Edward Hall (1977) would call *extensions*—physical objects and practices developed to extend people's innate capabilities. Musical instruments are an extension of people's capabilities to produced melody and harmony with the voice, just as the practice of writing is an extension of speaking and e-mail is a further extension of writing. The technologies and practices that serve as extensions are fundamental components of what anthropologists call culture, and thinking about cultural practices and objects *as extensions* focuses attention on nature-nurture dialectics.

In the United States it is commonly believed that musical talent is innate and that people either are or are not 'musical.' Evidence from other societies, however, suggests that musical abilities, like other abilities, are often largely due to the early habit formation of children that make certain activities easier, or makes them appear natural, for them. Incipient habits are shaped by the values and examples of core people around the child and are reinforced by praise when the child shows interest or ability in a valued activity. Talent also involves propensities that make an individual better suited for some activities over others. In sports it is easy to see that individuals born with certain body types (height for basketball, large size for football) may have a natural edge, but the activity has to be socially valued, and it still requires discipline and work (nurture). Having the voice to sing certain styles, e.g., opera or gospel, is like the sports example, where the physical make-up of the body plays a part. But innate talent is often much harder to pinpoint in the intellectual and creative realms, because we cannot easily see the particular "muscles of the mind" that aid in these areas. Was Mozart's genius innate, or was it the product of particularly early and intense training, ambition, and praise from his father that somehow combined just right to match the boy's *dispositions* (incipient habits + inborn propensities)?

Some societies do not even have the concept of innate musical talent; the Aymara of Peru and the Venda of South Africa generally think of musical and dance ability as being available to anyone who has the interest and who puts in time and effort. From firsthand experience, I have found that in societies where participatory music making and dance are a regular part of frequent valued social activities, the general level of musical competence, especially as regards relative pitch production (rendering intervals accurately) and having a good sense of time and rhythm, is generally high. In Shona communities in Zimbabwe, toddlers begin dancing and sometimes singing in family and community celebrations, and even before this, babies are danced on their mothers' backs. Although children and adolescents are excluded from some religious ceremonies, there are abundant occasions in which all ages are encouraged to participate in music and dance together. Good performance is enjoyed and praised, even if only with smiling eyes, for people of all ages at such events. Practice rarely makes perfect, but if everyone in a social group does a particular activity repeatedly from early childhood as a normal part of valued social occasions, and if doing the activity well elicits praise, it is likely that there will be a generally high level of competence.

The prominent ethnomusicologist John Blacking suggests that "although ethnomusicological research has provided timely warnings against over-generalization about human musicality, it has also contributed to arguments in favour of a species-specific musical competence. For example, studies of musical practice in sub-Saharan Africa and Southeast Asia show that in communities with cultural systems that value general musical competence, all normal human beings are proficient in dancing, singing and instrumental performance" (1992:302). Blacking goes on to argue that "musical ability is genetically inherited, but in the same way as the biological potentialities necessary for speech" (1992:302–3). Along with mental and physical disabilities, a prominent reason that individuals might not develop musical/dance competence is "social and cultural inhibition which deprives individuals of the interaction necessary to develop the capability. (This deprivation would be comparable to the atrophy of speech in children who have been isolated from the human intercourse necessary to develop their language potential)."

It follows that competence in performance will be lower among the general population in places where music and dance are assumed to be specialist activities not regularly practiced by everyone, and especially in places where the habit of connecting musical ability with the idea of in-born talent prevails. In spite of school music programs in the United States which involve many children, music is considered a specialist activity by the society at large. Ethnomusicologist Melinda Russell has shown that participation in school music programs falls off as students progress to higher grades and as the pressure to reach a specialist standard becomes more pronounced (personal communication). School music programs at all levels are geared toward presentational performances and do not involve collective music making among all ages as a normal part of valued social occasions—a normal part of being social. With the exception of singing in church, many middle-class North Americans stop making music altogether as they approach adulthood, and it is common to hear people in the United States say, "I don't know anything about music," or "I am not musical." Such statements would be surprising to people in societies where participatory music is common. These attitudes among North Americans are partially self-fulfilling descriptions, since they hinder musical participation and the continuous musical learning that results.

Like Blacking's, my argument is that social values that encourage general musical participation, and thus early musical/dance habit formation, are more important than innate ability for achieving musical competency; there is abundant ethnomusicological evidence to support this claim. I have found, however, that many of my students at the University of Illinois are adamantly reluctant to disconnect musical ability from inborn talent. In relation to innate musical ability, someone inevitably asks, "What about perfect pitch?" Here is what the *Harvard Dictionary of Music* has to say:

> Theories of absolute pitch [perfect pitch] assume that individuals with this ability possess an internal standard pitch in long-term memory. Some theories maintain that the ability is largely innate, but a few cases of apparently successful training have been reported. *The ability appears to be most easily acquired in childhood.* There is no general agreement as to whether absolute pitch is continuously distributed in the population or if there are distinct subgroups. Underlying neurological mechanisms have not been identified. (1986:2, emphasis added)

Our understanding of perfect pitch remains far from conclusive, but my reply to the students takes a different turn. I point out that I have never claimed that inborn mental-bodily propensities are not involved in shaping abilities and habit trajectories. But even if perfect pitch is an innate ability, it in no way guarantees general musical competency. As the same *Harvard Dictionary* author comments, "Most trained musicians have excellent relative pitch; only some have absolute pitch, which has more limited practical value" (1986:1).

The more important point, what I really want my students to know, is that tying musicality or any ability to innate talent is a hindrance and can be used as an excuse for not participating in activities like dance, music, and sports that, due to their universality in societies around the world, appear to be basic to being human. As suggested in the previous chapters, these activities offer alternative ways of knowing and developing the self, are prime activities for achieving flow states, and are key resources for connecting intimately with others. Beyond and amidst all of this, music making and dancing can be great fun. Cosmopolitan habits of thought about innate talent and the overvaluation of high musical specialization are culturally relative and might be rethought when perceived as obstacles to wider participation. An alternative to emphasizing innate talent would be to foster early musical/dance habit formation in our children—not only by providing them with lessons toward some future specialized ability but by making music/dancing *with* them *now* as a normal part of family and social life, underpinned by the belief that such activities, regardless of skill level, are valuable in and of themselves.

The Self and Identity

A number of people whom I know think of themselves as having some unchanging essence or core to which they add and subtract things—learn new skills, develop good habits and abilities, or change aspects of themselves that they don't like—according to conceptions of their 'true self.' This idea is itself a learned habit of thought based on social conceptions of personhood emphasizing innate characteristics; it is also learned as part of particular religious systems, for example, the idea of the soul as personal essence. Another way of thinking about *the self* is in terms of the physical body we are born with, which includes the mind, nervous system, and genes, plus the total collection of habits that guide everything we think and do.

The body we are born with and the social environment we are born into (including social conceptions of the body) shape our individual constellations of habits. If a girl is born with blond hair and delicate facial features in a society where blond hair and such features are considered beautiful, the child may learn early on, from the subtle as well as overt reactions of those around her, that she has a special and desirable appearance. She may also learn that she can gain preferential treatment because of her appearance. These experiences (of body + social environment) create certain habits in the girl such as the tendency to expect special treatment and to conceptualize herself in a particular way. Similarly, a girl born with a tall body may be guided by those around her to develop skills in basketball if she is growing up in a place where this sport is highly valued. Our bodies and the social environment operate in dialectical ways throughout a lifetime to shape habits of thought and practice.

In many cases, we develop habits without much direct awareness of them *as habits*. They develop so early or so slowly, often through *socialization* (modeling ourselves on those around us), that they seem natural, normal, or commonsensical. In North American society, thinking of oneself in terms of color, in terms of being American, in terms of being a boy or girl, and acting, talking, and walking in certain ways because of social models of masculinity and femininity are such old, subtly developed habits that we often don't notice them at all. These are the layers of habit that are often mistaken for a personal essence or core, yet they are learned and developed and can be changed with effort, just like the habits of painting, playing the guitar, and smoking.

Thinking about the self and personality in terms of constellations of habits is both realistic and analytically useful in that habits, like human life, are processes. The repetitiousness of habits offers a high degree of stability and continuity to living, yet as in the process of life, with each repetition there is the potential for growth or change. Thinking of the self in terms of habits offers a good middle path between overly static notions of self ("I was born that way") and the overly fluid conceptions ("I can fashion myself any way I choose") that have become popular in the so-called postmodern era.

The total constellations of habits that make up any individual are more numerous and varied than we normally think about. It is instructive to take ten or fifteen minutes to make a list of everything you have done, do, and are. For example: I am a man, a 'white' man, a thin man of medium height, a middle-aged man, a North American, an Italian American, an Illinoisian, a cosmopolitan, an English speaker, a Spanish speaker, a musician, a performer, a composer, a father, a brother, a husband, a son, a nephew, a cousin, a professor, an ethnomusicologist, a music fan, a writer, a reader, a kayaker, a cyclist, a skier, a former surfer, a pipe smoker, a dog lover, a homeowner, a taxpayer, a neighbor, a walker, a dancer, a singer, a swimmer, a sleeper, a coffee drinker, an eater, a daydreamer, a cook, a sailor, a beer drinker, a lawn mower, a carpenter, a repairman, a gardener's helper, a dishwasher, a movie watcher, a clothes washer, a traveler—the list could go on much longer. Each category includes more specific designations: a performer of Cajun music, zydeco music, old-time music, Andean music, Shona mbira music; a reader of academic books and articles as well as newspapers, magazines, maps, signs, and fiction; a professor who gives classes, grades papers, writes lectures and tests, attends faculty meetings and conferences. Each of these designations still comprises more specific habits which allow me to undertake the given activity; for example, consider all the discrete habits required to play any musical instrument or to swim. Taken together, all of these (and more) constellations of habit are who I am and guide what I do.

Nowadays people use the word *identity* as if it meant the same thing as *self*, yet it is important to differentiate the two terms conceptually because of the ways individual and collective identities function in the social world. The *self* is the composite of the total number of habits that determine the tendencies for everything we think, feel, experience, and do. In contrast, *identity* involves the *partial* and *variable* selection of habits and attributes that we use to represent ourselves to ourselves and to others, as well as those aspects that are perceived by ourselves and by others as salient. I would not consider any number of the habits that I listed above as relevant to think about my own identities or to present myself to others—for example, the fact that I am a walker, a swimmer, or a coffee drinker. I rarely represent myself as a dishwasher or lawn mower unless I am being criticized for not doing enough around the house, and being a taxpayer is relevant only when demanding my rights from City Hall. When we conceptualize or talk about our identities, we usually do not include all possible aspects of ourselves but rather highlight what is relevant or productive within a given situation while downplaying other aspects. People typically shape their self-presentation to fit their goals in particular situations and rarely reveal all the habits that constitute the self.

The strategies of self-presentation and 'self-selection,' however, are only part of the identity dynamic. People are also constantly being identified by others because of attributes and deep-seated habits operating below their own focal awareness but clearly noticeable to others. One time when I was playing banjo in a country bar in rural Indiana, I was immediately pegged as a college professor by a local woman in the group. I was dressed in jeans and a T-shirt and had said very little. The bar was not located anywhere near a college or university. What signs had I projected that allowed her to guess so easily and so accurately? I will never know. Social identities are based on some kind of iconicity—the foregrounding or recognition of similar habits or features that allow individuals to group themselves and to group others. While the substance of resemblance is inherent in the entities identified, iconicity is not natural or presocial. Any two objects or people will likely have a variety of similarities and differences, and people learn and sometimes choose to focus on some features rather than others depending on past experiences and goals in the situation, as well as aspects emphasized in the society.

In realizing our own identities, we tend to foreground aspects that are regarded as important by the people around us. In North American society, a good deal of emphasis is placed on occupation. One of the first questions adults ask when they first meet is "What do you do?" and so we learn to emphasize this aspect of our identity. In South Africa or the United States, people pay special attention to skin color as an important basis of identity because of the nature of racial discourse in those countries. In Ireland, being Catholic or Protestant is a key aspect of self-representation and perception. In a feminist music festival, gender is an aspect of identity that probably will be emphasized, whereas the fact that a person is also a walker, a taxpayer, a daydreamer, or a homeowner might not come up or be important. We choose to foreground certain aspects of ourselves (occupation, color, religion, gender, age) for self-presentation, or have those aspects chosen for us, depending on what is socially important in a given context and within the society at large.

Conceptualizing oneself as 'white' or as an 'American' is a habit of thought that is learned from the people around us when we are children and that, in turn, inspires other habits and behavior.[1] My skin isn't really white and Africans' skin isn't really black, but we learn to think of ourselves in these ways because of racial discourse and the very words employed. Borrowing from the French writer Michel Foucault, we might define a *discourse* as a relatively systematic constellation of habits of thought and expression which shape people's reality about a particular subject or realm of experience—racial discourse, nationalist discourse, the discourse of modernity, scientific discourse, ethnomusicological discourse. The premises (that skin color matters) and terms (*white, black*) of a discourse bring each other into existence and function in a systemic way to shape people's habits of thought about particular aspects of life. In the United States, the habits of thought and expression shaped by racial discourse are so powerful that they often influence major life decisions and conceptions of self such as who might be considered an eligible marriage partner or who is innately musical. Once such habits of thought become deeply entrenched, they frequently operate below focal awareness—that is, they are taken for granted and do not come up for consideration as to their origin, nature, or accuracy.

Learning to recognize and critically question the power that social discourses have on our senses of self and others (Does skin color really matter? What does it mean to be an 'American'?), is a crucial aspect of life's work. From this perspective, discursively produced categories like 'race,' 'ethnicity,' 'nation,' 'modern' should be understood *as subjects for social analysis rather than objective rubrics that can be used in the process of social analysis and description.* This distinction is crucial; discursively pro-

1. Highlighting the "nature" side of this process, psychologist Susan Gelman argues that for reasons of evolutionary adaptation humans have an innate propensity to essentialize (believe in inner essences of and thus iconicity among) the members of categories in certain domains, especially living species. But she also holds that "language guides children to notice and essentialize some categories more than others" (2003:15).

duced categories of social identity must be understood in relation to the discourses that produce the terms and the social and political functions of those discourses.

Another important variable in the dynamics of identity formation is whether we are interested in differentiating ourselves from or uniting ourselves with those we are interacting with. When trying to create a political alliance people might emphasize one or two aspects of the self—e.g., 'ethnicity' or 'race' in the civil rights movement; gender in the women's movement; 'class' and occupation in union organizing; or political orientation in party organizing. In the creation of such movements, the many differences that will necessarily exist among the people involved—whether or not they are also mutually smokers, dog lovers, heavy metal music fans, or tennis players—will probably not come into the conceptions of identity for movement membership, although more of these habits of the self may become important later as two members start becoming friends.

The conscious use of a few aspects of identity to unite people for political ends or social advancement has been called *strategic essentialism*. *Essentialism*, as I am using the term here, refers to the reduction of complex selves to a few emphasized aspects that are projected as fundamental and immutable. Early on in the women's movement, the complex and varied subjectivities of women were reduced to a set of stereotyped traits of 'the way women are.' These were specifically contrasted with a stereotyped patriarchic style in order to rally women. In Zimbabwe during the early 1960s, middle-class black nationalists began to emphasize color as the essential trait uniting Africans against the 'white' rulers and downplayed their class and cultural differences with the African majority. This strategy contrasted with earlier decades, when the 'black' elite had denied the importance of color and emphasized their class and cosmopolitan cultural identity in an effort to advance themselves in the colonial society (chapter 5). This is just one example of the way social groups can strategically use different facets of identity to serve political ends and how the emphasized aspects of self-representation can shift depending on circumstances.

The symbol *strategic essentialism* has typically been used for situations where social groups 'essentialize' themselves for political or social unification, and this is often both necessary and positive. But negative attitudes involving racism, classism, sexism, ageism, and xenophobia are also based on stereotyped or essentialist portrayals of social groups. The important questions for social analysis are, who is doing the essentializing and to what ends? The term *identity politics* refers to the strategic use of group identities for political ends as well as to the struggles over who has the right or ability to control public representations of particular groups that, in turn, affect the social status and life chances of group members. Political movements and situations almost always involve the component of identity politics, and identity politics often involve expressive cultural practices like music and dance as publicly recognized identity signs for particular groups (chapters 5 and 7).

Within hierarchical societies, for example, people of higher-status groups and classes typically essentialize the differences between themselves and members of lower classes and emphasize signs of identity that differentiate them. In earlier centuries in Europe there were actually laws that designated what colors and clothing styles the different social classes could wear. A parallel exists in the arts. The greater institutional support for, and value placed on, elite arts as opposed to popular and so-called folk arts in our society serves a similar function of marking class distinctions. The higher value placed on elite arts—e.g., the idea that classical music is somehow superior even if the majority of people don't listen to it—underwrites the higher value of the social groups that this art indexes.[2] Conversely, disparaging the arts and cultural practices that index dominated groups is part of a discourse that represents those groups as inferior. In the early and mid-twentieth century, musical styles associated with African Americans such as jazz and roots rock 'n' roll were often described as primitive, licentious, and dangerous in the mainstream media; rap received the same reception toward the end of the century. This process can have dangerous results, as we shall see in chapter 7.

Identity always involves the twin aspects of unifying ourselves (emphasizing similarities) with some people and differentiating ourselves from others. We do this for a host of practical and emotional reasons: creating labor unions, nation-states, political parties, armies, interest groups, fraternities and sororities, or cliques at school. Issues of personal, social, and economic security are at the heart of social group formation and identity.

2. In an exercise I did for years in my large music classes, I asked students to rank a series of recorded examples in terms of (an unspecified) social value and to indicate if the examples were linked to particular social groups (by age, educational and economic level, 'ethnicity,' residence), and finally to indicate which type of music they were most likely to listen to. The examples included a Beethoven string quartet and examples of country, rock, and rap. The great majority of students ranked Beethoven highest in social value and rock (first) and rap (second) as the types they listened to most. The majority also linked the styles to the social groups that might be expected— country to rural working-class people, classical to higher-class educated people, rock to youth, rap to African Americans and youth more generally.

Anthropologists such as Richard Adams have even suggested that people's need to be part of groups is an evolutionary feature because belonging enhances the potential for survival. Certainly the need to bond with others is present in babies, who require a relatively long period of care by those around them. Thus whether the need to bond with other humans is in the genes or is simply one of the first habits humans develop remains a question, but the answer would not change the basic drive to identify with others. The ongoing processes of identity formation and the strategic uses of identity categories remain a central problem for social and ethnomusicological analysis.

Art and Signs of Identity

In-group and out-group status are marked by a broad range of signs such as clothing styles, hairstyles, body decoration, speech styles, and ways of walking. As public articulations framed to receive special attention, often the arts are key rallying points for identity groups and central to representations of identity. Some markers of group identity, such as speech accents or gendered ways of walking, may be such old habits that they operate low in focal awareness most of the time. Other identity markers are consciously used for self-presentation and identity (e.g., clothing styles).

Likewise, artists who represent themselves and their group identity through their works probably also use conscious icons and indices of identity as well as other signs of identity that simply emerge unselfconsciously, from deep habit, as a product of who they are. For instance, in Bahia, northeastern Brazil, there are music-dance groups called *bloco afros* that consciously represent ties with their African heritage through carnival performances. They wear costumes and sing songs about places and events in Africa to emphasize that they are proud to be descendants of Africa for political reasons. The music that they play is called samba-reggae; it is a combination of samba, reggae, funk, and other rhythms derived from various African American styles of the New World, played in densely layered percussion ensembles. These signs of identification with the African Diaspora are consciously chosen and displayed. At the same time, the subtle aspects of rhythmic articulation and movement styles of the dancers are grounded in the fact that the performers actually grew up in the Afro-Brazilian community and learned to move and produce rhythms in certain ways because of this experience. These subtle yet profound indices of identity are products of deep socialization and emerge unselfconsciously in performance to communicate the same message of 'Africanness' and membership in the community just as the consciously chosen signs do.

Like facial expressions and body language when they are directly affected by the inner moods that they signify, signs of identity that result from one's actual experiences are what Peirce would call dicent indices—identity signs that are actually affected by the social position, experiences, and ingrained habits that they signify. Artists typically manipulate their 'materials'—be they paint, stone, words, musical sounds, or body movement—to create intended effects and meaning. Usually other dicent signs will be evident in the works that remain low in the artist's focal awareness but that emerged from his or her own habits and experiences. As in the bloco afro example, both types of identity signs may be operating in parallel.

In the reception of certain genres, people make evaluations based on the presence or absence of dicent indices, signs of authenticity. For example, the singer-songwriter genre, rap, autobiography, love poetry, realist paintings, and photographs are framed to be interpreted as actually having been affected by what is being represented and the actual experiences or identity of the artist. If, after reading a moving collection of love poetry, we learned that the poet had never been in love, the work itself might be reevaluated. Likewise, if we learned that a rapper whose work portrays life in inner-city gangs had grown up in a middle-class suburb and had never had experience with gangs, his status would probably be tarnished, because we expect dicent authenticity within this genre. In the art used to express existing identities, this dicent or causal relationship between the sign and its object is often considered important—we expect the authentic representation of a given social group or cultural position in art to have been directly affected by membership and experiences in that group or position.

In chapter 3 I mentioned a form of 1980s Peruvian popular music known as *chicha* that indexed 'modernity' through the inclusion of electronic studio audio art–like sounds. The main fan base for this music was the children of highland Andean migrants who had settled in the capital city of Lima on the coast. Although they were born in Lima, these teenagers were not accepted as Limeño because of prejudices against highlanders in the capital. Likewise, never having lived in the sierra, they were not considered and did not consider themselves highlanders although they were surrounded by Andean relatives and neighbors. A number of second-generation migrants told me, "I do not know who I am." Chicha music evolved as one answer to this identity crisis. The style indexed highland identity through its use of *wayno* (the most common highland genre) melodic elements. It also indexed urbanity through its use of cosmopolitan *cumbia* rhythm, and it indexed youth through the inclusion of electric guitars, bass, and keyboards. The texts of the songs were predominantly about young love but also commented on the lower-class status and aspirations of the migrant children. Fused together in a coherent musical style and sign vehicle, these different indices grew out of and expressed the complex identities of the fans; that is, chicha was a dicent index of their cultural position as Peruvians themselves recognized (see Turino 2008, chap. 4). But for younger migrant children growing up in this situation, chicha also provided a coherent icon of a *possible* way to understand their identity. The style provided a model for young children to come to grips with their highland heritage in combination with their coastal-Lima residence and class position; the "hip" popularity of the style among their older peers also helped them feel comfortable about who they were.

In the following chapter I provide similar examples of how music- and dance-signs were combined in new ways to create dicent indices of identity as well as icons of as yet nonexistent—i.e., *possible*—social identities in Zimbabwe. It is the semiotic density of music that makes it particularly useful in such processes. *Semiotic density refers relatively to the number of potential signs occurring simultaneously. Reading words on a printed page is less dense semiotically than hearing someone read the words aloud, since vocal tone, rhythm, inflection, and physical and facial gestures add a whole range of additional signs occurring simultaneously with the words. As the chicha example shows, songs have even greater semiotic density than the spoken word. Fused in a single sign vehicle and occurring simultaneously, the melodic elements indexed highland heritage, the rhythm indexed urbanity, the instrumentation indexed 'modernity' and youth; all of this was presented together with other signs rendered in the vocal style, words of the texts, and onstage, clothing, choreographic, and gesture styles. Music recordings, and to an even greater extent musical performance, have great potential for creating dense combinations of icons and indices to represent existing social identities and to provide models for *possible* ones.

The Culture Concept

One of the earliest and most famous definitions of the anthropological concept of *culture* comes from Edward B. Tylor in his 1871 work *Primi-*

tive Culture: "Culture or Civilization, taken in its wide ethnographic sense, is that complex whole which includes knowledge, belief, art, morals, law custom, and any other capabilities and habits acquired by man as a member of society." Until recent decades many anthropologists thought of culture in this unified and somewhat objectified way. Alfred Louis Kroeber (1876–1960), an important American anthropologist, took a particular interest in the culture concept. In his chapter "The Nature of Culture" (1963). he wrote that culture is "shared and supraindividual, culture can exist only when a society exists; and conversely every human society is accompanied by a culture." By supraindividual or *superorganic*, Kroeber meant that culture is inherited, that it patterns individuals, and it is independent of specific individuals. For example, most North Americans are born within the English-language speaking community, and the English language would be very much the same regardless of the specific individuals born into that community. In contrast to 'great man' theories of history, Kroeber argued that individual genius is shaped by the cultural patterns of the era and is not independent of those patterns.

More recent conceptions have moved away from the idea of culture as a unified whole and the idea that each society is accompanied by *a* culture; the focus on the supraindividual character of culture has been augmented by an interest in the dialectical interplay between individuals and broader cultural patterns. The concept of *habits* is helpful here. Just as the *self* is the composite of habits guiding everything an individual thinks and does, we can think of *cultural phenomena* as consisting of *habits of thought and practice shared among individuals* within social groups of varying sizes and specificity and along different lines of common experience and identification. Shared habits are often imitated from earlier generations. To help shift our understanding away from the idea of culture as a unified entity to the notion that everything in social life has a cultural component, I prefer to avoid the noun and use the adjectival form whenever possible— 'cultural realm,' 'cultural practices,' 'cultural group,' and so on—because the grammatical structure of our language can influence how we think about phenomena.

The term *culture* is often used in everyday speech as if it were a synonym for *society*—Peter is from culture X. The two terms really refer to different order of phenomena, and thus it is best to keep them distinct. *Society* refers to the networks and institutions of existing social roles and relations unified by structures of governance and/or common patterns of social organization. Sovereign states create the boundaries for most large-scale contemporary societies. The laws and economic systems defined by states are fundamental for structuring the social roles and relations of their citizens, although it is possible to have smaller societies, such as those of relatively autonomous indigenous peoples with their own systems of organization and governance, nested within a state's territory. The shared habits that facilitate communication and identification are fundamental to social relations, but cultural processes and society are not the same. We *belong to* social groups and *are part of* society, whereas the habits shared among actual groups of people—cultural phenomena—are part of and belong within *us*.

Thinking about cultural phenomena as comprising shared or similar habits among people leads to the realization that there will be no single unified culture for a given society. Since individuals develop habits from their personal experience, it follows that the habits people hold in common are derived from having similar experiences and being in similar social positions and circumstances in relation to the environment. Children born into wealthy families may have the similar experience of traveling abroad on vacations. These experiences may lead to common habits of thought such as that foreign travel is possible and desirable and that learning foreign languages is useful, and to a sense of the world as including very different people and places. It is no accident that cosmopolitanism used to be associated with the upper classes. Poor children who rarely even leave their inner-city neighborhood or rural village probably will not share these habits of thought about the broad and accessible nature of the world. Thus *within the same society* a whole series of habits involving foreign travel or easy access to material goods or the ability to command others (wealthy children see their parents do this) will unite the members of economic classes and will *culturally* distinguish one social class from another.

Other sets of habits form along gender lines. Because of the threat of sexual harassment and rape in our society, women develop a whole series of self-protective habits that influence their daily lives, such as not walking alone in dark isolated places or not riding a bike alone on isolated country roads, things that as a man I rarely even think about. The fact that women share this set of habits, along with many others that men do not share, binds them as a cultural group and distinguishes them from men. Thus while habits of thought about the possibility of foreign travel may culturally divide women from different economic classes and be shared among men and women of the same classes, the self-protective habits developed by women will culturally unite them across class lines and differentiate them from men in their own classes.

African Americans develop a whole set of other habits that lead them to identify with each other and that distinguish them from Euro-Americans. An older African American friend once told me that when her sons bought expensive items such as fancy wheels for their cars, she always insisted that they permanently keep the receipts of purchase in a file, that they make this a habit. The reason for keeping the receipts was so that if the police ever showed up and claimed the items were stolen her sons would be able to prove purchase. Experience in the black community had taught my friend that young black males were always suspect in the eyes of the authorities, and she wanted to protect her sons. Since I am a member of the dominant social group, such a thing would never occur to me, and my habits differ accordingly.

In his book *Race Matters,* Cornel West, a prominent intellectual and university professor, tells stories of being harassed by police. "Years ago, while driving from New York to teach at Williams College, I was stopped on fake charges of trafficking cocaine. When I told the police officer I was a professor of religion, he replied, 'yeah, and I'm the Flying Nun. Let's go, nigger!' I was stopped three times in my first ten days in Princeton for driving too slowly on a residential street with a speed limit of twenty-five miles per hour. (And my son, Clifton, already has similar memories at the tender age of fifteen)" (1994:xv).

While West and I probably have a variety of habits in common due to our occupation (preparing books for publication, preparing lectures, attending faculty meetings) and our habits of thought about the possibility of foreign travel are probably similar because we belong to the same social class, his experiences in other realms differ from mine because he is 'black' and I am 'white' in a society where skin color matters.

Cultural Cohorts and Cultural Formations

Within any society, each individual is a vector for cultural similarities and differences with others along a variety of habit trajectories because of similar or different experiences, social positioning, and aspects of the self. Thus rather than thinking about 'culture' as a unified entity, it is better to conceptualize the *cultural realm* in a more flexible way. Since people will identify with others because of shared habit trajectories, I suggest the terms *cultural cohort* or *identity cohort* to refer to social groupings that form along the lines of specific constellations of shared habit based in similarities of *parts* of the self. In our society, class, gender, occupation, and color are particularly salient parts of the self that strongly influence social position, experiences, and thus habits. Age is another prominent basis for the formation of cultural cohorts—"60s generation," "generation X." Other cultural/identity cohorts can form around interests and hobbies (bikers, football fans, bluegrass aficionados, kayakers) as well as political, religious, and ethical beliefs and activities. Because of the pluralistic nature of the self, each person will belong to a variety of cultural/identity cohorts having greater or lesser social salience and prominence in their lives: I share a number of habits with others of my generation because we grew up in similar historical circumstances (listened to the same popular music, were affected by the Vietnam War); I share attitudes about the possibility of foreign travel with both men and women of my social class; I have not developed the self-protective habits of women that operate across class lines; I do not keep the purchase receipts of expensive items, because it never occurs to me that the police will show up and accuse me of theft.

To this point I have been trying to break up the holistic conception of unified cultures so that we can understand how individuals within the same society group themselves and differentiate themselves from others along a variety of axes depending on the parts of the self that are salient for a given social situation. Within a society and even across societies, however, there are broadly shared constellations of habits that pervasively influence most aspects of individual selves. Usually learned during early socialization, these pervasive constellations of habits have the special force of time-depth within individual selves and lives. When a great many of these pervasive habits are common to groups of individuals, they serve as the basis of social group formation because they permit identification (iconicity) and ease of social interaction. Indeed, common habits such as speaking the same language help make social interaction possible; common experiences, and thus habits, also make it possible to correctly interpret the indexical cues that are fundamental to social interaction.

I use the term *cultural formation* to refer to a group of people who have in common a majority of habits that constitute most parts of each individual member's self. It is the *pervasiveness* and often the time-depth of habits influencing individual thought, practice, and decision making that distinguish *cultural formations* from *cultural cohorts*. Habits of the formation make up a kind of baseline for much of what individual members think and do. Speaking English, capitalist ethics, living with social hierarchies, driving on the right-hand side of the road, knowing what a red traffic light means, knowing that Thomas Jefferson was a founding father, knowing what an extended middle finger means, among myriad examples, are all habits that combine to define the cultural formation that pertains to many U.S. citizens. Regardless of whether we are relating to others in a given situation emphasizing our identities as women, African Americans, college professors, musicians, or kayakers (cohorts), we typically speak English, drive on the right, stop when the light turns red, and recognize the value of money for exchange (habits of the formation). We share a majority of habits with other members of our cultural formations; only certain specific aspects and habits of the self are highlighted to join (or be joined) with other members of our various cohorts.

Within a given formation, the members of different cohorts will be guided similarly by a majority of habits of the formation but will be distinguished *as cohorts* by the emphasis and development of selected habits. A middle-class person raised in the Chicago suburbs has probably grown up speaking English, has internalized many aspects of capitalist ethics, and has probably spent most of her "musical life" listening to commercial presentational and high fidelity musics. If, however, certain experiences make the woman question the suburban life she has been living, and through high fidelity recordings she becomes fascinated with old-time country music and begins to play it, she may well seek out other fans and players of this music (CD track 1). The old-time cohort is centered on participatory music making, but it also involves images and ideologies of 'folk' simplicity, 'roots' America, and rural community living (chapter 6). So several aspects of the woman's experiences have combined to attract her to this cohort. Playing old-time may be only one of many things that she does, or it may become the center of her life. In the latter case the social circle, ideologies, and activities of the cohort can become very prominent cultural influences. This does not mean, however, that she sheds all the habits she developed growing up in suburban Chicago. In fact, she will continue to share many of these habits of the formation with people from the suburbs, even if they have become equally active in other cohorts involving hip-hop, salsa, golf, sailing, or political activism.

The relationship between the concepts of *cultural cohort* and *cultural formation* thus should be understood in several basic ways. First, the habits of thought and practice that pertain to a cultural formation operate *across* specific cohorts, and in fact, formations underpin or *create the conditions* for the specific cultural cohorts that will emerge within that formation. For example, because of the history and legacy of slavery in the United States, the habit of associating skin color with social status led to the creation of cultural cohorts along color lines in the United States. The self-protective habits that partially define women as a separate cohort are necessary only in cultural formations where the habit of perpetrating violence against women exists. Similarly, the cohorts of university professors, kayakers, and bluegrass fanatics can exist only in formations where there are universities, kayaks, and bluegrass.

Second, cohorts are differentiated from the cultural formation by different *levels of shared habits of thought and meaning* attached to a particular object, institution, or practice. For example, the habit of recognizing "the Golden Arches" as an indexical sign for McDonald's restaurants and the idea of 'fast food' are features of the countrywide cultural formation of the United States (and the capitalist cosmopolitan formation; see below). Most North Americans share the *general* recognition of what this sign means. More specific attitudes and practices in relation to McDonald's and fast food, however, may pertain to, and differentiate, cultural cohorts. The members of an upper-class cohort who partially identify with each other around shared attitudes about 'refined taste' may feel distain for fast food restaurants and avoid them like the plague. Cultural cohorts that form around 'health food' or vegetarianism will also avoid McDonald's, but for different reasons from those of the dining connoisseurs. The members of a politically defined cohort that favors local businesses and food production and opposes capitalist massification may boycott McDonald's on these grounds. An age cohort that has learned to love "Happy Meals" and the toys offered may develop the habit of pestering their parents to stop every time the Golden Arches come into view. So here we have a social institution and sign vehicle (Golden Arches) generally recognized, and hence being a point of commonality, within the countrywide *formation*, while the same institution and sign vehicle generate different habits of thought and practice at the level of specific cultural cohorts.

Again, the general meaning of 'McDonald's' within the formation creates a necessary condition for the multiple reactions at the level of specific cohorts. A unified or holistic conception of *culture* obscures rather than clarifies the analysis of these more specific levels of social identification, practice, and meaning. Similarly, most North Americans will have a general notion about what a kayak or a banjo is, but only certain people will follow up on this general knowledge to develop the skills necessary to roll a kayak and take it down whitewater rivers or to play a banjo in the old-time frailing or three-finger bluegrass style (chapter 6; CD tracks 1 and 2). The value-guided emphasis on certain cultural items and ideas, and the personal investment of time, money, and energy to develop the habits necessary for using them in certain ways, is a common basis for occupational and interest-based cohorts against the backdrop of resources available within a given cultural formation.

For interest-based cohorts, conscious choice is involved in skill development and joining up with others who similarly value or take part in the activity. Freedom and awareness of choice, however, *are not* general definitional features that distinguish cohorts from formations. Individuals may be assigned by others or by circumstances to a gender-based, color-based, class-based, or occupational cohort against their wishes. Conversely, people may elect to change habits derived from the formation, although the difficulty of doing so often depends on the longevity of the habits as well as other features such as social support for making such a change. Cohorts that provide alternatives to basic tenets of the formation are an important source for such social support. Returning to the example described earlier, as the old-time cohort becomes central in the woman's life, the connected images of rural community and simplicity, and the valuing of such ideas among her friends in the scene, may influence her to try country living or take up subsistence farming or a craft (see chapter 6).

Middle-class old-time music-dance scenes in the United States originally emerged as the basis for a cultural cohort in conjunction with 1960s counterculture and back-to-the land ideologies, all of which were oppositional to basic tenets and tendencies of the capitalist cultural formation. Here the preconditions supplied by the broader formation were negative— "what we don't want to be." As discussed in chapter 6, this case suggests the various ways that the concepts of cultural cohorts and formations are useful for social analysis and praxis. In the old-time music scene, the same individuals share habits from the formation and oppositional habits from the cohort, a fact that explains what appear to be contradictions within the same individuals but simply derive from different spheres, and depths, of socialization in their own lives. But as this case also suggests, the old-time music-dance cohort provided models and support for certain members to profoundly change their lives.

The cohort and formation concepts are useful in other ways. For example, they provide tools for analyzing social movements that begin as cohorts but gather strength to the point of transforming a broader formation. Such is the case with the Nazi Party, which began as a small political cohort but developed an ideology that temporarily engulfed and redefined the cultural formation of Germany (chapter 7). While the outcome of this movement was disastrous, there are examples of cohorts that developed and gathered strength to transform a society along more positive lines; the civil rights movement of the 1950s and 1960s in the United States is one such example (also chapter 7).

Formation-based habits pertain broadly to most realms of life, whereas

cohort-based habits are more specific and situational. The distinction between cohorts and formations is thus a matter of degree in terms of the
prominence of the influence of a certain set of habits in given individuals'
lives and is not static. Religious beliefs and practices can be the basis of an
identity cohort within a broader cultural formation if, say, church members come together to worship on Sundays but still largely operate in relation to the habits of their larger regional or national formation during the
rest of the week. If the religious group isolates itself and its tenets become
the primary basis for living, however, it becomes a cultural formation (e.g.,
the Amish in Illinois). In cases where a cohort begins to function like an
emerging formation, its prominence as a formation will deepen with each
subsequent generation if its tenets and social style become the basis of
habit formation and socialization of the young.

Nested Cultural Formations

While the concept of cultural formation returns us closer to the original
broadly conceived anthropological meaning of the term *culture*, even
within a single society cultural formations should be understood in pluralistic terms. Any given individual belongs to a variety of *nested* cultural formations of lesser to greater size, specificity, and intimacy. At the smallest,
most specific end of the continuum, individual families may be thought of
as cultural formations insofar as there are specific habits that are unique
to and shared by its members *across* the more specific gender-, age-, oc-
cupation-, and interest-based cohorts that may exist within the family.
Families typically develop special words for things, ways of operating together, jokes, memories, and narratives about the family, all this based on
the strongly indexical nature of such intimate social units because of the
wealth of shared experiences. Families are a fundamental type of cultural
formation for social analysis because they are the cradle of early socialization and habit formation.

There may be regional cultural formations. A good example in the
United States is Cajun country in southwestern Louisiana, made unique
by the local form of French spoken there and Cajun music, dance, cuisine, festivals, and history. Regional cultural/identity formations may be
particularly pronounced in countries with weak centralized governments
and limited or relatively recent mass-media infrastructure; this is true for
Peru, Colombia, Brazil, and other Latin American states, as well as in Africa and Indonesia. This was also true formerly in the United States; in
1861, when having to choose between loyalty to his country and loyalty

to his state of Virginia, Robert E. Lee chose Virginia. In this fundamental life decision, Lee's primary identification with the nested regional formation took precedence over the larger (and, at the time, weaker) national cultural formation.

Because of the major influence of the state (governmental institutions and roles + territory) in people's experiences, however, cultural formations at the level of entire countries are often a primary type. Government-directed mass public education and laws, as well as attitudes encouraged by governments through the mass media, create broadly shared habits of thought and practice at the country level. When the cultural formation at the state level is particularly profound and comprises many shared habits among most citizens, it is a national-level formation. *Nation* typically refers to a cultural/identity unit that identifies itself in relation to political sovereignty, that is, to having or desiring its own state. Nations are often conceptualized in relation to a relatively unified countrywide cultural formation, but belonging to a nation is a subjective condition based on *national sentiment,* the feelings of belonging to this type of identity unit, whereas belonging to a state is an objective condition.[3]

Transstate Cultural Formations

As with Kroeber's definition cited earlier, people are in the habit of thinking of 'culture' as coterminous with a particular society or country. I have suggested that there are smaller nested cultural formations; I would also suggest that there are cultural formations that exist across country borders. *Immigrant communities, diasporas,* and *cosmopolitan formations* are three prominent transstate types, each with its own characteristics and dynamics.[4] The dispersed nature of transstate formations makes them more difficult to grasp, yet in light of the recent discourse emphasizing 'global' processes and culture, these concepts provide useful tools for contemporary cultural analysis.

Immigrant communities are a distinct type of cultural formation in that

---

3. Whether or not one has feelings of loyalty and belonging (national sentiment), people's membership in states is objectively marked by, e.g., the need of a passport to leave and return and the need to pay taxes, send one's children to school, and obey the laws.

4. This framework for transstate cultural formations is explained in more detail in my paper "Are We Global Yet? Discourse Analysis, Cultural Formations, and Zimbabwean Popular Music" (Turino 2004).

the members are dispersed geographically across state boundaries and combine habits based on models from their original homes and their new 'host' society home; they also create new habits based on their experiences as immigrants. Sometimes immigrants integrate themselves within their new host society on an individual basis and do not associate with others from 'home.' To exist as an immigrant community, people have to associate with each other on the basis of 'original home' identity and operate within community networks in the host country to a significant degree, such that the community forms an enclave and supplies prominent models for socialization. If assimilation is the goal and is possible and immigrants only occasionally identify themselves with others from 'home' (e.g., an annual German festival or Italian American celebration), and the original home is only a minor source for cultural habits, then immigrant status is likely to become the basis of a cultural cohort rather than a more pervasive formation.

Immigrant communities are bipolar in that they define themselves in relation to their original and new homes. *Diasporic formations* are distinct in that they combine habits from the original home and their new home *and* are influenced by the cultural models from other places in the diaspora. The diasporic sites are unified as a formation by at least symbolically emphasizing their allegiance to their original homeland and by social networks across the sites. Both immigrant and diasporic formations involve immigration, and both involve a subjective identification with the formation.

Like diasporas, *cosmopolitan cultural formations* involve prominent constellations of habits that are shared among widely dispersed groups in countries around the world; but unlike diasporas, cosmopolitan formations are not traced to any particular homeland. Unlike the other two types of transstate formations, cosmopolitans often do not subjectively identify with, or even recognize, cosmopolitanism as the basis of a cultural formation. Unlike the members of immigrant and diasporic formations, cosmopolitans are defined not by immigrant status but rather by the major adoption of cosmopolitan lifeways and habits of thought.

The most prominent cosmopolitan cultural formation in the world today was spread by European and U.S. colonialism; it is defined by habits of thought and practice derived from a combination of Christianity and capitalist ethos and practices under the umbrella discourse of modernity (see chapter 5). The members of this formation in Africa and certain countries in Asia and Latin America tend to be of the elites of those countries and often remain culturally distinct from the majority populations.[5] In countries like Zimbabwe and Peru, people whose habits are largely based in this *modernist-capitalist* cosmopolitan formation are a minority—like small cultural islands. They are linked to cosmopolitans elsewhere in the formation—in England, France, and the United States but also to cosmopolitans in other African, Latin American, and Asian countries—through travel, cosmopolitan communication systems like the Internet, and educational and social institutions; cosmopolitans typically study, travel, and live for some time abroad. As in any cultural formation, however, the primary basis for links with cosmopolitans elsewhere in the formation is the shared habits of thought, practice, and communication which make social interaction attractive—people are drawn to others who are culturally similar.

In the cold war period, the modernist-socialist cosmopolitan formation provided a competitive alternative to the capitalist formation, and currently the Islamic formation is a prominent basis for another form of cosmopolitanism. Thus just as there are multiple diasporas existing in the world (African Diaspora, Indian Diaspora, Jewish Diaspora, etc.), there are also multiple cosmopolitan formations. Because of the growing prominence of the capitalist-cosmopolitan formation, especially in the post-Soviet era, the members of this group have begun to define their lifeways as 'global,' that is, universal. This is in part a description of the increasing spread of the capitalist formation and in part an ideological move that helps naturalize its spread. However, unless a particular cultural practice, technology, or habit of thought is truly universal—that is, involving everyone everywhere—'global' is not an accurate description and is more like wishful thinking.[6]

5. This elite status derived from the colonial system. The members of this group were socialized through cosmopolitan education in missionary and colonial-government schools, served in intermediary posts between the colonizers and colonized masses, took the reins of state in the postcolonial period, and are the people who are able to benefit most from foreign aid and economic alliances in the contemporary period because of their cosmopolitan connections. That is, they are the people cosmopolitans elsewhere are most likely to deal with.

6. While the political organization of the peoples of the world under the state system is global, involvement with the Internet and capitalist investment possibilities are not, in spite of popular advertising slogans like "global investing." The major record companies also describe themselves through slogans and advertising as 'global' in scope; see Turino 2004.

For any given individual, the models for habit formation, thought and practice are multiple. A monolingual Spanish-speaking Mexican in Chicago may well learn to use cosmopolitan technologies like the Internet and e-mail and to dance diasporic traditions such as salsa, but if the majority of habits that determine his everyday thoughts, interactions, and practices are guided by models from his original home and from the immigrant community in Chicago, then much of what he does may be best understood in relation to the dynamics of the Mexican (American) immigrant-community formation. Few individuals fit neatly into any single analytical cubbyhole in everything they think and do. The more eclectic a person's experiences are, the more eclectic her habits, and thus the *more* tools we will need to understand her patterns of decision making and social action and interaction. This is precisely the point of the models I am offering here; unitary notions of culture or of Bourdieu's *habitus* (see below) do not provide enough tools for analysis and description. The concepts of nested cultural formations and the formation-cohort distinction are meant as concepts for analyzing and describing specific instances, as well as general *tendencies,* of social thought and practice. They are meant to break up holistic notions of *culture* and to be used in varied combinations and ways to help us understand the fluidity, and indeed messiness, of social life and identities. Finally, they are simply analytical concepts and should not be mistaken for ontological categories.

Models for Socialization

Following Pierre Bourdieu's general formulation (1977), the overall model for social life being sketched here is like this: A person's internalized dispositions and habits (Bourdieu uses the term *habitus*) are products of relations to the conditions around her and her concrete experiences in and of the environment. Habits and dispositions guide what we think, do, and make (practices). Our practices and the things we produce affect, to greater or lesser degrees, our environment, which in turn affects our dispositions, which in turn affect our practices, which in turn affect external conditions, and so on. Our practices thus become the mediators between the internalized constellations of habit and the social and physical world around us.

Bourdieu's model appears circular and, some have claimed, too mechanical, static, and unconscious. Yet I believe that there is room for dynamism and individual agency within this framework. While most of the habits that make up the self are shared with others—are *social habits*—in relation to given formations and cohorts, no two individuals' social positioning, experiences, and genetic makeup are identical. Moreover, life is full of chance experiences, and their effects on people will vary according to their own *internal contexts. Consequently, each individual is a somewhat distinctive constellation of habits—this model of self, identity, and cultural phenomena maintains a place for individual uniqueness and by extension the cultural uniqueness of specific groups. The practices that emerge from the unique aspects of individuals and groups in relation to novel circumstances affect the social and physical environment in new ways, which in turn affect the internalized habits and dispositions of individuals in new ways, and thus it is here where there is room for innovation, creativity, and transformations at the individual and group levels.

The value of conceptualizing the *self, identity,* and *culture* in terms of habits is this: Habits have specific histories, create material effects, and over time gain relative stability. They are real, existing forces at the level of both the individual and society. On the other hand, habits are not set in stone; they can and do continually change, and they are the result of circumstances and experiences in conjunction with biological capacities and propensities. Even if, as Susan Gelman suggests, the human propensity to essentialize is hardwired, harmful social habits like racism can be changed because of conscious effort such as civil rights legislation or more or less gradually through experiences such as gaining a new friend of another 'race.'

Like overly static conceptions of an unchanging core self, earlier anthropological writings discussed cultures as unified, homogeneous, and stable wholes. Recent postmodern approaches have gone to the other extreme and describe culture and identity as extremely fluid social constructions, almost as if people could make them up as they went along. Using habits as the fulcrum for thinking about the self, identity, and cultural phenomena, it is possible to locate a more realistic middle ground between overly fluid and overly static conceptions of individuals and social life. Since people develop habits by imitating those around them, this approach clarifies how individual selves are socially constituted, just as cultural cohorts and cultural formations are necessarily constituted, and perhaps transformed, by the specific experiences and habits of individual members of the group. To provide an example of this cultural dynamism, the following chapter describes the emergence of a new cultural formation in Zimbabwe and traces the rise of the presentational and high fidelity fields in a place where there was only participatory music making a century ago.

5 Participatory, Presentational, and High Fidelity Music in Zimbabwe

Musical life in Shona villages of Murehwa District, northeastern Zimbabwe, is centered on community participation as a primary goal of performance. The ceremonies, beer parties, and other musical events renew bonds among Shona community members as well as with their ancestors, who remain vital spiritual forces in people's lives. Until the early twentieth century, group participatory performance was the main type of music making in Zimbabwe; drumming, hosho (shakers), and lamellaphones such as the mbira[1] were used to accompany communal dancing, singing, and handclapping. Singing or playing indigenous instruments like the musical bow or mbira alone or in small informal groups for personal enjoyment was the only other form of music making that existed. Indigenous participatory music making is still vital among African peasants and among members of the working class who reside in cities.

With the coming of British colonizers at the end of the nineteenth century and European and North American missionaries in the decades to follow, however, cosmopolitan styles of popular music, musical values, and presentational modes of performance were introduced. Indigenous Zimbabweans first learned presentational performance as a value, idea, and practice in missionary and government schools, and it initially per-

---

1. A variety of regional lamellaphone ('thumb piano') traditions exist in Zimbabwe, mbira, karimba, and matepe among them. While belonging to the same family, these instruments differ in terms of key arrangements, playing techniques, and repertories. Switching from one to another is akin to shifting between a guitar and a mandolin in that some playing techniques transfer but tunings and fingerings differ.

tained to middle-class Africans[2] who performed "concert" music as amateur specialists in township recreation halls during the 1940s and 1950s. Beginning in the late 1950s, members of the cosmopolitan African middle class spearheaded a cultural nationalist movement that involved indigenous musicians and dancers in presentational performance during political rallies—a trend that was continued by the Zimbabwean government after independence from settler rule in 1980. Meanwhile, in the 1960s and 1970s, young urban Zimbabweans created a new style of popular music. They performed indigenous drumming and mbira music with rock instrumentation in nightclubs for listening and participatory dancing; due to a variety of factors during the 1960s, young urban Zimbabweans began to consider the possibility of music as a professional career for the first time.

The history of high fidelity recording in Zimbabwe intersects at various points with the main musical trajectories that I describe below. The middle-class African "concert" performers initially learned cosmopolitan popular styles from the United States and England from recordings imported through South Africa. During the 1940s and 1950s, a handful of the most successful Zimbabwean musicians made commercial recordings with South African companies such as Gallo because Zimbabwe did not yet have a record industry. In Zimbabwe, the high fidelity recording of middle-class presentational styles and indigenous participatory traditions was actually initiated by the colonial government. In the cold war period after World War II, with nationalist movements sweeping Africa, the white settler government was particularly concerned about controlling information flows. One of the state-controlled radio stations was specifically directed at African listeners. Its personnel began to record single-issue 78rpm disks of regional mbira and dance-drumming music, itinerant acoustic guitarists, and middle-class popular music groups in an attempt to attract the full range of African listeners to the station and to keep them from tuning in to 'subversive' foreign stations. Between 1955 and 1970 a huge and

---

2. In Zimbabwe, the term *African* is used to refer to 'black' people and *European* to refer to 'white' people even if, in the latter case, the family has lived in Zimbabwe for generations. The term *settler* is also used to refer to Zimbabwean families of European extraction. The two major African groups in Zimbabwe are the Shona and the Ndebele. I worked in the Shona region, and my references to 'African' traditions will be restricted to this group. Note, finally, that before the name Zimbabwe became official with independence in 1980, the colony was referred to as Rhodesia and Southern Rhodesia at different points in its history, and the capital city of Harare was Salisbury. Here I will primarily use contemporary place-names for the sake of simplicity.

fairly stylistically comprehensive library of African music recordings for broadcast was amassed.[3] The first commercial Zimbabwean record company opened its doors in 1959, and several more were to follow. The local record industry flowered during the 1970s and 1980s with vinyl 45rpm and long-playing records of local popular artists and guitar bands such as the Harare Mambos, Thomas Mapfumo, Oliver M'tukudzi, the Green Arrows, and many others. By the new millennium, however, dreams of professional success and stardom, inspired by the Zimbabwean recording industry and by cosmopolitan interest in African music as 'world music' abroad during the 1980s and 1990s, were dashed by the economic collapse of the country.

By the time I conducted research in Zimbabwe in the late twentieth century there were many styles and modes of music making. In this chapter I discuss indigenous Shona participatory performance and the development of presentational styles during the colonial and postindependence periods. Presentational performance, high fidelity recording, and musical professionalism all emerged as ideas and practices with the rise of a new African cosmopolitan cultural formation in Zimbabwe. In this chapter I sketch the processes by which this cultural formation came to coexist alongside the indigenous cultural formations. The chapter concludes with an example of the transformations that occur when participatory traditions are adapted for professional stage performance, in this case by the National Dance Company after 1980.

Indigenous Shona and Cosmopolitan Cultural Formations

The term *Shona* refers to the majority language spoken in Zimbabwe and is used as a shorthand for the people who speak it. The term does not suggest a unified cultural formation, however. There were a variety of regionally based social groups — 'tribes.' Moreover, British and white-settler colonialism led to class stratification and a variety of different cultural positions within the African population. As a part of the colonial process, mission schools were established to convert indigenous Zimbabweans to Christianity and to modernist-cosmopolitan lifeways. Children in mission schools and families living on mission station land (e.g., through women's social clubs) were actively taught cosmopolitan styles of hygiene, dress, cuisine,

3. This collection is currently housed at the Zimbabwe National Archives and remains a fundamental source for understanding the musical history of the country.

values regarding work, money, and 'progress,' monogamous nuclear family structures (indigenous Shona are polygamous), Christian beliefs, ideas about democracy and nation, how to read, write, and do math, as well as how to read, arrange, and perform presentational choral music, among many other facets of life. Education and adoption of cosmopolitan cultural style became the primary avenue for class mobility within the African population.

After several generations—that is, after cosmopolitan habits were internalized by Zimbabweans as the basis for socializing their own children—a distinct African middle-class cosmopolitan cultural formation began to emerge. Here I am making a distinction between an early phase of colonialism when Africans imitated 'foreign' 'external' models of practice and a later phase when cosmopolitan habits became deeply internalized, 'commonsense' aspects of Zimbabweans themselves. It was during the second phase, when cosmopolitan habits became basic to socialization *within* the group—parents to children—that a new cultural formation emerged. Note that this shift occurred within different Zimbabwean families at different times throughout the twentieth century and through the present. As the shift from imitation to the internal generation of cosmopolitan habits occurs, individual family formations become part of the broader cosmopolitan formation (see chapter 4).

The small African middle class was distinctive, economically, socially, and culturally, both from the white settlers (also a small minority) and from the African peasant and working-class majority. As one prominent example of this distinctiveness, African middle-class artists developed their own forms of presentational music that was modeled on cosmopolitan popular styles but by the 1940s and 1950s had become distinctly local. Basic to cosmopolitanism as a type of cultural formation, members in any given site will have many habits in common with people elsewhere in the formation (wearing tuxedos, saving money, reading music notation), and yet cosmopolitanism is always simultaneously *local* and *translocal*; people in each local site will develop a somewhat distinctive combination of habits drawn from the cosmopolitan formation and the local environment. The presentational musical styles favored by the cosmopolitan African middle class are a case in point.

Meanwhile in many rural areas and in the working-class urban townships, indigenous Shona beliefs, practices, and art forms are maintained as a normal part of life. During the colonial period, apartheid structures legally separated the country into 'white' and 'black' areas. Rural African families were restricted to reservationlike regions known as 'tribal trust lands,' where they continued to practice subsistence agriculture, maintain indigenous family structures and spiritual beliefs, and practice indigenous styles of music and dance. Cities were designated as 'white' areas, and Africans who came to work there were segregated in the 'black' townships that surrounded the cities. Many members of this emergent working class also maintained indigenous lifeways as a matter of course. A central pillar of indigenous Shona cultural formations is a set of spiritual beliefs involving ongoing relationships with family and clan ancestors who people believe intervene in their everyday lives. In the contemporary period, indigenous Shona lifeways remain vibrant in rural communities but also among some working-class people who live most of the time in or around cities.

For the sake of description, in this chapter I distinguish between two prominent African cultural formations that presently coexist in central and northern Zimbabwe: the indigenous-Shona cultural formation and the modernist-capitalist cosmopolitan formation.[4] Of course the situation is not as neat as this distinction suggests; many individuals internalize habits drawn from both indigenous and cosmopolitan models to varying degrees, and moreover, they are conscious of doing so (see Turino 2000:35–41). For example, the same individual might go to a cosmopolitan medical doctor and, if this failed to bring about a cure, to a diviner or indigenous healer. A cosmopolitan Zimbabwean who firmly believes in the scientific method might also retain a belief in the power of witchcraft. This should come as no surprise; as suggested in the previous chapter, individuals the world over are always complex combinations of habits of thought and action influenced by the various models that they have grown up with. Nonetheless, in Zimbabwe coexisting indigenous and capitalist-cosmopolitan cultural formations provide the major models and hence major tendencies for decision making and for living.

4. Unless specified otherwise, when I use the term *cosmopolitan* in this chapter I am specifically referring to the modernist-capitalist formation, which is the primary one in Zimbabwe. During the Liberation War of the 1970s, nationalist leaders were briefly involved with modernist-socialist cosmopolitanism—a prominent competing formation during the cold war years—via China and the Soviet Union. Other transstate cultural formations exist in Zimbabwe; for example, there is a small enclave of people of the Indian Diaspora. But having been introduced by the early colonists and diffused by missionaries for much of the twentieth century, modernist-capitalist cosmopolitanism provided the oldest and most influential transstate cultural models throughout the country.

Zimbabweans are aware of this cultural divide. Using the word *Western* instead of *cosmopolitan,* one of my mbira teachers, Chris Mhlanga, told me: "We have got two groups here in Zimbabwe. I think in Africa each country is divided into two: those who like Western culture, who want their own [indigenous African] culture to be abolished, and those who stay with their own culture who don't want their culture to be abolished" (quoted in Turino 2000:32). A number of people made similar categorical statements to me, yet these same individuals in other conversations would emphasize that many Zimbabweans are complex combinations of ideas and practices drawn from both 'Western' and indigenous models. I do not think that there is a contradiction between these two types of assertions; each is correct in its own way. Given the model of the self, identity, and culture presented in the previous chapter, I would suggest that each Zimbabwean is fundamentally socialized within a particular cultural formation which provides bedrock bases for decision making, thoughts, and practices. But through lifelong experiences individuals also pick up new habits in the environment, which, after the early twentieth century, increasingly included cosmopolitan elements.

Thus, given the spiritual orientation of Shona society, people socialized within indigenous communities will tend to consider what their ancestors will think about a particular decision or action. For example, Mhlanga once told me that when he was contemplating the use of an electric grinder (a cosmopolitan innovation) to make mbira, he consulted his ancestor about the appropriateness of this decision. Because of the ethos of extended family relationships, people in the indigenous formation often feel a responsibility to help extended kin who are in need, and they will prioritize this over nuclear family capital accumulation. Someone raised in a capitalist-cosmopolitan household, on the other hand, might prioritize saving money for his business, his children's education, or future financial security. Indeed several African cosmopolitan friends who lived in Harare told me that they actually avoided visits from extended kin and were reluctant to visit the rural family home so as not to feel financial pressure from relatives. Likewise, for cosmopolitans the decision to use a particular tool will probably be based on its efficacy alone without considering what one's deceased grandfather would think about it.

Any of these individuals might combine cosmopolitan and indigenous habits, but the point is that basic tendencies for decision making and for living will be grounded in the cultural formation in which one was originally socialized. In the musical realm, indigenous and cosmopolitan values and approaches can be distinguished largely along the lines of the participatory and presentational fields of music making.

Indigenous Participatory Music in Murehwa

The central and northern parts of Zimbabwe are on a high plateau; Murehwa is a beautiful region dotted with small mountains, outcrops, and streams. The villagers are primarily subsistence farmers and herders, but Murehwa is only sixty kilometers from the capital city Harare, and good roads make travel back and forth easy. People from rural areas have long gone to the city to seek cash employment. Because of the apartheidlike colonial system prior to African majority rule in 1980, however, black Zimbabweans were relocated to 'tribal trust lands' and were not allowed to own homes in the city or land in regions legally designated as 'white' for much of the colonial period. Consequently, they formed the habit of considering their rural places of residence 'home,' even if they lived much of the time in the urban townships. In addition, the Shona concept of *musha* links people to their rural homes. *Musha* means 'home,' but it also refers to the place where one's parents and ancestors are buried. Thus land is not considered just an economic resource or commodity; one's musha has a spiritual essence because it is the place where one's ancestors reside, and in indigenous spiritual beliefs, one's ancestors remain actively engaged with the living.

In Murehwa most musical events are family-sponsored ceremonies for ancestors usually between one to three generations back or for a relative who died the previous year (grave ceremonies). Weddings, funerals, and beer parties are also common musical occasions. While most Shona ceremonies are not scheduled within an annual festival cycle as among the Aymara of Peru, in a given region they are equally frequent, especially in good harvest years. Events typically go all night and may last several days and nights depending on the wishes of the ancestors.

A Bira Ceremony in Mhembere Village, Murehwa, March 1993

Bira refers to a ceremony held to contact one's ancestors; families sponsor these events for a variety of reasons. Someone in the family may be sick or having some type of difficulty and a diviner has established that a particular ancestor is causing the problem to draw attention to some misdeed or ritual oversight within the family. In such cases a ceremony will be held to consult with that ancestor. Other families simply hold ceremonies periodically to stay in touch with, consult, or honor particular ancestors. Ancestors attend the ceremony through the body of a person who serves as the spirit's medium; an ancestor who chooses to return will select a person who will serve as her medium for life.[5]

After a date had been set for a bira in Murehwa during March 1993, the host went to visit certain musicians to invite them to the ceremony. Most people in the village, each with his or her own musical skills, will attend the bira, but the host must make sure that certain core musicians are involved. Unlike the customary prescription of specific instruments and genres for given Aymara festivals in Conima (see Turino 1993), in Murehwa there are decisions to be made. Music and dance are used as a means of attracting a given ancestor to the ceremony. It is important to have the type of music that the ancestor enjoyed while she or he was living, and even the specific pieces played in the way she liked them. Thus the host must ensure that musicians attend who can play the intended ancestor's favorite instruments and music. In Murehwa there are two types of music-dance that are typically used to attract ancestors: *dandanda* played with two drums, hosho, call-and-response singing, and dancing; and music performed with mbira, hosho, singing, and dancing. Only certain people know how to drum dandanda or play mbira, so these individuals must be specially invited, and of course the intended ancestor's spirit medium must also be present at the bira.

A week before the ceremony, the family brewed a special 'seven-day beer' and made other preparations. The ceremony was scheduled for Friday night. Two young men from the village who play mbira arrived with their instruments early, around four o'clock, and other neighbors and family members began arriving slowly as evening came on. Women in the family were attending to the food over a fire. Boys were gathering wood for a bonfire that would be kept going all night. The drummers arrived around six o'clock and set down their drums inside the round kitchen building, where the bira would be held. At this point some people began moving inside while others remained outside talking and drinking bottled beer purchased by the host. People were relaxed and casual.

5. Not everyone who dies comes back to earth through the body of a medium. An ancestor who does decide to come back, however, makes himself or herself known to the person, typically a family member, whom the spirit has chosen as medium. People learn that they have been selected as medium in a variety of ways, for example through dreams, through physical ailments that a diviner determines are caused by the ancestor, or simply by becoming possessed.

Around seven, the mbira players sat down against the wall inside the round house and began playing, and someone picked up a pair of hosho to accompany them. One mbira player performed the basic *kushaura* (to lead) part, and the other played the *kutsinhira* (to follow), which is specially designed to interlock with the first part. Often this interlocking is done simply by playing the same pitches of the same mbira part one beat behind so that the two players consistently alternate pitches.[6] After settling in, the mbira musicians played through a number of pieces slowly and softly, almost tentatively as if they were just warming up; most people were just sitting around or talking quietly together. One woman did a few dance moves, as if in jest, as she crossed the room; otherwise the music did not draw much attention.

Around eight more people arrived, and more began to come in and sit down around the circumference of the round kitchen house, men on one side, women on the other. The mbiras and hosho were still going, and every so often a man or woman would briefly get up to dance alone in a gentle way and then sit down again. Some people were softly clapping the basic pulse with the mbira music; occasionally someone might clap a more intricate pattern; a few people sang softly with the music, almost as if they were singing to themselves; others sat silently or talked together.

Around nine-thirty the mbira players stopped and the dandanda drummers took over; it was known that the ancestor who was required at this ceremony favored dandanda music (CD track 6). More people entered the house, until it became quite crowded. The volume and power of the drums focused attention. One drummer played the basic rolling 12/8 core pattern while the other played varied patterns that interlocked with the other's ground part. A number of women picked up a single hosho. Similar to the way Conimeño panpipes are played in Peru, each woman played half of a single 12/8 pattern interlocking with the other half played by another woman. One of the women began a song loudly, and the men and women divided up to sing two parts in call and response. Each antiphonal phrase was basically twelve beats long, but the two parts were extended slightly so that they overlapped. As the song got going, others began to sing variations on the basic phrases, creating new layers of sound accompanied by additional whistles and women's ululations. The song was performed for a long time, and more people got up to dance in the center of the round house. More songs followed in close succession, and the singing, drumming,

6. Certain pieces have different kutsinhira parts that are specially composed to interlock with the first part.

hosho playing, and dancing intensified. People subtly watched the dancing woman who was the medium of the intended ancestor. As she began to show physical signs of being possessed by the spirit, people encircled her, dancing and singing with greater energy. At one point the medium stopped dancing and her body jerked as if being struck; the spirit had entered her. Others continued singing and dancing around her to heightened ululations—the room was electric.

The medium was led out of the house by an attendant as the music and dancing continued inside. After a time the medium came back into the house dressed in a black robe and carrying an ax. The music subsided, and she was guided to a mat in the center of the room, where she sat surrounded by the hosts and other elders. The host clapped his hands in greeting, welcomed the ancestor with a long speech, and then offered snuff and seven-day beer. The ancestor spoke, telling the people about certain problems that had occurred between two brothers in the family, admonishing them regarding their behavior, and instructing them how to correct it. The people listened quietly as if they were children being scolded by a parent—which was, in fact, what was happening.

When the conversation with the ancestor concluded, the drums, hosho, singing, and dancing began again, and people participated at will. Some people began going outside for air or to stand around the fire. Sometime later the medium went outside—the ancestor had left—but the rest of the people kept up with their celebration, which would go all night. Around one o'clock, the drummers took a break and the mbira players took over again. This time there was more dancing, singing, and clapping to the music. By around three a.m. some people began slipping away to their homes, but many stayed. The dancing and singing diminished as people got tired, but the musicians kept playing, and those dedicated to keeping the ceremony alive participated with clapping, singing, and dancing. Some people slept where they sat. Around five a.m., the drummers took over and the dancing and singing picked up again. The performance once again intensified gradually until dawn.

Characteristics of Shona Participatory Music Making

Many friends in Zimbabwe commented that the music and dance in ceremonies are at their absolute best between five a.m. and dawn. During this time people's energy is rekindled as dawn approaches and the end of the night's vigil is in sight. In my experience five to dawn is indeed a particularly intense time musically and in terms of the closeness felt among participants who supported each other through the long night. In participatory events, the element of time is important, as is the effort and sacrifice involved in supporting the ceremony by playing and dancing when one would rather have been home in bed.[7]

In Shona village ceremonies there are a variety of roles within a musical performance, ranging from highly skilled drummers, mbira players, singers, and dancers to neophyte singers, dancers, and people who can only clap the basic pulse. Playing the all-important hosho, or shakers, constitutes a middle ground in regard to the level of specialization required. In contrast to the Aymara of Conima, musical roles in Shona villages are determined not strictly by gender but rather by skill; on a few occasions I have seen women take over the drumming from men who were not considered to be doing well. Thus, also unlike Conima (see chapter 2), in Shona ceremonies distinctions in skill and specialization *are* articulated publicly. Someone who is not fulfilling a specialized role adequately will be more or less gently replaced by someone who can, and in fairly rapid order.

In indigenous Shona society, people have developed a tradition in which the most highly skilled drummer or mbira player can enter in and be challenged within the same performance as a neophyte who can only clap the basic pulse. The improvisatory techniques of Aymara wind players in Conima, Peru, create a similar situation in which there are spaces for different levels of expertise within the same tradition and performance (*requinteando,* see chapter 2). Conimeños, however, place less emphasis on specialization than Shona musicians do, and more emphasis on articulating egalitarian relations within performance. Nonetheless, on these issues the Shona and Aymara cases differ in degree rather than in kind. Musical practices in both places suggest that successful participatory performance should cater to different levels of competence as well as different types of musical interests. The traditions in both places provide challenges to people particularly interested in expanding their technical capabilities while simultaneously allowing easy access to people who have less investment in musical performance per se or whose interest in musical participation is primarily out of feelings of social responsibility. In both cases,

---

7. The *jerusarema* dance group I performed with actually had a song boasting about staying up all night, with a slot where the names of members who had done so would be sung. The song was typically sung during the three-to-five-a.m. period, and the names of people falling asleep at the time would be inserted to remind them of their duty to remain awake.

musical performance provides the skill-challenge balance for flow experiences at different levels of expertise.

Rather than understanding neophyte contributions to Shona performance as secondary or incidental to the 'real' music produced by the specialist mbira players or drummers, as cosmopolitans might, some friends in Zimbabwe told me that they actually thought about this the other way around. That is, the core specialists were not the stars of the situation singled out from secondary participants or audience but the ones responsible for maintaining a solid rhythmic groove and a melodic-harmonic foundation that made fuller participation both possible and enjoyable. The *real* music comes only when everyone is sonically, kinesically, and socially engaged. As in Conima, the music is a gestalt of all these things. Yet this in no way diminishes the importance of the specialist core of a Shona ceremonial performance; it simply suggests that the emphasis ultimately goes to the collective experience rather than to the individuals who make the experience possible. Indeed the skilled and knowledgeable drummers, mbira players, and hosho players are crucial to inspiring full and creative participation, because they carry the burden of laying down and maintaining the stylistic foundation upon which other contributions depend. The same is true for the core musicians in Conimeño wind ensembles.

Like much participatory music, dandanda and mbira songs are relatively short (twenty-four or forty-eight beats respectively; CD tracks 5 and 6) and are repeated with the same rhythmic feel for long periods of time. Major musical contrasts are not present, and intensity in dynamics and tempo rises and falls in a rather organic way throughout an event, depending on the needs and energy of the participants. Shona drums and hosho provide rhythmic drive for dancing, and the percussion strokes are arranged to fall slightly before and after the basic pulse. These arrangements of slightly early and late percussion attacks create a special rhythmic tension that provides power and energy for singing and dancing.[8] The hosho also create sonic density, an aura of buzzy sound around the entire performance; the bottlecaps fastened to mbira boards and resonators create the same effect. As in Aymara wind performance, textural density is created, here by vocal layering and overlap. Also similar to Aymara wind performance, unison singing will be structured in wide intonational bands (relative to cosmopolitan tuning), with some people singing slightly sharp

8. These aspects of microtiming are central to what Charles Keil refers to as "participatory discrepancies" (1987).

and others slightly flat of the median melodic line. This preference is also exhibited in the tuning of mbira: unison and octave pitches are purposefully tuned slightly off so as to create complex overtones, *beats,* which add to the density and overlapping sound. Aymara panpipes are tuned 'wide' to create precisely the same effect.

The interlocking, or *hocketing,* technique of Andean double-row panpipes is also basic to Shona music at a variety of levels. Again, *interlocking* refers to placing one's pitches or percussion strokes in the rests or unaccented spaces of other people's parts so that some type of alternation or musical dialogue occurs. The two mbira parts are designed to interlock pitches; women play half of the full hosho pattern, interlocking with their neighbors, who complete the pattern. Call-and-response singing, common in Zimbabwe and African music generally, is a type of interlocking practice at the macro level of formal organization. Interlocking also affects improvised singing at more subtle levels. Especially in mbira music, people will devise vocal and handclapping parts that will place pitches or claps in the spaces of the parts being sung or clapped around them. When I get North American audiences or classes to clap along with the music I am playing, they almost invariably join in unison on my basic accented pulses. Unison performance is certainly one way to join with others. In African (and African American) settings, however, it is just as likely that if a number of people are clapping a basic part, others will join in with interlocking parts to add rhythmic dynamism and interest. Interlocking is as deeply ingrained a habit among African and African Diaspora groups as unison is for most Euro-Americans.

The lead dandanda drummer interlocks strokes with the ground drum part, but he or she also plays off the movements of dancers. The drummer may focus on a particular dancer and play patterns that double (sound in unison with) his or her body accents. The drummer is just as likely to improvise interlocking patterns that accent the *un*accented rhythmic patterns of a dancer's body. Dancers contribute percussive parts with the slapping of their feet (some may wear leg rattles). Likewise dancers move different parts of their body simultaneously to create multiple rhythmic parts, and these may be in unison with or, alternatively, in interlocking relationships to selected drum, mbira, or vocal parts. They may interlock their own different body patterns or dance in unison or interlock with other dancers. Here it becomes clear that the arbitrary linguistic distinction in English between *music* and *dance* actually distorts the fact that they are simply different roles within the overall gestalt of a unified performance combining movement and sound.

Interlocking is important for creating feelings of intimacy, familiarity, and mutual attention among participants; it results as people closely listen to, watch, and directly respond to those around them. Both in Conima and Murehwa, a given song is performed in a highly repetitive manner for a long time. Rather than creating boredom, repetition and long duration create *opportunity* within participatory performance. Certain *ground* parts have to be sustained without much alteration to keep the music going: hosho parts, the basic dandanda drum part, the basic dandanda melody, the *kushaura* mbira part, and people clapping the basic pulse function in this way. Other people, however, add *elaboration parts* over these foundations, and it is here where the greatest dynamism occurs.

What typically happens in a bira performance is that an individual who is singing may begin to listen to the man on his right and devise a part that specifically interlocks with his. After a number of repetitions, he might start listening to a woman across the room who is singing something particularly interesting, and he devises a part that fits with what she is doing. A particular dancer may then catch this singer's eye; her body patterns may inspire yet another rhythmic-vocal line, and he will sing with her for a while. If no one else catches his attention, he may then revert to a stock melody that comes from the mbira piece that is being played, and he might focus on the sound of the mbira for a while. As this singer's attention shifts to different individuals in the room and he begins to sing with them, eye contact and gesture as well as what he is singing indicate that he has intimately joined that person; others typically reciprocate and may shift what they are doing to complement his part, and so it goes.

Through dancing, singing, handclapping, and elaboration instrumental parts, many people in the room are operating in this same way, so that throughout a long performance, people's focus will continually change and there will be a shifting kaleidoscope of different intimate relationships realized through sound and motion. Dumisani Maraire once told me that in Shona musical performance it is important to repeat the same pattern or variation for a long time and that if you change too quickly you will not get everything that the variation has to offer. Another way to interpret Dumi's remark is that if a person changes her musical part or body patterns too quickly, it will not allow others the chance to focus and lock in with her. To change the pattern soon after someone has joined you is like turning your back during a conversation. As with good social relationships, these complex musical relationships can be built only on the basis of a *security in constancy*.

When people create parts that interlock well with the parts of peo[

around them it is not only musically satisfying but also socially and spiritu-ally satisfying—it feels wonderful. A person's presence and musical contribu-tions create immediate responses from those around her. When the perfor-mance is cooking, the synchronicity in sound and motion is a confirmation, direct and unspoken, that the participant has been seen, heard, understood, and is a valued member of the group. Long performances and extended repetition offer the opportunity to connect with a number of people in this direct, unspoken way that seems to exclude any possibility of duplicity—for those moments, at least, people are truthfully intimately connected.[9] In the shifting webs of intimacy produced through attentive, energetic interlock-ing performance, the individual parts create a greater whole.

As written here, this seems like a metaphor for good social life, but *in the doing* it is not metaphoric but actual: successful participatory performance *is* good social life. In the moment, the experience is just what it feels like. After the ceremony is over, the feelings are partially remembered and help maintain or improve day-to-day relationships within the community, for a while, until the next ceremony or festival offers this potential again. Music making of this sort remains vital among Shona peasants and members of the working class who maintain indigenous religious beliefs and lifeways, but over the course of the twentieth century other modes of music making emerged in Zimbabwe within a different cultural formation.

The Rise of Cosmopolitanism and Concert Music in Zimbabwe

Missionaries established schools throughout the Zimbabwean territory to Christianize and 'civilize' the indigenous populations; access to mis-sion land, healthcare, and other inducements were initially used to attract people to the schools and church. The children who grew up on mission station land, in African purchase areas,[10] or in white households where their parents worked as domestics learned English and began to internal-

9. I would suggest that these observations about synchrony and feelings of social intimacy also pertain to team sports. Well-timed passing in basketball or soccer, for example, operates very much like musical interlocking and can create the same effects at the level of feeling.

10. Colonial Zimbabwe, known as Rhodesia, was legally divided into white and black areas, with the best agricultural land going to white settlers. As noted earlier, Africans were limited to communal reserves known as 'tribal trust lands,' but a certain amount of rural land was designated for African purchase; these areas became the domain of the African middle class, the only people with enough capital to buy land.

ize cosmopolitan ideas and lifeways—e.g., Christianity, the idea of working for wages, the value of accumulating money, styles of speaking and dressing, a taste for British food and American or British popular music, ballroom dancing, European-styled weddings, the ideas of nationhood and democracy. The dramatic nature of these new habits for Zimbabweans is evident given that they did not even use money before the white settlers arrived and did not have an indigenous word for 'nation.'

Early in the twentieth century, the influential colonialist Cecil Rhodes promised Africans that they could move up in colonial society through European-styled education and cultural attainment with his famous dictum "Equal rights for all civilized men." Mission-schooled Africans took this promise seriously. Color remained the ultimate determiner of social, economic, and political rights until 1980; during the colonial period there was a two-tiered class system, with elite Africans still being lower in the hierarchy than working-class white settlers. Social status within the African population, however, was defined in terms of the degree of education and 'civilization' obtained, which resulted in better employment as teachers, clerks, foremen, and small businessmen. Thus a new African middle class began to emerge that emphasized the attainment of cosmopolitan social style and lifeways as the basis of a distinctive class position and aspirations. Coming from African families but educated and socialized in a new way, the people who began to form the African middle class accurately felt themselves to be different from both the indigenous majority of Shona peasants and workers as well as from the white settlers who ruled the country.

The first generation of black Zimbabweans who came into close contact with white settlers learned from, and *imitated*, their mission-school teachers and employers in the hope of economic improvement. By the second and third generations, however, members of the African middle class were not simply imitating European and American lifeways but were developing cosmopolitan habits based on the models of their African parents, teachers, and neighbors and the other members of the middle class with whom they came in contact. It is with these subsequent generations that a distinctive Zimbabwean site of the capitalist cosmopolitan formation began to emerge: when the models for cosmopolitan socialization came from within the African population itself.

The African middle class developed expressive styles and cultural practices that combined habits from the different groups around them but that were sometimes distinctively their own. They spoke English with an accent blending British and local speech styles with an attention to clarity and refinement that differentiated them from bilingual peasants and workers. They attended Christian churches and went to medical doctors when they got sick, although some may still have believed in witchcraft and might have tried indigenous healers when 'Western' medicine failed. They began to value the practice of saving money for their own economic improvement and for their children, although some may still have bowed to the pressure of indigenous custom and provided for needy extended kin. European-styled weddings were preferred, and many African cosmopolitans publicly eschewed the indigenous practice of polygamy, but some continued to practice it clandestinely.

By its very nature, cosmopolitanism is eclectic, always combining cultural resources and habits from various sites within the formation, as well as unique aspects of a specific locale. The members of the African Zimbabwean cosmopolitan formation thus created unique combinations of habits that distinguished them from cosmopolitan settlers in Zimbabwe and from African peasants, as well as from other cosmopolitan sites elsewhere in the world. Yet with each subsequent generation they became more firmly a part of the broader capitalist formation as its habits became the major internally generated basis for socialization.

"Concert"

Already in the 1930s, school graduates who had moved to the urban townships in search of better employment began to develop a new urban-popular concert musical genre. In school, Africans learned to read Western music notation and were trained to sing in European-styled four-part tonal harmony. They learned to value clear diction when singing and transparent textures as well as musical arrangements that emphasized contrasts in dynamics and voicing and well-balanced closed forms (CD track 8). In school events they became accustomed to and came to value presentational performance. In the African townships around Harare (then Salisbury), the African graduates who enjoyed music formed singing groups, usually vocal quartets or quintets, initially as a recreational activity. They also began to team up with instrumentalists who learned cosmopolitan wind instruments in the Police Band or with others who had learned guitar, bass, and drums.

The "concert" style[11] that emerged combined jazz-inflected instrumen-

---

11. A few Zimbabweans that I spoke with used *concert* to refer to the middle-class tradition that I discuss here. There was no standard designation for this style, so I have adopted the term "concert" (in quotes) as a matter of convenience.

tal accompaniment (sax, trumpet, guitar and/or piano, bass, traps), with suave African American vocal styles and harmonies popularized by groups like the Mills Brothers and the Ink Spots.[12] It is striking but appropriate that "concert" performers should choose these groups as primary models. They were African American performers, but unlike the music of many other African Americans of the day, recordings of the Mills Brothers and the Ink Spots had 'crossed over' into mainstream cosmopolitan music markets. Moreover, the smooth, sophisticated musical style, mode of dress, and choreography that made them popular with cosmopolitans generally precisely matched middle-class Africans' sensibilities, musical values, and sense of themselves.

When Zimbabwean "concert" artists modeled themselves on the Mills Brothers, the Ink Spots, and jazz musicians from England, the United States, and South Africa, they were imitating the recordings of performers from other countries but *not* from another 'culture.' The styles and artists that served as the models for "concert" were part of the same cosmopolitan cultural formation of which the African middle class was also a part. This interpretation is supported by the fact that "concert" groups kept abreast of cosmopolitan musical trends and incorporated a variety of styles once they were popular within the formation. Thus performers like Portuguese-Brazilian-Hollywood star Carmen Miranda also influenced Zimbabwean "concert" performers, as did genres such as 'rumba' (the widely diffused version of the Cuban son) and cha-cha once these had become cosmopolitan mainstays. It could be argued that these artists and styles were taken up by Zimbabwean middle-class artists because they were the ones made available by the transstate recording industry, but U.S. country music (e.g., Jimmie Rodgers) and rural blues were also widely available and, in fact, were adopted by working-class itinerant guitarists in Zimbabwe but not by middle-class "concert" performers. "Concert" artists gravitated toward sophisticated or refined models that resonated with their class-based musical values and sense of themselves.

"Concert" performers such as the Bantu Actors and De Black Evening Follies (CD track 9) were specialist amateurs with solid day jobs. They performed what amounted to variety shows including comic skits, dance numbers, and popular cosmopolitan musical styles of the day in township

12. The music of the Mills Brothers and the Ink Spots might be described as smooth, light, jazzy, or swing influenced; these were the popular songs of their day. Their vocals were almost silky and impeccably arranged. A good example of the Mills Brothers is their hit from 1943, "Paper Doll."

recreation halls for silent, attentive, well-dressed middle-class audiences. The songs and choreography were either learned from foreign recordings and films or modeled on them with altered melodies and new lyrics in indigenous languages, sometimes on subjects of particular African middle-class concern (e.g., the Epworth Theatrical Strutters' song "Education Is Good"). Kenneth Mattaka, the leader of the Bantu Actors and one of the founders of the Zimbabwean "concert" tradition, compared his group with the participatory music making that went on in the rural areas: "We brought in now better singing, where we could read notes, we could read staff notation. You see, then that became the difference. . . . In those days, people used to appreciate it if you sing good songs. You know, musical, and all the parts in, and all the harmony. Educated people used to appreciate that. The *makwaya* [a rural style] was just a shouting sort of singing, different, not well composed" (quoted in Turino 2000:128). It was clear from this and other comments Mattaka made to me that he preferred the middle-class performance style and considered it superior to indigenous Shona music making.

People who attended the concerts emphasized with pride the polite, sophisticated music and atmosphere. A number of them stated that the atmosphere was so refined that "you could bring your mother-in-law." The people who had been involved with this musical tradition also emphasized that the audiences were always very polite and attentive to the performers; during performances the audience was so quiet that "you could hear a pin drop." Here is the description of one concert performer: "There was the stage, and, you the singers, the entertainers, were on stage. The audience, they sat quietly. They came dressed up in their best. People brought their wives! Their mothers-in-law!! To a concert which went on from eight o'clock to half past eleven. And it was an evening that had a lot of class" (quoted in Turino 2000:136).

The "concert" tradition represented a radical contrast with participatory music events taking place elsewhere in Zimbabwe. In bira ceremonies, people are packed together in small kitchen huts, people singing, dancing, clapping, ululating, accompanied by loud drumming and hosho; the sound and motion are dense and intense. The same rhythmic groove goes on all night. There are no artist-audience distinctions. The middle-class concerts were ideal presentational events. According to artists of the golden era of "concert" (1940s–1964), the audiences were all a performer could hope for: they were still, polite, quiet, attentive, and appreciative. For their part, the concert artists arranged their performances so that they contained a good deal of variety to keep the audiences attentive and entertained. Musical and dance numbers were alternated with comic and dramatic skits. Musical variety was also emphasized, for example alternating a Mills Brothers–style presentation with a 'Latin' number, to please audiences.

Cosmopolitan musical values, first learned in mission schools, formed the basis that guided performance (CD track 8). Mattaka emphasized the importance of reading music and careful vocal arrangements in standard European harmony. High fidelity recordings I have heard of the style document the tight vocal and instrumental arrangements, clear textures, and closed, balanced forms that middle-class Zimbabweans favored. Instrumental introductions and solos between sung verses were also used to provide contrast within a song, as is common in presentational and high fidelity popular music generally (CD track 9).

Both the musical style and the social style exhibited during the concerts closely resembled middle-class popular music and musical events elsewhere in the capitalist cosmopolitan formation during the period. Nonetheless, the humor of the comic skits, some of the themes in song texts, lyrics in local indigenous languages as well as in English, subtle aspects of the rhythms and instrumental solos, the accent of the singing, and the choreographic movement were all also distinctly Zimbabwean. Zimbabwean "concert" music and 'African jazz' can easily be distinguished from the models that come from elsewhere in the formation. Such is the nature of cosmopolitanism. Each local site of a given formation will share much in common with other sites, hence its existence *as* a formation, and yet will be distinguished by stylistic tints that characterize a given locale.

Presentational music and high fidelity recordings were introduced and adopted in Zimbabwe initially in the context of colonialism. But these fields became local modes of music making among the cosmopolitan African middle class. That is, presentational performance and listening to high fidelity recordings were 'organic' or dicent practices that emerged with the emergence of a new site of the capitalist cosmopolitan formation in Zimbabwe. I want to emphasize that when members of the middle class sang in Mills Brothers or Carmen Miranda style, or performed jazz and rumba, they were not being traitors to 'authentic' Zimbabwean culture or pretending to be something they were not. The "concert" style, and the values that guided it, authentically emerged from and expressed the cultural position of its artists and audiences; it was a dicent index of their particular sensibilities, directly affected by those sensibilities.

This important point is sometimes difficult to grasp because people habitually think of countries as having a single culture—as if *societies* and *cultures* were synonymous or coterminous. As suggested in chapter 4 and illustrated here, this is often not the case. Moreover, because of stereotypes about 'genuine' African music and 'culture,' it is sometimes difficult to grasp the idea that ballroom dancing and jazz have become authentic local practices among a certain portion of the population in places like Zimbabwe. The idea of *cosmopolitanism*—as a type of transstate cultural formation with common habits of thought and practice shared among groups of people in widely dispersed locales—explains how styles like jazz, rock, and rap can be genuinely local in a variety of places at the same time.

To this day in Zimbabwe, presentational performance and high fidelity recording exist side by side with indigenous participatory music making, although different social groups place different value on these fields. As Mattaka emphasized, "educated people" particularly value presentational music. He was specifically referring to African cosmopolitans. It was the members of this cultural formation who became the leaders of the cultural nationalist movement in Zimbabwe in the 1950s and of government after independence in 1980. Because of their own cosmopolitan dispositions, the political leaders emphasized presentational music making in party and government arts programs; because of their nationalist goals, they involved indigenous dancers and musicians in the presentational field.

Nationalism and Presentational Performance of Indigenous Dance

While "concert" and African jazz was being performed inside township recreation halls for middle-class Africans, outside in the market area of Mbare Township burial societies and other working-class regional associations gathered on Sundays and during evenings to perform the indigenous dance-drumming traditions that came from their rural homes.[13] These participatory music-dance events were held for recreational and social reasons in the townships, much as music making and dance were experienced at home. During the 1959 to 1963 period, however, these migrant groups became involved in presentational stage performance within the context of a cultural nationalist movement designed to unite the different regions of the country within a new nation.

The colonial territory that became Zimbabwe is inhabited by a variety of social groups, each with its own dialect or language and its own

13. This township for housing African workers is located just outside the capital city and was known as Harare during the colonial period. The township was renamed Mbare after 1980, just as the capital was renamed Harare.

instruments and dance-drumming traditions. The Korekore populate a broad band across the north; the Zezuru live in the central region surrounding what became Harare; the Karanga live in the south-central area; the Manyika are located in the central-eastern region; the Ndau inhabit southeastern Zimbabwe. These are all considered subgroups of the Shona. The Kalanga, located southwest of Bulawayo, Zimbabwe's second largest city, are sometimes classified as a Shona group, whereas the Ndebele are the main non-Shona group; they are located around Bulawayo.[14]

Because Africans who migrated to Harare for jobs could not own residences, they were 'temporarily' housed in the black townships surrounding the city. Once there they began to associate with others from their rural home regions, at first informally and then by forming burial societies and regional associations.[15] As a primary social activity, members of these organizations would perform the dance-drumming traditions originating in their rural homes in the open market area of Mbare Township during times of leisure. Whereas formerly these dances were largely restricted to, and only known in, their original rural locations, through migrant performance in Mbare they became more widely indexical of their regions and the social groups that performed them. The militaristic dance-drumming tradition *muchongoyo* was performed by Ndau migrants from southeastern Zimbabwe. The Zezuru became associated with mbira music and dance as well as recreational *shangara* dance drumming. Karanga migrants performed and became known for their fast foot-tapping line dance known as *mbakumba,* the Korekore became known for *dhinhe,* and the Murehwa area for the playful *jerusarema* dance-drumming tradition.[16]

When the colonial government's African-Service Radio began recording single-disc issues of indigenous music for broadcast after the mid-1950s, it was often these migrant associations that they recorded—located near the radio studios in Harare, they were the groups and traditions easiest to find and record.[17] The migrant associations and burial societies that recorded typically included the region in their name, e.g., the Murehwa Jerusarema

14. Ndebele speakers represent a significantly different indigenous African cultural formation in Zimbabwe. I did not conduct research among this group, however, so my discussion is basically Shona-centric.

15. Burial societies were like grassroots insurance organizations. Collective dues were used to pay for the transport of deceased members back to their rural homes and for funerals.

16. See Turino 2000:68–77 for fuller descriptions of these dances.

17. Some recording was also done by mobile units in the rural areas.

Club and Burial Society. Radio play of these high fidelity recordings further spread and cemented the indexical associations of a given region or social group with their performance traditions among Zimbabweans generally. As mentioned in chapter 1, the mass media often create 'mass indices'—indexical signs that are similarly interpreted by many people, in this case because of common associations through radio broadcasts.

While the creation of mass indices is actually the goal of advertisers and political propagandists, with the African-Service Radio recordings it was simply a byproduct of the colonial state's real agenda—attracting the different African groups to tune in to, and stay tuned to, government-controlled programming. Truly, the white Rhodesian settlers must have felt their privileged way of life threatened from various sides during the post–World War II era. The war against Hitler's racism and imperialism led people in the Allied countries to recognize and question these problems in their own societies; this recognition spawned more liberal attitudes, which aided nationalist movements in British colonies as well as the rise of the civil rights movement in the United States (chapter 7). At the same time, the cold war was raging, and the Rhodesian government was particularly concerned that 'our Africans' not tune in to Radio Moscow or some other source of 'communist propaganda.'

By the mid-1950s, members of the African middle class had become frustrated with their attempts at upward social mobility within colonial society through their attainment of education and 'civilization' (Rhodes's promise). In the post–World War II era, nationalist movements were arising all over Africa. Zimbabwean cosmopolitans likewise turned to a nationalist strategy and began demanding voting and equal economic rights. Within the modernist cosmopolitan formation during that period, political legitimacy was often conceptualized in terms of 'national' popular sovereignty. That is, according to widely held nationalist ideas, each identifiable sociocultural group—each 'nation'—had a right to its own territory and government (chapter 4). As in many African countries, the problem was that a single, unified 'nation' did not exist in the Zimbabwean territory; rather there were a number of semi-autonomous social groups within the county's boundaries that had been created by colonialism. By the logic of nationalist discourse, each of these groups—the Korekore, Zezuru, Karanga, etc.—could have claimed 'national' status, but the cosmopolitan leadership chose to adopt the colonial boundaries to define their country. Thus Zimbabwean nationalists had two tasks before them if they were to arrive as a legitimate nation-state: they had to gain control of their own state, but they also had to unify the different groups in order to create a nation to go with it. The processes of creating and/or maintaining 'national' identification and sentiment are frequently referred to as *cultural nationalism*, and it is in the 'nation building' aspect of nationalist movements that music and dance often play a prominent role.

A number of eyewitness accounts suggest that it was only after Robert Mugabe returned from Ghana in 1960 and became publicity secretary of the budding National Democratic Party (NDP) that cultural nationalist programs were initiated. President Kwame Nkrumah had invited literate Africans to Ghana to teach, work, and learn about that country's recently successful nationalist movement. It was in Ghana that Mugabe began to understand colonialism in Marxist terms and learned that nationalist movements needed broad-based popular support to succeed. Nathan Shamuyarira, a committed nationalist and observer at that time, noted

> The NDP added one important factor that had been singularly missing in Rhodesian nationalism: *emotion*. Nationalism is basically emotional, and has to be to succeed. At times—particularly in early years—*it should be blind and blinkered* if it is to establish its principles. . . .
>
> The work of building emotional appeal was left to the NDP, particularly one of its able new officers, Robert G. Mugabe. . . .
>
> Thudding drums, ululation by women dressed in national costumes, and ancestral prayers began to feature at meetings more prominently than before. (1965:67–68, my emphasis)

I interpret this emphasis on emotion in combination with the comment about nationalism's needing to be "blind and blinkered" as a suggestion that the leaders should minimalize symbolic, propositional language about the movement, which would raise questions and engender debate. This, in fact, is precisely what the nationalist leaders did; they emphasized indexical signs—thudding drums, national costumes, ancestral prayers—intended to make people *feel* that they belonged without inspiring symbolic analysis of what and whom they were joining up with (see Turino 2000:184–86).

Under Mugabe's direction, the NDP and, after it was banned, the subsequent nationalist party, Zimbabwe African People's Union (ZAPU), held numerous mass rallies in the townships around Harare. Stages were erected, and party officials were introduced to the masses with short speeches about the party, the movement, and the Zimbabwean *nation*, but significantly, the main activities at these rallies involved music and dance. Indigenous dance groups—usually the migrant associations near at hand—performed jerusarema, muchongoyo, mbakuma, shangara, and mbira music, among other traditions. Each of these dances indexed and was meant to appeal to the people from those regions.

The same groups were juxtaposed onstage repetitively, rally after rally, such that new indexical associations began to form in people's minds. As suggested in chapter 1, one of the potentials of indexical signs is that they can have a *semantic snowballing* component; they can collect new associational meanings while retaining earlier associations. Thus, in addition to being indices of their original regions, the various indigenous dances began to be associated with each other as a canon of 'traditional Zimbabwean dance,' and they came to be indexically linked to the party and the 'Zimbabwean nation' through the short speeches inserted between performances at the rallies. In addition to the indigenous dances, "concert" performers such as the Cool Four and De Black Evening Follies, as well as guitar bands, were featured in the rallies to appeal to, and index, urban cosmopolitans. African middle-class journalists covering these rallies noted that the performances combined "the new and the old," the 'traditional' and the 'modern,' and this was precisely the image of the new nation that the leaders intended (e.g., see Supiya 1962:8).

The nationalist leaders had been socialized within the cosmopolitan formation and had grown up with the concept of *nation.* Their problem, however, was how to create a perceivable model of this abstract concept for the bulk of a population that had not internalized the idea of this type of identity. The rallies were specifically designed to be experiential models of what the *possible* Zimbabwean nation would be—would look, sound, and feel like. Using preexisting music/dance indices of the different social groups and regions as well as linguistic signs, the semiotic equation is something like this:

The rallies =
> Korekore index + Zezuru index + Ndau index + Murehwa index + Karanga index + cosmopolitan music indices + 'ZAPU' (linguistic index for the party) + leaders (indices of the party) + symbols *about* the party and 'Zimbabwean nation'
> = an icon *of* the unified, collective, 'traditional but modern' nation

Notice that different sign types played specific roles in the creation of 'rally-as-icon-of-the-nation.' Music-dance indices signified and concretely linked people to their original regions or to modernist cosmopolitanism; in this regard, the "reality function" of indexical signs was important. As indexical signs, the performance traditions were also *metonymic, the part standing for the whole. The symbols *about* the nation and party, delivered in brief speeches, were necessary to recontextualize the regional and cosmopolitan indices as signs connected to the ideas of party and nation. That is, the symbols were necessary to create the *general* context for (re)interpreting the other signs and these events as a whole. With all these semiotic elements put together, the rallies were meant to function as icons, in that they were intended to create an overall image of what the as yet nonexistent nation would be.

Because belonging to a 'nation' is a subjective condition, the symbol has to be imbued with emotion to get people to invest in the new identity unit, as Shamuyarira observed. Although *presentational* stage performances constituted the central rally activity, these events typically ended with a mass *participatory* singing of what would become the national anthem, "God Bless Africa," and with mass chanting of slogans such as "ZAPU, ZAPU, Freedom!" The presentational activities were designed and controlled to create an icon of the *possible* nation, and the participatory activities were meant to arouse emotional investment in the idea as experiential fact. Eyewitness Shamuyaririra concludes: "The whole square was a sea of some 15,000 to 20,000 cheering and cheerful black faces. The emotional impact of such gatherings went far beyond claiming to rule the country— it was an ordinary man's participation in creating something new, a new nation" (1965:68). Imagine the experience of singing or chanting in sync with twenty thousand other people; the emotional effect of social bonding must have been powerful indeed.

The Rise of Indigenous Guitar-Band Music

Years of government repression after 1963 led to a banning of the nationalist parties and the rallies. War between the Rhodesian state and the armies of the two major nationalist parties (ZAPU and ZANU) followed, and mass nationalist events would not be held again until African majority rule and independence were established in 1980. Nonetheless, the seeds of cultural nationalism had been sown, and this led to a new interest in indigenous Shona music and dance *among African cosmopolitans* who largely resided in urban areas. It should be remembered that many indigenous communities had never lost interest in their own practices, and thus for them such processes of 'renewal' and 'cultural renaissance' were largely irrelevant.[18] But among young African urbanites, cultural nationalism helped create new habits of thought and taste. They learned to value selected indices of Shona lifeways as a part of a new type of local cosmopolitan subjectivity that, according to an explicit nationalist discourse, should blend the 'best' aspects of local indigenous lifeways with the 'best of the modern.' Precisely mirroring this emerging subject position, during the 1960s and 1970s new uniquely Zimbabwean styles of music were created fusing indigenous genres, such as drumming and mbira music, with cosmopolitan 'rock' instruments such as electric guitars, bass, keyboards, and drum kit.

The rise of musical professionalism and a quest for stylistic originality was the other primary influence that led to the creation of this unique Zimbabwean guitar-band style. In 1957, the colonial liquor laws that had prohibited Africans from buying cosmopolitan types of alcohol (whisky, gin, bottled beer, etc.) were liberalized. This led to the opening of nightclubs where African guitar bands were hired, sometimes for extended engagements. In 1959 the first Zimbabwean record company went into business; by the 1970s, a relatively healthy capitalist recording industry was selling an array of high fidelity recordings of popular local electric-guitar bands. To compete effectively, groups began to experiment with a variety of different styles to see which would hit with audiences and the record-buying public. Thomas Mapfumo, one of the founders of the indigenous-based electric style, once told me that the combination of indigenous genres with 'modern' instruments was effective because it appealed to the greatest number of people. The electric instrumentation, he said, attracted young urbanites, while the indigenous musical base appealed to older people and rural people—it had something for everyone. Beginning in a rock-cover band, Mapfumo went on to specialize in indigenous-based guitar-band music and became one of Zimbabwe's most successful musicians.

The combination of nightclubs and a new recording industry—in conjunction with the cosmopolitan rock boom of the 1960s and journalistic tales of fabulous rock-star wealth abroad—inspired young Zimbabweans to consider professional careers in music in substantial numbers for the first time in the country's history. The ideas of musical *activity* as a career and as a salable commodity instigated revolutionary changes in the very conceptions of what music is and is about. The idea of musical/dance pro-

---

18. Nationalist party documents frequently referred to their cultural programs as inspiring 'cultural renaissance,' 'renewal,' and 'revival.'

fessionalism was also supported by government initiatives during both the colonial and postindependence periods.

The National Dance Company

Soon after independence, the Zimbabwean Ministry of Education and Culture established the National Dance Company (NDC). The official goals for the company were to "revive, *develop*, and promote the traditional dance and music of Zimbabwe," to develop an appreciation for the aesthetic contributions of Africa to world dance, and to serve as an ambassador of culture in international and national arenas (Welsh-Asante 1993:241, my emphasis; Turino 2000:321). Modeled on similar nationalist—'folkloric'—dance companies in many countries in and beyond Africa (e.g., Mexico's Ballet Folklórico), the company was a product of modernist-cosmopolitan thinking. Aimed at international and national arenas, the performances were shaped for cosmopolitan audiences. The goal to "revive" indigenous dance came directly out of nationalist discourse and a broader modernist discourse asserting that 'the traditional' had declined due to colonialism and modernity—in spite of the fact that these dances were still going strong in rural villages and in the townships. But it is the goal of 'developing' indigenous dances that I want to concentrate on here. Under the guidance of cosmopolitan artistic directors, 'development' most basically meant the transformation of *participatory* traditions into fixed *presentational* forms specifically arranged for nonparticipating audiences.[19]

The Ministry of Education and Culture arranged for foreign experts Peggy Harper of Britain and African American dancer, choreographer, and scholar Kariamu Welsh-Asante to direct the company along with Zimbabwean Shesby Matiure, who was a music-dance expert trained at Kwanongoma College in Bulawayo. The directors of the company chose 'master teacher-performers' for each of the regional dances. Each master taught his regional dance to the other teachers and then to a troupe of younger dancers who were selected for the company through formal auditions.

19. The muchongoyo dance is the exception to this statement. Unlike dances to mbira music, or the shangara, mbakumba, dhine, dandanda, and jerusarema dances, muchongoyo was a presentational tradition to begin with. That is, while the young men of an Ndau village can choose to learn and participate in this dance, when it was and is performed in village settings it involves highly controlled choreography that is performed for an audience of onlookers. The other traditions that were taken up by the NDC have the looser quality of participatory social dancing.

Subsidized by the government, these dancers became the first full-time professionals in the indigenous dance field in Zimbabwe; other professional companies were later spawned from the NDC.

This professional, highly rehearsed ensemble took up the national canon of indigenous dances and music that had been established in the rallies of early 1960s—shangara, mbakumba, dhinhe, muchongoyo, jerusarema, mbira—and the company also presented choral music. The original selection of the canon in the early 1960s had largely been based on criteria of regional representation and convenience; these were the traditions performed by regional migrant groups in the townships, and the 'master teachers' were often from these same ensembles. As just discussed, the initial process of shifting the indexical associations of these dances from region to 'nation' was through the repeated juxtaposition of the different migrant groups on rally stages. With the NDC, however, the indexical shift from region to 'nation' was fortified in that, for the first time, the same troupe of performers did all the representative dances and labeled them 'national'—these indexical signs of regional and cultural diversity were not only united within the same events but now also united within the same bodies of the dancers.

Whereas in participatory events one or two dances and rhythmic grooves will be performed all night, Welsh-Asante designed the NDC stage performances to provide dynamic contrasts. To judge from the printed programs, a typical performance began gently with "Mbira dance" and then developed in intensity with shangara, dhinhe, and mbakumba to the intermission. The second half again began gently with a choral selection. This might be followed with one of Welsh-Asante's own pieces such as "Earth Movers," set to the music of Quincy Jones, or "Wonder's Suite," which was a jazz suite inspired by the music of Stevie Wonder. At this point a musical selection on mbira was used to create a pause before the energetic finale of muchongoyo and jerusarema. The inclusion of Welsh-Asante's own compositions among the indigenous dance numbers projected combined images of the 'traditional' and the 'modern' in ways similar to the 1960s nationalist rallies.

The artistic directors of the NDC stressed high specialization and professionalism, and as Deputy Minister of Culture Stephen Chifunyise remarked, Welsh-Asante had "done a commendable job of organizing and restructuring these traditional dances for the concert stage" (personal communication, quoted in Turino 2000:325). Emmanuel Ribiero, who worked with the company between 1982 and 1990, however, had a different goal in mind. He argued that the company's performances should remain true to

FIGURE 5.1 Jerusarema dancers in a beer hall in Mbare Township.

the original style as done in the villages where the dances came from. Ribiero told me that the emphasis on stagework, showmanship, and 'artistic development,' as well as the fact that the group was not rooted in any given locale, led to major changes in the dances to the point where local people sometimes rejected the NDC versions of *their* dances (Turino 2000:326). The NDC's version of jerusarema is a good case in point.

Jerusarema is a playful recreational dance from the Murehwa District (fig. 5.1). It is accompanied by a drummer playing two tall differently pitched drums, and by hosho. The men stand on one side of a circle playing a hallmark rhythm with wooden clappers while singing and yodeling. The women stand in the opposite semicircle moving gently to the music. Then taking turns at will, one or more pairs of male and female dancers enter the center of the circle to dance. The music and dance are arranged in alternating "on" and "off" sections, eight beats each. The men play the clappers and the drums intensify with patterns that mirror the dancers' movements in the "on" sections. In the "off" sections the drummer plays a quiet holding pattern and the woodblocks are silent (CD track 10).

During the "off" sections, the men and women who have entered the center as partners face each other, doing a gentle step to the music as if resting. For the "on" sections, individual dancers do a variety of formulaic moves associated with this dance or may invent playful movements that mime certain things going on in the celebration. For example, one time at a *guva* (grave ceremony) two dancers went into the center and pretended to dig a grave, and one lay down in it in a humorous way; at a school graduation party, one of the dancers mimed someone reading and writing, to the delight of the other participants. Among the most standard formulaic moves during "on" sections, men face their partners squatting down low with one knee bent forward while the other leg moves in and out behind the dancer; the arms do a kind of breaststroke motion. This choreography mimes the movement of a field mouse through tall grass, which explains an alternative name for the dance, *mbende* (field mouse). Often during the "on" sections, the men and women in the circle approach and retreat from each other with a variety of subtle rhythmic body gestures directed at the partner. Sometimes, as a joke, the man and woman might execute a very subtle pelvic thrust toward the other, but the members of the jerusarema burial society that I joined emphasized that this movement should be done only "late at night after the children have gone to bed." Publicly modest, my friends from Murehwa felt that this "off-color" joke was usually inappropriate.

Jerusarema was often used as the finale for NDC performances because of its exciting music and lively character. In the NDC version, the spontaneous, improvisatory character of the dance and the repertoire of moves were greatly reduced. Dancers "went in" in set pairs and a set order. The field mouse movement became a centerpiece of the choreography, and, strikingly, the "on" sections were repeatedly punctuated with a dramatic pelvic thrust between the male and female dancers. When I asked Patrick Nyandoro, one of the original members of the Murehwa Jerusarema Club and Burial Society, about the NDC version of his dance, the following conversation ensued:

NYANDORO: They can do it, but they don't do it to detail. That group, they can just pretend to show the people it is like this, but that's not it.

TURINO: What are some of the differences?

NYANDORO: The difference is that playing [with] your own group, you know how to do it. Yes. You see, like those who were in the National Dance Company, jerusarema, [they were] doing it so very badly, it is not how we play it. They just come together [gesturing the pelvic thrust], that's not it.

TURINO: You mean when the man and woman . . .

NYANDORO: Yes, that's not it. It shows something that is not so good to the people. You can play there, a woman and a man. We dance together, but we don't show [that motion]. You do your styles, and she does her styles, you finish together. (interview 1992)

It is not hard to understand why this sexual move became a centerpiece of the NDC version. It creates excitement—it is good show business—and it fits stereotypic images of sexualized African dances just as muchongoyo fits cosmopolitan stereotypes of African warriors. What upset my friends from Murehwa most, however, was that as part of their duties during the 1980s, NDC dancers taught their versions of the 'national dances' to schoolchildren to promote the canon in different parts of the country. I myself found it startling to see young boys and girls execute a dramatic pelvic thrust toward each other when they danced jerusarema. People from Murehwa felt even more strongly that *their* dance and, by indexical extension, they themselves were being misrepresented in a way they found disturbing.

The NDC performed for visiting dignitaries and on foreign tours for other cosmopolitans around the world. During the 1980s, the NDC also performed in state-sponsored festivals and on TV, and in conjunction with their work in the public schools, they diffused their choreography as the 'official' versions of the dances. Given the original goal of 'preserving' indigenous dances, it is significant that the artistic directors, with the exception of Ribiero, did not attempt to maintain the playful, more spontaneous ethos of the original participatory traditions. There is no malice in this. Due to deeply socialized habits of thought and value, most cultural groups feel that their own lifeways are the best, most logical, most 'commonsensical' way to proceed. For the African middle-class leaders and the cosmopolitan 'experts' directing the NDC, hiring and training professional dancers who could consistently render preplanned, controlled choreography that would be effective for presentational performances simply made sense given the cosmopolitan audiences they had in mind. The only problem is when one social group has more power and resources at its disposal to influence the public representations and habits of other groups.[20] This occurred in Zimbabwe between the white settlers and the African population during the colonial period, and similarly between the cosmopolitan African leadership and 'the masses' after 1980, as the jerusarema example indicates.

Meanwhile, peasants and working-class people who maintain indigenous religious beliefs and lifeways still value participatory music making

20. *Identity politics* or the politics of representation was introduced in chapter 4 and returns as a fundamental issue in chapter 7.

and styles most highly—necessary for bringing ancestors into ceremonies, necessary for community bonding, necessary for individual catharsis and fun. In spite of the diffusion of the NDC's version of jerusarema, the Murehwa burial society still performs its version every Sunday afternoon as a social activity in Mbare Township, as it has done since the early 1950s. The same individuals, however, might participate in jerusarema or in a bira one week and go to a government-sponsored music-dance festival where indigenous traditions are performed onstage in a presentational manner the next. They might also participate in a bira one weekend and the next weekend go to a nightclub where guitar bands perform arrangements of mbira and jerusarema music onstage for participatory dancing. By now everyone is listening to many local indigenous and cosmopolitan styles on the radio and high fidelity recordings—mbira, gospel, rap, country, rock, guitar-band renditions of mbira and dance-drumming music, Zimbabwean versions of rumba, among many other styles. In terms of styles, performance contexts, and modes of engagement, Zimbabweans have many more musical resources now than they did in the late nineteenth century. This is all to the good as long as all fields continue to be equally valued and available for the contributions they can make to social life.

6 Old-Time Music and Dance
Cohorts and Cultural Formations

I was in a jug band in suburban northern New Jersey during high school in the 1960s. We got together weekly in my basement for what ultimately amounted to a party. I played guitar and a four-string banjo tuned like the high strings of a guitar. There might have been another guitar player, but most of the friends who came played found percussion instruments like washboard, spoons, and pots, as well as kazoos and a washtub bass that we made. Jay blew bass lines on the jug. We all sang. I remember performing for a couple of high school events, although I don't remember the reaction. There were some big-name jug bands we admired, like Jim Kweskin's, performing in Greenwich Village nightclubs and on records, but we never thought about making it ourselves. Our band was simply about getting together in my basement; it was just something to do.

The mainstream 'folk revival' that began in the late 1950s in the United States had multiple causes and effects and antecedents dating back to the late nineteenth century. It led to a new star system including the likes of the Kingston Trio, Peter, Paul, and Mary, Joan Baez, and the early Bob Dylan, who were involved with presentational and high fidelity music making. It also created new fans and practitioners for genres like singer-songwriter, old-time string band music, bluegrass, and acoustic blues. But perhaps one of the most pervasive effects was that it led to *participatory* music making all over the country—groups like our basement jug band. Seeped in its own, in many ways troubling, romanticism of the past and of America's own exotics (Appalachians, African Americans), the great folk scare of the 1960s still had many important positive effects. Especially for those of us growing up in suburban America of the 1950s and 1960s there was a vaguely felt need to connect—with place, a past, and other people.

The term *folk revival* is curious because it was not really so much a revival of something that had died as it was an *adoption* of certain musical influences, styles, and imagery by urban and suburban middle-class Americans from other social groups and regions— especially rural and working-class southerners and African Americans. The movement represented more of a transference than a revival. *Folk revival,* like the term *folk* itself, suggests a particular discursive construction of these groups by people who are outside the groups in question. The discourse that brings the idea of 'the folk' into existence is historically tied to nationalist projects, and more broadly to the discourse of modernity, which needs the concepts of 'folk' and 'traditional' to stand in binary contrast to the conception of 'modern' as a cultural category; that is, we understand 'modern culture' only in relation to what it is not—the 'folk' and 'traditional.' As Foucault suggested, *discourses*—systems of premises and concepts that shape thinking about a certain realm—bring their own terms into existence and are sustained by the commonsense adoption of those terms. The symbols *folk* and *traditional,* as currently understood, make sense only in relation to the broader premises of the discourse of modernity.[1] Because of the prevalence of this discourse within the capitalist cosmopolitan formation, middle-class 'folkies' are attracted to the 'folk' and 'folk music' because they represent an idealized alternative to modernist, capitalist lifeways and society.

At the beginning of the twentieth century, 60 percent of the population in the United States lived in or around locations with fewer than 2,500 inhabitants, and most were involved with farming; by 2000 52 percent of Americans lived in suburbs (Caplow, Hicks, and Wattenberg 2001). As compared with both rural towns and urban neighborhoods, suburbs were curious, socially diffuse places. When I was a child in the 1950s, the only adult I ever saw walking the roads of our town, outside the shopping center, was a man who was considered with some suspicion to be "an artist" and an eccentric. True, our town was formerly a rural truck-farming area turned bedroom community and was spread out. But it is not overstating the case to say that, as far as our adult role models were concerned, life

1. In chapter 1 it was explained that because the sign-object relations of symbols are established through other symbols (words), the strongest indexical associations with a given symbol are the other words of its definition or, in this case, the broader linguistic context of the discourse.

was compartmentalized in private homes, cars, classrooms, and stores; most *real* men mysteriously left town every day to work in New York. An adult male walking the roads on a weekday was an oddity and was suspect. Many suburbs still have this compartmentalized, car-dependent quality (see Kunstler 1993).

For those of us already interested in making music in grammar school, rock 'n' roll was the option of choice. Garage-band three-chord wonders like the Kingsmen's "Louie Louie" were encouraging, but stars such as the Beatles, the Stones, and the Jefferson Airplane seemed so big and so far from anything we could hope to do. Then there were Pete Seeger and Bob Dylan. They were also big, and were powerful examples because of their success. I still remember the first time I heard Dylan: I was on the back porch listening to records with my older sister Susanne. At the time I wasn't cognizant of his verbal or stylistic prowess; all I could think was "If he can sing like that and actually make records, then I can sing too. Hell, I can sing better than *that!*" It was very liberating. With the exception of Baez, Peter, Paul, and Mary, and few others, the aesthetics of the 'folk revival' actually celebrated everyman voices and instrumental abilities; many of the songs were easy to learn and play. Pete Seeger had been trying to wrestle singing and playing away from the professionals for years in a country where great importance is placed on specialization and professionalism. Through a lifetime of tireless effort he, and others who followed, succeeded in opening up a variety of musical scenes that have enriched many people's lives—I count myself, my son, and many of our friends who play old-time string band music among them.

In fundamental ways, the mainstream 'folk revival' was a result of a mainstream need to make music without pressured comparison to the stars—to have music back for connecting with places, a past, and other people, with *home,* however it is conceived. Music is certainly not the only way that people can do this, but *participatory* music and dance have special qualities and characteristics for creating solid feelings of community and identity. Sounding together articulates and realizes a special way of being together, and the style of particular sounds—whether rap, punk, country, or old-time—carries specific indexical meanings that further define the nature and identity of the community being brought forth through performance. Participatory music-dance traditions exist the world over, and this suggests that they fulfill some basic human needs and desires. The 'folk revival' suggests that in times and places where such traditions don't easily exist, as in suburban America of the 1960s, people will find a way back to participatory music making even if, as in our case, it was initially through presentational and high fidelity models.[2]

People growing up in Shona and Aymara villages hear the music used at festivals and ceremonies and are danced on their mother's back before they can walk. The events in which they experience music and dance are often among the most exciting, significant, and pleasurable times of their lives, and these associations grow richer and richer with the passing of years. By the time people actively begin participating in music and dance, they already have established habits of movement, rhythmic sense, vocal production, and an implicit understanding of how to perform. The basis for achieving synchrony in performance is already set through common experience and socialization from the time they are babies. People growing up in cultural formations where participatory music and dance are at the center of social life are socialized to participate competently. This is nurture, not nature, at work.

The same is probably true for North American children growing up in dedicated Christian families that attend musical churches each week. In the United States there are many other similar instances where children are deeply socialized with particular styles of music integrally wedded to ceremonies and events that bond the particular community. Ellen Koskoff (2001), for example, describes vibrant music making in the Lubavitcher Hasidim community of Brooklyn. Children who grow up in families involved with Cajun music in Louisiana have ample opportunities to participate in music and dance within community settings on a frequent basis, as do Texas-Mexicans, among whom weddings, anniversaries, and major birthdays are celebrated with community-specific music and dance styles—mariachi, conjunto, polka—involving children at a young age.

Many middle-class Euro-Americans in the suburbs, however, do not grow up with strong communal music making and dance experiences in community settings or in the home. School, especially in the early years, is a common context for music making, but unfortunately this does not prove to be a compelling experience for many kids. Positive musical associations grow up largely around commercially produced popular music

---

2. I first became involved with the 'folk revival' in primary school through a friend's older brother, Clem Bianchi, who played in a Kingston Trio–type ensemble. Here I am largely offering a personal interpretation of the phenomenon as it affected me. There is a large literature on U.S. folk revivals. For a variety of historical views see Denisoff 1971, De Turk and Poulin 1967, Klein 1980, Whistnat 1983, Lieberman 1989, Rosenberg 1993, Filene 2000.

styles. These styles, and the artists who perform them, can certainly be important to individual identities and bond groups of friends, especially during the teenage years. They also serve as models for the multitude of teenage rock bands that exist in almost every town in the country. But the processes of early musical socialization are not tied to actual music making in the commercial popular styles that are significant to the children, nor are they tied to significant occasions that socialize the children to make music with adults within broader communities.

As humorously depicted by Steve Martin in the opening of his movie *The Jerk,* there is a stereotype that white Americans don't have any rhythm, any soul, or even any 'ethnicity'—"white men can't jump." In a literal sense, this stereotype is as erroneous as the one that holds that dark skin is tied to natural rhythm as some type of genetic endowment. The fact is that many children growing up in middle-class white suburbs simply do not have the same opportunities that Shona and Aymara village children do for early music and dance socialization within deeply meaningful communal events. I think some people growing up in white suburban America in the 1950s and 1960s at least intuitively felt this lack. The 'folk revival' was one response to a need for participatory music making and dance and for emblems that would tie individuals to the idea of community and to what was deeply and alternatively American. For my part, I remember that my initial attraction to the five-string banjo at an early age was the result of my conscious belief that it was *the* American Instrument (Gura and Bollman 1999). I was looking for something, and I wasn't alone.

Cultural Cohorts, Cultural Formations, and the Idea of Authenticity

Square and contra dancing accompanied by old-time string band music, or at least fiddle-driven music, is still performed on a regular basis in communities throughout North America. I would distinguish between two types of settings. In regions as diverse as upstate New York, southern Missouri, the southeastern United States, and Cape Breton, Canada, I have experienced dances attended by local, rural people; these events and music are simply part of the community's social life over time. The second type of setting, one in which I have participated in Brattleboro, Vermont; Austin, Texas; and the Midwest circuit of Illinois, Indiana, Ohio, and the St. Louis area, involves white middle-class participants, often of urban or suburban extraction; these dance-music scenes originally were influenced by the 'folk revival.' The adults currently involved with the 'revivalist' setting typically did not grow up with old-time music and dance as a basic part of community life; they came to it on their own because of an attraction to the style as well as the imagery and the participatory ethics that surround it. They also are often not originally from the places they find themselves dancing in.

The basic distinction between these two types of settings hinges on whether the music and dance are normal and long-standing features of the community or regional cultural formation or whether they are the basis for the creation of a cultural cohort (chapter 4). The difference is fundamental. In the first type of setting mentioned, the dances are part of a broader community cultural formation, and the people within that formation would interact in various ways even if the dances didn't exist. In these situations, people grow up with the music and dance styles, and the habits needed to perform them in culturally appropriate ways are formed at an early age, such that there tends to be little self-consciousness about performance and creative license. In places where music and dance styles are part of the broader formation, there is coherence between the values guiding performance and the general patterns and values of social life. As mentioned in chapter 2, Aymara musical ensembles and the sounds they create grow out of and articulate more general patterns of egalitarian social relations. Likewise, when old-time is a normal part of community life, attitudes about gender roles, religion, and social etiquette that guide everyday life will inform attitudes, behavior, and style at rural community square dances.[3] As in Shona and Aymara villages, a child growing up with old-time music and dance as part of the cultural formation will have different types of longer-standing indexical associations with performance—home, family, neighbors, first experiences courting, etc.—from those of the first-generation members of a revivalist-inspired cohort.

In the middle-class scenes, old-time music and dance are the basis of a cultural cohort that comes together for those activities; the 'contra dance community,' as people like to call it, is mainly a community in relation to the dance and music. This is not an "imagined community," to use

3. In such places, the music and dance styles will probably not be referred to as 'old-time,' but for the sake of convenience I will use this term for the comparison of the two types of settings. In some rural communities in southern Missouri and North Carolina, the style and terminology have shifted toward bluegrass.

Benedict Anderson's (1983) celebrated phrase; it is an intentional interest group that forms around particular activities, a particular style complex, as well as a particular discourse about the style and activity which, in this case, involves notions of 'folk' community and 'traditional' Americanness. For many middle-class participants, dance events stand in stark contrast to their everyday lives (e.g., as computer programmers, teachers, office workers) and social networks. Moreover, as I illustrate below, the style of interaction and values of the middle-class old-time cohort stand in stark opposition to basic tenets of the capitalist cultural formation which prominently influenced participants' socialization. Within given individuals, the tensions between the habits of the capitalist formation and the habits of the intentional cohort lead to interesting dynamics and, sometimes, paradoxes. Yet the importance of the old-time cohort for many of its members is precisely that it provides a temporary alternative to the values and lifeways of the 'modern' capitalist formation.

The same dedicated members of the cohort travel for miles from Indiana, Illinois, Missouri, Ohio, to attend dance weekends held annually in different locations, which are a special time-out-of-time and an opportunity to experience flow and join with likeminded people. During the weekends, or even at the local regular dances, the community isn't imagined but actual; nonetheless, it is sporadic, temporary, and geographically diffuse. For many, middle-class contra dance and old-time music scenes are enveloped in their own ideologies of purity and authenticity that are drawn from revivalist and folkloristic discourses about the 'folk.' These attendant ideas are part of the attraction but paradoxically define core middle-class cosmopolitan participants as outsiders to the *real* 'folk' tradition, and thus sometimes create an odd wannabe or purist self-consciousness. Because I use an electric pickup on my banjo at dances I have sometimes been scolded: "That's not the old-timey way" (why are microphones more authentic?). My response to such quagmires is simply to consider middle-class scenes (weekly local dances, dance weekends, old-time festivals like Cliff Top) as part of a unique and separate tradition with its own evolving values, practices, styles, and participants.

Thus, in contrasting the settings where old-time is a basic part of a community formation as opposed to being a cohort I am not suggesting that one is more *authentic* than the other. The styles, practices, and values in both types of settings can be dicent articulations of the distinct cultural positions of participants and thus equally authentic. As suggested in chapter 1, given practices that serve as signs of identity may be understood as authentic when they are the result of habits that are actually part of the person producing those signs.[4] By this logic, and in spite of revivalist discourses to the contrary, if I only imitated the style and repertory of southern banjo players from the 1920s, I would be operating inauthentically. Since I am not of that time and place, my music and style would not be coming out of my own range of experiences and habits and thus would not be a good representation of who I am. Learning from recordings of older banjo players is part of my experience and habit base, but I have also studied south Indian vina, Peruvian charango, and Shona mbira, play Cajun accordion, and grew up with rock and 'folk revival' music. I am a cosmopolitan, and the banjo compositions that come out of this diversity of musical experience are more authentically me and representative of my cosmopolitan old-time music cohort than if I simply imitated Dock Boggs's style.

If authenticity is linked to dicent signs, then both the rural community-based and the middle-class old-time traditions can be equally authentic, or true, to the people who practice and enjoy them; they are simply distinct traditions. I realize that there is a fine line between the argument I am making here and ones used to justify cultural appropriation, where members of dominant groups take up the traditions of less powerful groups and ultimately claim them as their own. This problem is partially alleviated, however, precisely by being clear about the nature of the tradition being performed, that is, by stating directly that middle-class old-time is a distinct tradition not to be confused with, or represented as, southern rural lifeways.

A useful variable for thinking about differences within and across both types of settings is the length of time a given person has been involved with old-time music and dance. Longevity of socialization within and investment to the activity influences the degree of competence, comfort, and creative freedom during performance. Usually people who grow up with a style are simply more comfortable than those who did not, because the habits of performance were formed at an early age. In this regard, children and teenagers who are currently active in the middle-class cohort may well have grown up with old-time music and dance in their hometown or regional circuit due to the influence of their parents. For them,

4. The signs stand for the habits that constitute individual and group identities, and those same habits directly influence the signs and thus are dicent, or causally connected.

playing old-time at home and with friends and going to dances and dance weekends are normal parts of family life and custom. That is, these practices are part of their *family cultural formation,* and this second generation approaches the music and dance in ways more similar to people where old-time is part of community or regional formations.[5]

Although influenced by the attitudes of their parents, members of the second generation and other younger members in the cohort seem less concerned with the ideology of the 'folk revival' and issues of purity and preservation. Old-time is simply a type of music-dance they grew up participating in. Old-time is one of many styles they have access to as members of the broader capitalist cosmopolitan formation. Freed from ideologies of 'folk' authenticity, and since eclecticism is itself a value in this cosmopolitan formation, second-generation musicians tend to be more varied and experimental in their approach to instrumentation, style, and repertory than are hard-core 'revivalists.' Even in what I am calling the first generation of the 'revival' there are some musicians who favor a freer, eclectic approach over 'historic preservation.' In recognition of this creative tendency within the cohort, at the Cliff Top Festival, a major countrywide event for the middle-class cohort, besides the standard fiddle and banjo contests there is a special contest for experimental bands and performers.

From this point on I will concentrate on middle-class old-time music and dance. Like the 'revival' itself, this case offers the opportunity to study a participatory tradition that was created out of the needs of people who wanted but did not necessarily grow up with possibilities for collective music making and dancing. The analysis of the processes, successes, and drawbacks of this cohort sheds light on the possibilities of creating participatory music-making and dance scenes within the capitalist cosmopolitan formation.

The Emergence of Middle-Class Old-Time

Old-time music was a music industry designation devised in the 1920s as one less offensive alternative to *hillbilly* to refer to recordings of early country musicians.[6] It was also a term used by music preservationists to refer

5. See chapter 4 for a discussion of these nested cultural formations.

6. In October 1925, Okeh Records instituted the 45000 "Old Time Tunes" record series; see A. Green 1965:215.

to southern 'mountain music.'[7] String bands that recorded in the 1920s included fiddles as the main melodic instrument accompanied by five-string banjos, often in clawhammer or frailing style,[8] guitar, and perhaps other instruments like mandolins, autoharps, harmonicas, and even piano or accordion, in a somewhat ad hoc fashion. Sentimental and minstrel songs and tunes were recorded as were blues- and ragtime-derived pieces and square dance tunes typically in AABB form with each section composed of eight 4/4 measures. On the dance tunes, bands created dense textures with the melody instruments playing in unison or heterophony, a dense, rhythmic fiddle technique (bearing down on the bow often across two strings simultaneously) and frailing banjo technique, against a harmonic accompaniment and bass lines played on the guitar. Highlighted solos were usually not included, although instrumental sections were alternated with vocals when singing was involved.

The early string-band music that was recorded grew out of rural musical styles from Georgia, the Carolinas, the Virginias, Kentucky, and Tennessee, as well as the Ozarks and Texas—music that was often used for community square and line dancing. The performers who recorded 'old-time tunes' were often local amateur musicians. Other early fiddlers who recorded, such as John Carson, had also made regional names for themselves in fiddle conventions and contests and campaigning for politicians.[9] Some banjoists had gained professional experience through performing in medicine shows and circuses.

Indeed the five-string banjo, originally an African-derived African American instrument during the colonial period, burst into American popular culture in the context of professional blackface minstrel shows

7. For example, see the poster for the White Top Music Festival, 1931, in David Whistnat's book *All That Is Native and Fine* (1983:189).

8. *Clawhammer*, or *frailing*, refers to a right-hand banjo technique in which the hand literally takes the shape of a claw. It is a melodic style in which the pitches are produced by striking down on a given string with the fingernail of the right index finger and the thumb playing the fifth, drone, string in a quarter-note, two-eighth-note rhythm (the fifth string sounding on the final eighth note of this pattern). Other melody notes are played by dropping the thumb down to other strings. It is a rhythmic, percussive style that contrasts with the three-finger "up" picking style made famous in bluegrass by Earl Scruggs.

9. Whistnant writes, "John A. Burrison has established that there were fiddlers' conventions in Atlanta as early as 1899 and that an annual one was established in 1913. Bill C. Malone says fiddlers' contests 'have been held in the South at least since the late 1730s'" (1983:18).

initially in northern cities after the 1830s. The banjo in its contemporary form, old-time banjo performance technique (frailing), and a portion of the contemporary old-time repertoire (e.g., "Old Dan Tucker," "Yellow Rose of Texas") came into existence or were taken up by white performers in the context of minstrel theater—a tradition that at least partially functioned to rationalize slavery and promulgate racist stereotypes. So much for 'folk' purity, if one wants to base such ideas on noncommercial rural origins. As an indexical sign, the banjo has a long, complex, and in some ways troubling history—as troubling and as vibrant as the history of the United States itself. Like much of the best in American music, it was African derived, initially African American, and then subsequently adopted and dialectically developed by both black and white performers in various local amateur and professional urban-popular traditions. Given its winding history and various associations in different times and places, the banjo is "the American Instrument," insofar as it is a useful index of our musical and social history (see Linn 1991; Conway 1995).

Old-time string band music is relatively unknown in the contemporary United States. It tends to be confused with a commercial country style that grew out of it in the late 1940s known as bluegrass. As developed by Bill Monroe and his group The Bluegrass Boys (hence the genre name), bluegrass used much of the same instrumentation: fiddle, banjo, guitar, with the mandolin becoming a central lead instrument because Monroe was a mandolin player. Bluegrass bands also added the string bass as a standard part of the rhythm section. As discussed in chapter 2, bluegrass is a presentational and high fidelity music in which virtuosic soloing, clearer textures against homophonic accompaniment, and carefully arranged two- to four-part harmony singing in high ranges became hallmarks. Providing another hallmark of the style, Earl Scruggs, a member of the Bluegrass Boys in the late 1940s, popularized a rapid-fire virtuosic style of three-finger banjo picking, which, although less self-sufficient rhythmically, produced a much clearer timbre than did the old-time frailing technique (compare CD tracks 1 and 2). Bluegrass has remained familiar in American popular culture because it was featured in the theme song of the *Beverly Hillbillies* TV show (performed by Lester Flatt and Earl Scruggs) and in the movies *Bonnie and Clyde* (Flatt and Scruggs's "Foggy Mountain Breakdown") and *Deliverance,* among others. Old-time music finally got a boost from Hollywood, however, with the Cohen brothers' film *Oh Brother Where Art Thou* and the major motion pictures *Song Catcher* and *Cold Mountain.* Both old-time and bluegrass were taken up by 'folk revivalists' in the late 1950s.

The middle-class old-time string band style is partially based on the "hillbilly" recordings of the 1920s, groups like the Skillet Lickers, Charlie Poole and the North Carolina Ramblers, and Al Hopkins and the Hill Billies (one source for this genre name; see Malone 1985; Peterson 1997). The 1952 reissuing of part of Harry Smith's hillbilly record collection by Folkways as *Anthology of American Folk Music* also helped shape the canon for the old-time 'revival.' This record included medicine show and Grand Ole Opry performer Uncle Dave Macon, the Carter Family, Dock Boggs, and Clarence Ashley among many others, and it provided the first opportunity for many urban and suburban dwellers to hear old-time performers. By the late 1950s, some of the more industrious—Mike Seeger, John Cohen, Ralph Rinzler among them—traveled in the rural South to learn from and record the early country recording artists they came to know from Smith's collection, as well as other community musicians at festivals and in their homes. These and other young enthusiasts also introduced southern artists to the 'folk revival' through organizing concert and festival appearances outside the musicians' home regions.

Rinzler became part of the Greenbriar Boys, an early connection between bluegrass and the 'revival.' Mike Seeger (Pete's brother) and John Cohen along with Tom Paley (replaced by Tracey Schwartz in 1962) formed the New Lost City Ramblers in 1958. Their goal was to reproduce the style of the early country musicians captured on the 78rpm recordings, which they did in presentational performances and on high fidelity records. The New Lost City Ramblers provided the first model for the old-time revival. By 1965, Alan Jabbour, a PhD student from Jacksonville, Florida, began studying and recording southern fiddle music in Virginia, West Virginia, and North Carolina. In 1966, Jabbour formed the Hollow Rock String Band with fellow graduate students and university employees at Duke and the University of North Carolina–Chapel Hill—Bert Levy, a medical student from Long Island, on mandolin; Tommy Thompson, philosophy, on banjo, and Bobbie Thompson from Jacksonville, art instructor at Duke, on guitar. Even more than the Ramblers, with its 1967 record Hollow Rock began the process of creating the contemporary countrywide old-time tune canon— pieces that I encountered among middle-class players in upstate New York, Brattleboro, Vermont, Austin, Texas, and the Midwest alike between 1974 and 2002: "Over the Waterfall," "Dinah," "Money Musk" "Cabin Creek," and "Kitchen Girl." That middle-class old-time scenes as distantly removed as Vermont and Texas should share a core of the same tunes suggests the emergence of a single geographically dispersed tradition at least partially inspired by high fidelity recordings.

Another band to contribute to the middle-class, panregional old-time music canon was the Fuzzy Mountain String Band, also based in the Chapel Hill area. In 1994, three members of this band, Bill Hicks, Blanton Owen, and Sharon Sandomirsky, wrote in the notes of a reissued CD of their music:

> Informal music making was a regular thing at Tommy and Bobbie Thompson's house near Durham, N.C. in the mid 1960s. Alan Jabbour, Bertram Levy, Tommy and Bobbie eventually formed the influential Hollow Rock String Band out of those jam sessions, and in 1967 another handful of regulars decided to form a band of their own which they called the Fuzzy Mountain String Band. Dave Crowder and JoAnn "Claire June" Stokes provided guitar accompaniment to the fiddling of Malcolm Owen and Dick Zaffron, who also played mandolin on occasion. Eric Olsen played melody on the five-string banjo. . . .
>
> We played for our own enjoyment, mostly in living rooms and parlors, with an occasional paying job, folk festival, or fiddler's convention thrown in to complicate the works.[10]

Fuzzy Mountain met the people from Rounder Records at a festival and recorded two vinyl LPs in 1971 and 1972. The band members say that the first was recorded on a two-track tape recorder in living rooms and the second, although recorded at a radio studio, still consisted of "live takes." Their emphasis on homegrown informal music making and electronically unadulterated *high fidelity* recording is noteworthy—both as eyewitness description and as illustrating key values in the scene. There are no ambitions for stardom or professional success here; the group emerged organically out of informal participatory music sessions, got recorded somewhat by accident, and initially recorded in the same living rooms that they had begun playing in—high fidelity.

Nonetheless, in budding old-time music scenes around the country, Fuzzy Mountain did become well known through its records. Even more than Hollow Rock, many of the tunes on its albums entered the middle-class old-time music canon: "Sally Ann," "The 28th of January," "Ebenezer," "Old Mother Flanagan," "Wild Hog in the Woods," "Pretty Little Dog," "Frosty Morning," "Bonaparte's Retreat," "West Fork Girls," "Fire on the Mountain," "Bonaparte Crossing the Rhine," "Santa Anna's Retreat," "Shortening Bread," "The Falls of Richmond," "Barlow Knife," "Fisher's Hornpipe." Middle-class players in upstate New York, Vermont,

---

10. Notes, *The Fuzzy Mountain String Band*, Rounder CD 11571.

Texas, and Illinois with whom I played after 1974 were equally familiar with these tunes.

For me personally, and for many in the middle-class cohort, the most important new group of this period was the Highwoods String Band from Ithaca, New York. The group formed in 1972 out of the Fat City Stringband—Walt Koken and Bob Potts on twin fiddles and Mac Benford on banjo—which had been performing out in Berkeley. In Ithaca they added Doug Dorschug on guitar and Jenny Cleland on upright bass. As compared with the Ramblers, Hollow Rock, and Fuzzy Mountain, all quite traditionalist and straightforward in their approach, Highwoods created a new direction in the scene. Although bass was standard in bluegrass, its addition in an old-time band was new and added a strong rhythmic drive that was matched by the rhythmic and, for the time, wild twin fiddles. Echoing my experience, Mike Seeger described the band's impact: "Highwoods Stringband was undoubtedly the band that most directly influenced the current revival of southern string band music. Historically, the revival of traditional string music progressed from Pete Seeger's playing of some traditional banjo tunes and songs in the 1940s and 50s, to the broad-ranging traditionalist approach of the new Lost City Ramblers, to the fiddle tunes of Hollow Rock in the 1960s, to the rhythmic, loose-as-a-goose style evolved by Highwoods."[11] Fellow Rambler John Cohen writes "The throb of Jenny's bass fiddle added something never heard on old records—although the sound was inherent in Bluegrass. It was the old-time response to the big beat of rock'n'roll."[12]

While Highwoods did not contribute as much to the panregional canon of tunes as did its predecessors, it created a model for a freer, more rhythmically driving old-time sound that has been followed by such groups as Bubba George, the Horseflies (also out of upstate New York), the Freight Hoppers out of Bryson City, North Carolina, the Heartbeats, the Renegades, Rayna Gellert, and others. While many people in old-time scenes around the country maintain the traditionalist approach of groups like Hollow Rock, the Highwoods String Band opened up a space for younger players to experiment and push the limits of old-time (e.g., the Horseflies' use of synthesizers and reggae rhythms). By now the use of stand-up bass is a standard option for old-time string bands, as are the goal of creating rhythmic drive, the addition of more syncopated rhythms, and even improvisation and the composition of new tunes in the old-time style. Co-

11. Notes, *The Highwoods String Band, Feed Your Babies Onions*, Rounder C 11569.
12. Ibid.

hen's observation is useful; for younger players after the 1970s, Highwoods created a model that fit with the aesthetics of people who had grown up with rock and roll, a model that suggested flexibility and creativity within a scene that formerly had been more strictly concerned with the imitation and reproduction of older music. The key point here is that with the Highwoods, new cohort-specific styles and orientations began to emerge that were dicent articulations of the eclectic experiences of the middle-class cosmopolitans active in the scene. Highwoods stylistically set the stage for a new musical tradition: middle-class old-time.

Highwoods folded, but the members kept playing at home; I encountered them several years ago at the Cliff Top festival in West Virginia jamming in the parking lot. Walt Koken concludes, "Ironically, the more well known we became as a band, the less necessary we were to the growing old-time music scene, since one of the messages of the music is to do it yourself—unplug it, and take it home! So we did!"[13]

Why Old-Time? Searching for Simplicity and Community

Why old-time for the musically dedicated people who choose it over more mainstream styles like rock or jazz or bluegrass or hip hop? There are probably myriad reasons for given individuals, but I believe that there are some basic aspects that many of us share. Contemporary old-time is a well-developed participatory tradition in terms of the variety of musical challenges, the wealth and attractiveness of the tunes and dances themselves, and the informal, homegrown, participatory communal imagery that surrounds it. As Koken says, "Do it yourself, unplug it and take it home." The music and dance are facets of, and both iconic and indexical for, a much broader set of values that are held in common by many participants in middle-class old-time dance and music scenes.

The style is originally grounded in rural community music making; it continues to have this indexical meaning for contemporary middle-class participants, and this has proven attractive for people looking for an alternative community. For example, the Heartbeats dedicate their CD *Spinning World* "to old-time music, its community and family for enriching our lives and *for giving us a place to be.*"[14] As Ralph Linton observed long ago, 'revivalist' (what he called "nativist") movements are often the result of a dissatisfaction or discomfort with contemporary society (1943). Old-time

13. Ibid.
14. Notes, Green Linnet Records, GLCD 2111, 1993, my emphasis.

is iconic of a simpler, preindustrial life. This aspect *is* imagined, since by the turn of the twentieth century northern capitalist industrial expansion had already begun to deeply affect the rural south (Whistnat 1983; O'Brien 2001), and rural life never was easy or simple to begin with.[15] Nonetheless, the relatively simple, straightforward style of the music and dance are perceived by many middle-class participants as iconic—a portrait of the possible—for simple rural life. In regard to 'folk music' generally, David De Turk and A. Poulin note that "the way of life it represents is an alternative to suburbia in so far as it offers a simple and authentic way. Thus it is a singular bid for sane simplicity" (1967:22). In his interviews with old-time revivalists, Raymond Allen found that

> Most informants feel that the lyrics and feelings purveyed by old-time music symbolize [sic] the essence of an older era—an unhurried, rural existence close to nature. They admitted a certain attraction to rural living, although they varied in their desire to adopt such a lifestyle. New Jersey-born Steve Feldman, for example, had rejected the trappings of modern city life in favor of rural Tennessee: "Country living suits me more than living in the city and this crazy technological world we're in. And old-time hits the nail on the head in terms of *a place I'd rather be living in.* It just brings back the essence of a simple life. *The music is a smaller part of the larger whole,* which is really my turning away from city life."

Allen continues: "Other musicians preferred city living but felt that old-time music enabled them to experience vicariously the pleasures of country life. As fiddler Karen Hirshon reflects: 'Old-time music is a nice way to be connected to the farm without getting up at five in the morning'" (quoted in Allen 1981:65–81). As I argue in chapter 8, cohorts can be valuable precisely because they allow for gradual ("part-time") changes in habit and cultural orientation, whereas the idea of completely changing one's lifeways might appear too daunting.

Pierre Bourdieu has persuasively shown in his book *Distinction: A Social Critique of a Judgement of Taste* (1984) that there is often a great deal of coherence among the habits and dispositions that constitute individual

---

15. Following his vivid descriptions of frontier life in Texas and farther east, T. R. Fehrenbach (1983:300) concludes, "This life was hard, dirty, terribly monotonous, lonely, and damagingly narrow during the brutal years. Few of the Americans who later eulogized it would care to relive it."

selves. People drawn to old-time music and dance often share many habits, dispositions, and attitudes because the attraction to old-time is part of broader patterns of coherence within these individual selves. As Feldman remarked, old-time is a part of "the larger whole" of the people involved.

As I suggested in chapter 1, one of the basic functions of art is to imagine *the possible* and make such imaginings patent in perceivable, experiential forms. Old-time music and dance have provided the basis for an experience of alternative community settings within the capitalist-cosmopolitan formation, and this is especially true of the dance weekends that I describe below. The elements taken or imagined from the past or from rural life to create contemporary utopian moments, however, are *selective*. Cosmopolitan participants in old-time music and dance scenes typically do not adhere to fundamentalist Christianity or to the political conservatism that might be found in rural communities where old-time music and dance make up part of the formation (e.g., places in southern Missouri that I have visited). Members of the middle-class cohort also tend to eschew the gender and 'racial' hierarchies that characterized an earlier America and that remain in place still. The racist attitudes inherent in some of the minstrel show contributions to old-time, and expressed on some early hillbilly recordings, are selectively forgotten.

There is a political correctness and even squeaky-clean quality to some of these scenes that Charlie Poole and his North Carolina Ramblers might have found overbearing—NO SMOKING, even outside within fifty feet of anyone, no [open] drinking; at one contra dance I heard a woman scolded for wearing perfume! While these aspects fit with the images of wholesomeness that might be associated with a simpler rural life, it is more about the type of community settings participants prefer themselves—e.g., a chance to listen and dance to music and socialize outside of bars. To be fair, there is a variety within and across local scenes regarding such attitudes, but it is equally fair to say that, as in any cultural unit, there are widely shared values and attitudes that create social coherence. In the case of intentional cohorts it is shared values, attitudes, and predispositions that bring people to the group in the first place and keep them involved.

Social inclusiveness is basic to the ethics of the contra dance and old-time music cohort; beyond the participatory frame that characterizes these activities, social inclusiveness also fits with the liberal attitudes of most scene members. Anyone, regardless of color, creed, sexual orientation, personal style, or skill level, is welcomed. At a recent dance weekend at a park in rural central Indiana, hardly a hotbed of liberalism, two transvesti
attended the Saturday night dance. This is not particularly usual, so I as

them where they were from (I assumed nearby Bloomington or Indianapolis). It turned out that they were from the little town down the road from the park. A friend had told them about the dance, and so they came. No one outwardly seemed to notice anything unusual; they were made welcome and apparently had a good time dancing with different people throughout the night. Regardless of this open attitude, the vast majority (95 percent?) of people who are regulars are white and middle class.

While there is a history of black banjo and fiddle players and string bands in the south, and African Americans are certainly welcome, few participate as old-time musicians and dancers in contemporary middle-class scenes (one to three at most dances in the Midwest). Thus by default, membership in this cohort is characterized by color as well as class. This seems paradoxical given the liberal, inclusive attitudes within the old-time cohort, and, in fact, conscious attempts have been made to link contemporary old-time with African American as well as Anglo-American roots.[16] Yet the image of whiteness pervades as a practical fact. Whiteness fits with the romanticized Appalachian imagery surrounding the music and dance that was propagated, intentionally or not, by the 1960s 'folk revival,' and that was part of white-nationalist interest in old-time and Appalachia throughout the twentieth century. Around 1925, none other than Henry Ford sponsored fiddle contests and 'country dancing.' He saw these arts as an antidote to what he perceived as the ills of modern society brought on not by the system of mass industrial production and consumption that he helped ignite (!) but by cities, jazz, immigrants, and African Americans (Peterson 1997:59–61). I wonder whether the images of whiteness that surround old-time might not be part of the attraction for contemporary participants. The historically faulty constructions of country music and old-time as pure Anglo-American traditions[17] may help white middle-class participants feel a stronger sense of belonging and ownership, to feel that it is *their* ethnic tradition, at a time when prestige in American popular

16. For example, Cecelia Conway's *African Banjo Echoes in Appalachia: A Study of Folk Traditions* (1995). In addition, there have been workshops at scholarly meetings and festivals where African lute (e.g., xalam and ngoni) players were juxtaposed with banjoists to illustrate the connection.

17. The history of the banjo, as but one example, illustrates that musicians, instruments, and practices from African and African American heritage have influenced country music since the colonial period. Jimmie Rodgers, the first singing star of country, sang blues songs and even recorded a track with Louis Armstrong. Conversely blues, jazz, rock, and gospel have been deeply influenced by musicians, instruments, and musical orientations from European and Euro-American heritage. A detailed look

music and 'world music' is so strongly linked to African heritage and when "being ethnic" itself has cachet. Searching for and celebrating cultural roots, however this is defined, is certainly one force that draws people to the old-time music and dance cohort.

The Participatory Nature of Old-Time Music and Dance

More than any other single feature, I think, it is the participatory aspect of old-time string-band music and dance that attracts people to the cohort. When considered as part of the same performance,[18] this music and dance share many features with the Aymara and Shona traditions described earlier. At root, all three are defined by a participatory ethos—the expectation that if you attend a fiesta, ceremony, or a contra dance, you can and, in fact, *should* participate actively in the music making or dance. Like other successful participatory traditions, there are a range of performance roles in old-time music and dance that can attract people with different interests and skill levels. People who have never attended a middle-class contra or square dance before are invited to join in and after a short time can participate without too many train wrecks. This is possible because of the nature of the dance itself as well as the role of the caller.[19]

A dance is usually divided into two or three sets, each comprising four or five different squares or contras and ending with a waltz. In our area, as in many regions, contras are the most popular, and only one or two squares may be called during an entire evening.[20] Contra dances are done

at most American popular forms illustrates continual interchange between these and other social groups (e.g., Latin Americans).

18. Although playing string-band music happens in settings not involving dance such as in jams, at home, and in presentations, and contra and square dancing is not always accompanied by the types of string bands I will describe (other instrumentation such as a piano or accordion with fiddle is possible), here I will consider contexts where old-time string band music and dance form a unity.

19. At a community dance I attended in Cape Breton, there was no caller. The particular dance choreography was cued by the tune played. Square dancing was part of the community cultural formation and everyone present knew the conventions; thus a caller was not required.

20. See Phil Jamison, "Old-Time Square Dancing in the 21st Century: Dare to Be Square" (2004:8–12), for a critical discussion of the competition between square and contra dancers and the ultimate victory of contra dance. John Bealle describes the Bloomington, Indiana, scene as historically having been more open to both types of dance (2005).

FIGURE 6.1 Contra dancers at the Hyde Park Dance, Chicago, December 6, 2003. Photo by Paul Watkins. Used by permission.

in two long opposing lines; four couples make up squares. For both types, individual dances are original arrangements of a series of formulaic figures and movements—do-say-do, grand right and left, allemande right and left, sashay your partner, swing your partner, promenade, right and left hand stars, pass through, hay and half hay, among others of increasingly complexity. Once in motion, the lines or squares become a blur of weaving, spinning bodies in synchrony to the music and the guiding words of the caller (see figure 6.1).

Although most dances are organized around sets of partners, in contras the pairs move up and down, ultimately dancing with all the members of the opposite sex in the line and interacting with the members of the same sex in complementary fashion. One has a sense of moving, and actually dancing, with everyone in the lines, which helps create the communal feelings that people in the old-time scene seem to cherish. Even if you go to a dance with a wife or boyfriend, it is customary to change partners for each dance; this is so that single people will not be excluded and to foster interaction within the group as a whole. Contra dancers use the word *flow* to describe the feeling that they get when the dancing is good. Although they may not be aware of Csikszentmihalyi's theoretical elaboration of this term, they are in fact referring to the same phenomenon; going through the proper sequence of dance figures requires attention, but if the caller is good she will choose dances that match the competence of the dancers in the room so as to balance challenge with their abilities—a primary foundation for achieving flow.

Typically arising out of the ranks of experienced dancers, callers have their own repertories of dances, ranging from easy ones that involve simple combinations of the most basic moves to advanced dances that comprise intricate combinations of more esoteric, and in some cases original, figures. Before each dance begins, the caller teaches and walks people through a complete cycle of the dance without music. A good caller is also able to gauge the abilities of the participants and if there is a sizable number of beginners will choose her dances accordingly. She can start the evening off with two or three dances that recombine the same movements with only one or two new figures added per dance and in this way slowly build knowledge and confidence among beginners. Everyone learns new figures in this way, and people who have been dancing for some time know a sizable repertory of dance formulas. Even with simple choreography, experienced dancers can add their own flourishes and playful embellishments to keep the dancing interesting, much as an expert Aymara panpipe player might improvise a harmony to his partner's melody (*requinteando*) on a piece he has played many times. When the room is mainly filled with experienced dancers, the caller is challenged to bring out his most original and innovative pieces, and he will depend on expert dancers to guide the less experienced once the dance is in motion—in most dances it is common to see experts bodily steering neophytes through particular moves when they get lost. Thus, callers and expert dancers are like the core musicians in Aymara and Shona participatory events, who have the special responsibility of guiding the performance so that the maximum number of people can join in and feel comfortable.

There are always new dance figures to learn, and there are also subtle points of style that can be improved. Thus, new challenges are available even for the most seasoned dancers, and a good deal of emphasis is placed on learning within these scenes; workshops are often included during dance weekends or preceding a local dance. If further challenge is required, a dedicated dancer can begin to collect and arrange dances in order to become a caller—often starting off by "sitting in" and calling a few during events where there are other callers who can carry the evening. Similarly, I know a number of people who entered the scene as dancers but with time became interested in learning to play the music, so as to be able to participate in different ways.

While playing music is perhaps more specialized than dancing (but not calling), the instruments in a typical old-time string band—string bass, guitar, banjo, fiddle, sometimes mandolin—are graded in difficulty. The bass and guitar parts are technically quite simple, although a solid rhythmic feel is crucial. Most old-time songs use three or at most four chords in three or four keys (D, A, G, and A minor being most common); the bassist can simply play the root and fifth of each chord, and the guitar player can get by with a basic bass-strum-alternate bass-strum righthand pattern. People who have not played music before can begin to participate in old-time fairly rapidly after mastering some basics of these instruments. At the opposite end of the spectrum, the fiddle, the main melody-carrying instrument, is quite challenging and requires a good deal of practice before one can begin to join in jam sessions or play dances. The clawhammer style of banjo and mandolin represent a middle ground in terms of difficulty. Like fiddlers, banjo and mandolin players must learn and help carry the tunes, but these fretted instruments are easy to play in tune, and the righthand clawhammer or mandolin flat-picking techniques are easier than bowing.

Each instrument has its own series of graded challenges that can keep players interested and learning for years. There are always new tunes to master. Bass and guitar players can add new bass runs, rhythmic patterns, and timbral variations (e.g., slap bass), as well as playing substitution chords to add new flavor to old tunes (not always appreciated by the more traditionalist melody players). The guitar player who is deeply into the music but tired of this role can take up banjo or fiddle. Banjo players and fiddlers add improvised and formulaic variations to standard tunes to keep them ever fresh and interesting. Thus, as in most musical traditions, there is a constantly expanding ceiling of challenges that can be matched to increasing abilities, fundamental to experiencing flow. I became involved in different dance scenes strictly as a musician. Although I enjoy couple dancing (especially Cajun and zydeco) and like squares, I am not overly attracted to contras. Nonetheless, over the years I have danced some when not playing. Like me, others in the scene may have preferences for some activities over others but may be able to switch roles and participate in different ways during the same occasion.

Performance Events

In my Midwestern region, the middle-class contra dance scene is divided into two types of events. Weekly or biweekly dances are held in a number of towns and cities in Ohio, Indiana, Illinois, and Missouri, attended largely by locals. Some of these local groups also sponsor dance weekends—Jan Jam in Urbana; Swing into Spring and Sugar Hill in Bloomington, Indiana; Kimswick outside of St. Louis; Pigtown Fling in Cincinnati; Breaking Up Thanksgiving in Chicago. These dance weekends define an annual calendar and a regional network, attracting many of the same committed dancers and musicians year after year.

In Urbana a contra dance with live string band or fiddle-led music is held every other Friday night at Philips Recreational Center, a building of the Urbana Park District. The dance is held in a gymlike room with fluorescent lighting, chairs set up along one side, and risers for the band at the end of the hall; outside this room there is a loungelike hallway with comfortable chairs. About twenty to thirty regulars and newcomers attend. A core of experienced dancers, who rotate organizational roles (hiring bands, publicity, setting up the room and PA) attend regularly and keep the dance going year to year. A fair number of newcomers and beginning dancers attend, which influences the dynamic in terms of what and how musicians can play, the speed and complexity of the dances called, and in fact, who attends.

After the band has set up on stage and the PA has been balanced, the caller, mike in hand, begins the dance evening by calling people out on the floor: "Come on out now and form two lines [or four if there are a lot of people] for a contra dance," or "form your squares." The caller then walks the dancers through a complete cycle of the dance without music, stopping to help individuals if they are confused. Once the caller is comfortable that the dancers know what to do, she may ask the band leader (usually the fiddler) for the name of the pieces that they will play or simply signal the band members to begin. For some dances, the caller might request a special type of tune (a smooth piece or a tune with a lot of bounce) or guide the band in terms of tempo. Sometimes after the dance has begun, a caller may signal the band to speed up or slow down if things are not going well, and he also signals the band one or two repetitions before the dance will end. The musicians also may alter their tempos without prompting if they observe that the dancers seem to be dragging or are having to move too fast. This flexibility is one advantage to having live musicians, as opposed to using recordings, in participatory events (figure 6.2). If the caller perceives major confusion on the floor, she may stop the dance and re-teach the choreography, but this happens infrequently and is a sign that she didn't gauge the dancers' readiness or abilities correctly before begin-

FIGURE 6.2 Euphor String Band at the Hyde Park Dance: Matt Turino fiddle, Michael Shapiro guitar, Michael Valiant bass, Tom Turino banjo. Photo by Paul Watkins. Used by permission.

ning. Thus, the caller has a role like that of a conductor and bears the main responsibility for the success of a dance. Callers and bands have particular reputations within our regional network, and good ones, advertised on the annual calendar and in the newspaper, help attract dancers.

People who attend our local dance include faculty, staff, and students from the university as well as other people from town. Couples, families, and groups of friends attend together, and there are usually a few high school– and college-age dancers and children running about, as well as single people, mostly ranging from their thirties to their sixties. There is a constant turnover of new faces, people trying it out for the first time who have come with friends or who read about the dance in the paper. These people are welcomed by the old hands in part because of the scene's participatory ethos but also because the regular dancers hope that the scene will grow and some of the newcomers will stick. People who really love dancing have found that it has changed their lives and want to share this, almost with a missionary zeal. Bolder newcomers join right in on the first dance, not knowing what is coming; others sit on the side watching. After a person has sat out a few, an experienced person will invite him to dance and will take the responsibility of guiding him once the music has started. The constant infusion of newcomers makes it necessary for the caller to spend more time teaching the dances, slowing the pace of the whole evening, and calling more basic dances. It also makes it necessary for bands to play clearly structured tunes at slower tempos.

Local dances differ in size and the balance of experienced and inexperienced dancers. For example, the dances in Bloomington, Indiana, seems to attract a higher number of local experienced dancers than do ours, and the dance in Chicago is somewhere in the middle; both tend to be larger than ours. Each week a different band and caller are hired. Urbana-Champaign has a number of people who call and between two and four string bands that rotate with other bands and callers from as far away as St. Louis, Cincinnati, Bloomington, and Chicago. Sometimes "pick-up" bands involving people from different places play. Because of a resurgence of the number of people playing old-time in our town recently, jams preceding or concurrent with the dance have begun to take place in a back room of the building for people more interested in playing than dancing; individuals move between these two activities. Some enthusiastic long-time contra and square dancers and old-time musicians in town do not go to the biweekly dance regularly but travel distances to dance weekends and old-time music festivals.

If local dances are the training ground and mainstay, dance weekends are the high points in our regional network. Because of distances and the commitment of staying for two or three days, the weekends mainly attract the most dedicated dancers and musicians, and thus the overall level of performance tends to be higher and more flexible as compared to our local dance. Many people bring their families, so people of all ages attend. My favorite weekend is Sugar Hill, which is held in a park and campground outside Bloomington, Indiana, in August. People begin arriving on Friday afternoon to set up their tents before the communal potluck dinner and evening dance. At registration for the dance there are sign-up sheets for the different tasks such as cooking and cleanup for the subsequent communal breakfasts, lunches, and dinners. There is also a sign-up sheet for bands and pick-up bands to play for the Friday and Saturday night dances. Usually there are more bands that want to play than there are slots (about four per evening), so names are drawn from a hat around suppertime. Although for certain dance weekends well-known bands are hired, groups are not paid at Sugar Hill. This is a particularly fun dance to play because of the consistently high energy of the dancing. It is also a place for bands to establish a regional reputation—often other gigs will come out of a successful performance at Sugar Hill. There is also a time-slot sign-up sheet for callers, who rotate throughout the evening.

On Friday evening, people begin to gather around the building where the kitchen is housed and where the meals and dance will take place. Many of the participants know each other from past years and other dances and so sit down together and catch up. People take out their instruments, and small informal sessions happen around the outdoor picnic tables; established and pickup bands hoping to play get together to run through tunes. A buffet dinner is served, and most people join friends and family to eat. After dinner the PA system and large room are prepared for the dance. Dancing begins around eight o'clock, and the hall fills up immediately. Each caller and band has an hour or ninety-minute slot, with a break afterward for the next band to set up. Through the evening the energy of the dancing picks up, with the peak occurring between ten and midnight. Often the dancing will go to four in the morning or until dawn, with a decreasing number of younger and enthusiastic middle-age dancers carrying on; after around one, pick-up bands take over to power through the wee hours. The exhaustion of dancing and playing for long stints all night is a primary part of the cathartic experience that bonds the group and separates these events from normal life; the effect is very much akin to the experience of all-night bira ceremonies in Zimbabwe.

During the day on Saturday people socialize, take walks or bike rides around the park, and gather at the beach on the lake to swim and sunbathe. Jam sessions occur in the area surrounding the main building throughout the day, some of them lasting for many hours with different musicians filtering in and out. Fiddlers form the nucleus of these sessions, with between one and six fiddlers leading the tunes. There are a number of highly skilled old-time musicians in Bloomington who have played together for years and know many tunes in common. They provide such a strong musical core that others who might not know this particular repertory can join in without derailing the music. The sessions often take the form of concentric rings, with the core musicians, who have played together, at the center and increasingly less experienced musicians in the outer rings. As the afternoon moves toward evening, people begin returning from their various activities and gather around the jams to listen and socialize. If a particularly good jam is going, it often continues throughout the night in parallel to the Saturday night dance, although this varies from year to year.

By Sunday morning people are truly exhausted and equally elated. A final breakfast is prepared by the volunteers, and people sit with old friends and new friends they have made at this event. By this time a true sense of community and good fellow feeling has been created among the participants; this is not an "imagined community" but at this moment a deeply felt actual community, experienced briefly, to be renewed at the next dance weekend.

Participatory Music and Dance: Summary Conclusions

Formula, Improvisation, and Flow

Participatory traditions offer the conditions for flow for people at all skill levels. I suggest that many people are attracted to participatory performance for this very reason. Yet even within the same participatory activity there can be a number of approaches to reaching flow. In the middle-class old-time string-band tradition, many fiddlers and banjoists hardly vary a tune at all from repetition to repetition and purposefully try to keep the piece the same as the way they learned it. In my experience with such players, they are constantly learning new tunes, which are not regarded as models for variation and improvisation but rather are considered set musical items. Here closely circumscribed habitual performance provides comfort, while rendering the tune precisely and continually learning and playing new and increasingly difficult or esoteric tunes provide the challenge. This approach, which results in the most repetitive, predictable music, seems popular especially with beginning and intermediate dancers and callers. It is also helpful in old-time jams during which people, usually the fiddlers, take turns cuing tunes without considering whether other participants know them or not. Players who are intent on continually building their personal repertoires will know more of the tunes and be able to join in at jams comfortably.

My own approach, and that of other like-minded old-time players, is quite different. I have been playing clawhammer banjo for about thirty years, yet I have a relatively small repertoire of tunes. I am not interested in constantly learning new tunes unless they are substantially different from the ones I already know. Rather, I am more interested in composing tunes or in developing new formulaic variations on the thirty or so tunes that I regularly play. Most of the formulas I play are so habitual, as is the process of variation, that my general mental state while playing is largely "automatic pilot," although continual variations, which almost seem to happen by themselves, usually hold my interest. When playing a single piece for a long time during a dance, however, I sometimes get bored and consciously decide to vary something or try something new. At that point I am out of the habitual mode of performance and play with a different type of attention to what I am doing, but once I have repeated or worked with the new ideas for a few repetitions, the comfort-challenge balance is restored and I get back to flow, and so the process goes.

In jams I frequently do not know the tunes being played, and so after grasping the basic skeleton of the piece during the first several repetitions, I often use formulas or improvise to play with the basic melody. This is how I enjoy playing, but I have found that it sometimes annoys musicians who value the detailed, accurate rendering of tunes. In such cases I back off, play more softly, and concentrate on learning the melody, but probably I won't stay in that jam very long. Because banjoists have to retune for every key change, jams often stay in the same key for long periods. Old-time tunes in the same key can be structurally and melodically quite similar; hence even fairly small melodic details are often very important for distinguishing one tune from another. Some musicians also consider detailed rendering of the tunes to be important signs of competence and insider status. My manner of playing obscures such details, even on tunes I know, but if the fiddler core is strong my elaborations are sometimes appreciated. It just depends on who is in the jam.

My main role as the banjoist in our string band during dances is rhythmic. I particularly enjoy adding a good deal of syncopation, an overall swing feel, and playing with the time. In our local dances, where many of the dancers are inexperienced, I have received some complaints (both directly and indirectly) for (over)doing this, as well as for playing too fast. In this context, I find that I often have to hold back my own desires and preferences for the sake of the dancers. By contrast, when our band has played at dance weekends or other scenes where there is a greater proportion of experienced dancers, our rhythmic approach has generated enthusiasm. The overriding participatory ethos of contra dancing requires musicians to limit their own creativity and enjoyment to match the skill levels of the callers and dancers, just as experienced dancers must limit what they do to make a partner who is a newcomer feel comfortable. Such are the priorities of participatory traditions that I mentioned earlier. When we play at Sugar Hill, the dancers are so good and provide so much energy that our band soars. We play faster, improvise more, and are simply inspired by the movement in the hall. This close synergy between musicians and dancers has led me to think of the music and dance simply as different interrelated roles within the same performance complex.

Having learned his old-time repertory and approach from me initially, my fiddler son Matt plays in a style that is thoroughly formulaic. For a given tune he has learned my formulas and added many of his own, such that frequently he remembers only vaguely what the basic tune is. In contrast to my way of playing, however, Matt says that what he likes best is to continually go out on a limb by doing something he has never done before, because he likes the challenge of having to find a way out of a problem he has created for himself during performance. He consciously favors improvisation and spends more time improvising during performances than I do. We also play in presentational contexts, and Matt's improvisatory approach seems to work well for listening audiences. It is significant, however, that in our local contra dances, when his improvisations obscure the basic structure of the tune, especially if he blurs the A and B parts of the AABB form, we get complaints from less experienced callers and dancers, who find the music hard to follow and so lose their place in the dance. When he was younger, I sometimes had to remind Matt to stick to the tune more closely than he normally liked to do. In these participatory events extended improvisation is a problem, whereas formulaic variation and more limited intensive improvisation, if the rhythm is not altered too much, does not seem to cause a problem for dancers.

Shona mbira players exhibit the same type of range of approaches described for old-time musicians. One of my main teachers, Chris Mhlanga, repeatedly told me that he thinks of mbira pieces as being rather set—the basic ostinato pattern plus a limited number of stock formulaic variations—and that this material should not be altered during bira performances. He feels that there is little room for improvisation in mbira music, and he himself does not improvise. His reasons include the fact that if one mbira player improvises too much or plays formulas unknown to the other mbira players, the close interlocking relationship between the *kushaura* and *kutsinhira* parts will be lost. He also noted that the ancestors like the music to be played in the way they knew it when they were living, and if this is altered too much, they may not be attracted into their medium during a ceremony. Thus, whereas in the contra dance scene the ability of the callers and dancers limits the degree of improvisation and variation in the music, in mbira music it is the nature of interlocking parts and the desires of the ancestors that limits novelty.

Mhlanga told me, however, that in contrast to the *core* mbira parts, there is a great deal of room for formulaic variation and improvisation in the singing that the mbira supports. When I would come up with variations on the mbira and check their acceptability with him, he would typically instruct me to play the pieces just as he had taught them. When I checked vocal lines with him, he told me that they were fine and that, in fact, each musician should have his own vocal lines to sing with the different pieces. In Mhlanga's approach, mbira playing is a relatively circumscribed *core* part, and singing is a more open *elaboration* part, and the two may be combined by the same musician to achieve the comfort-challenge balance that creates flow.

Another of my teachers, Mr. T. Chigamba, represents another approach; his playing involved almost constant formulaic variation with some improvisation—parallel to the way I play banjo. This was so habitual for him that he had difficulty playing a piece in the same way for many consecutive cycles, which made learning from him difficult. Since he typically plays with his children and they know his repertory of formulas, this did not prove to be a problem. The Chigamba case points up the importance of the longevity of musical relationships as crucial for allowing greater variation and improvisation in participatory traditions. The same is true for my son and me, who know each other's moves so well that we can follow each other even in improvisatory sections, since these are typically extensions of things we have done before.

There are mbira players who, like my son, emphasize improvisation and, in addition, virtuosic display. As Berliner noted in his book *Soul of Mbira*, however, this type of "hot" playing, typically involving younger musicians, is sometimes frowned upon for all the reasons expressed by Chris Mhlanga. Virtuosic display is often counterproductive in participatory contexts, whereas it is crucial to successful presentational performance. Likewise, other Shona musicians, such as the late Dumisani Maraire, were of the opinion that formulaic variations should not be changed too quickly, because this does not give other participants a chance to lock in with a given variation with their own clapped, vocal, or dance parts. It would be like trying to have a meaningful dialogue with someone who keeps changing the subject. Again, participatory values limit what musicians can do, because music making is as much about social relations and fostering participation as it is about sound production and the creative drives of particular musicians. Those who wish to prioritize their own creative urges would do better to perform in presentational contexts.

In the least variable or improvisatory of the traditions I have studied, Aymara panpipe performance, two or three pieces are collectively composed during rehearsals by a small group of musicians for the festival that will begin the following day. A given genre has a number of stock formulas that are plugged in to new compositions especially as introductions and at cadences, as well as sometimes within the sections organized in AABBCC form. These formulas, plus a great deal of internal repetition across sections, allow community members who have never heard the piece before to pick it up quickly during the festival performance itself.

A key value of Aymara music making, explicitly stated, is that individuals should not stand out from the ensemble sound, and as in the other participatory traditions I have discussed, there is no place for highlighted soloing. As mentioned in chapter 2, however, in panpipe performance there is a technique known as *requinteando* in which one member of an interlocking pair improvises or plays formulas with the melodic segments performed by his partner. These spaces for variation and improvisation are very short and must not stand out. In fact, *requinteando* lines make a negligible contribution to the overall ensemble sound. I believe that the main reason for the practice is to provide a creative space for advanced panpipe players so that their interest and the skill-challenge balance can be maintained to enhance opportunities for flow within pieces that are closely circumscribed for easy access.

Organization of Social Spaces

In line with the guiding principle of creating comfort for many types of individuals, participatory occasions usually include different spaces that vary according to focal attention of the group and responsibility to participate. It is interesting that for bira ceremonies in Zimbabwe and contra dances in Urbana the physical space is structured in a very similar way. In Zimbabwe, people verbally make the distinction between "inside the house" and "outside the house" to designate musical genres and ceremonial activities. At a bira, spirit possession takes place inside the small, round kitchen house packed with people and alive with music and dance. People inside the house most definitely feel the responsibility of focusing on the ceremony and participating musically. Outside the house the hosts keep a bonfire going all night, sometimes with benches around it. People who are tired or who do not want to concentrate on the ceremonial activities can stay outside and socialize more casually.

If you are sitting inside the hall where a contra dance is taking place, there is a pressure to participate created by the constant invitations to dance. As Miriam Larson, a young dancer, put it, "Contra dancing isn't about performing for others, so you don't want a lot of people sitting around watching if they are not going to dance." At contra dances there is usually a social space outside the dance hall where people who do not want to dance can interact in other ways. In the recreation center in Urbana, there is a hallway with chairs where people can comfortably socialize without the pressure of invitations. There are also smaller rooms open down another hallway where musicians can play while the dancing is going on in the main hall. Similarly, at Sugar Hill dancing takes place inside a hall, socializing takes place on the porch and picnic tables surrounding the main entrance, and jams take place at picnic tables a little further removed from the entrance to the hall. In Aymara festivals there are also a variety of activities that people pass in and out of. The circle of musicians forms the focal point of the event, with dancers moving around them. Beyond these two circles, community members stand around drinking, eating, and socializing and, at will, get up to dance, or take up an instrument and join the inner circles.

At bira ceremonies, Aymara festivals, and contra dances, then, there are a variety of social spaces and activities to choose from. Each of the spaces has its own etiquette and levels of pressure to participate. This structuring of social spaces allows for the fullest attendance at the event as a whole in that there are a variety of niches where people with different interests and personalities can find an interesting and comfortable place. Some people come to the Urbana contra dance and dance weekends just to be with family members or friends but do not play music and don't like to dance. Others prefer playing and are attracted to events where an old-time jam is likely to occur, whereas for committed dancers (the majority), the main dance constitutes the core of the event. At a bira, family members and neighbors who, for whatever reason, do not have the energy for the inside-the-house activities can still support the ceremony but largely remain outside in a more casual setting. Often the same people will move between the different spaces and activities for variety or to rest during long events.

Cultural Formations and Cohorts

Beyond the stylistic details of the music and dance, the Aymara, Shona, and middle-class old-time cases differ in one fundamental respect. Shona bira ceremonies and Aymara festivals are at the center of social life in these two societies; they are integral activities of these *cultural formations*. The result is that the values expressed and modes of practice within these musical events are consistent with broader patterns of social life; people do not feel contradictions between these activities and the values that guide rest of their lives. Middle-class old-time music and dance scenes, like many other participatory traditions in the United States, are so far out on the margins that many people in the towns where the dances occur do not even know they exist.

Contra dancing and old-time music are the basis of a *cultural cohort*—a social group that forms around the activity itself. This cohort provides an alternative, temporary "place to be," as participants put it; the cohort is sometimes deeply valued precisely because it provides an alternative to 'modern' capitalist lifeways. While these scenes stand in opposition to the broader cultural formation, the people involved also have internalized values from the broader formation—e.g., the higher value of presentational and recorded music and artists in the star system—and thus old-time musicians may feel a tension or at times harbor doubts about the artistic validity of what they are doing unless they can tour or record. Professional standing and material production are highly valued within the capitalist formation. Participatory traditions do not sit well with these values; there is not much money to be made, and thus these activities are bound to remain marginal unless the basic values of the cultural formation are altered.

In fact, local string bands do record, and within the social network of old-time music there is a mini–star system of professional recording and touring artists, although this flies in the face of what the music and dancing are about for most people. Here we see the pull between habits of the cultural formation and those unique to this particular cohort—a tension within individual actors themselves. When we use the *formation* and *cohort* concepts, it becomes clear why cohorts that grow up within the capitalist formation but are set in opposition to it—punk, old-time, hip hop, hippie counterculture, political art—often appear to be riddled with contradictions and 'sellouts.' Within the capitalist formation, success is judged in terms of money and fame. In the value systems of these cohorts, money and fame, or signing with a major label, are judged as selling out and failure. Values derived from socialization within the formation tend to be deeper and older and will continue to influence given individuals even when the same people are dedicated to a cohort that rejects the very same habits and values. Yet this situation does not negate the potential importance of cohorts as models for living and social action.

As suggested in chapter 4, the distinction between cohorts and formations is a matter of degree in terms of the prominence of influence in given individuals' lives. As the example I gave, a religious group can be the basis of a cohort within a broader formation if, for the most part, the members still operate in relation to the habits of thought and practice of the formation. If the group isolates itself and its tenets become the primary basis for living, however, it becomes a distinct cultural formation. For some, old-time music became part of broader way of life involving a choice to live in a rural area, work at a handcraft or subsistence agriculture, and avoid mass media, mass consumption, and new technologies. In such cases what began as a cohort started to function as the basis for an alternative 'back to the land' cultural formation.

The example of second-generation members of the old-time cohort illustrates a different dynamic. When the practices of a cohort are passed down to a new generation as part of family cultural formations, the conceptual lines between cohort and formation begin to blur—or better said, ideas and activities that begin in a cohort become part of a cultural formation at the level of the family. Theoretically, if enough family formations are deeply influenced by the habits of thought and practice of a cohort, this can set the stage for the creation of a new formation at a broader level than the family. Family formations thus can provide a bridge between cohorts and the creation of new larger cultural formations. Given these possibilities, cohorts can be, and have been, forces for broader patterns of social innovation.

Time and Participatory Traditions

Time, transmission across generations, is required for new cultural practices and styles to take on the rich indexical meanings and depth of the habits of a cultural formation. Time is key to the power of participatory traditions in another way. Dancing all night for two nights in a row is crucial to the unique experience of contra dance weekends, as is playing and dancing all night at a bira. Aymara festivals last for days, and the exhaustion and different types of interactions that result are part of the joyous effect that they create. These events bring groups of people together for extended periods of time through intense participatory activities where people experience *each other* in heightened physical-sonic ways that provide a powerful sense of identity and unity beyond normal social interactions. These events are a time out of normal everyday time; they are, at their foundation, a celebration and experiencing of the social group itself and for this reason, perhaps more than any other, are highly fulfilling and meaningful. Most humans have a need to deeply connect with others; participatory music and dance events are an age-old and humanly universal way to realize this experience, and they are open to everybody. Old-time music and dance scenes, and the 'folk revival' more broadly, suggest that even in cultural formations where such opportunities are not readily available, some people will create them or seek them out.

7 Music and Political Movements

On April 10, 1865, only a day after General Robert E. Lee had surrendered and four days before Abraham Lincoln was shot, a huge crowd of boisterous celebrants assembled at the White House and called for a speech. Lincoln came to a second-story window and said, "I have always thought 'Dixie' one of the best tunes I have ever heard. Our adversaries over the way attempted to appropriate it, but I insisted yesterday that we had fairly captured it [tremendous applause]. I presented the question to the Attorney General, and he gave his legal opinion that it is our lawful prize. I now request the band favor me with its performance" (quoted in Cornelius 2004:37).

With so much suffering and bloodshed, now matched by joy at war's end, why did Lincoln respond to the crowd's demand for a speech with a song? How could Dan Emmett's minstrel ditty, originally a rationalization for slavery and a product of 'vulgar' popular theater in Northern cities, be considered a prize worth winning? What was it that was being captured and controlled here?

Some people think of music simply as entertainment, something to be enjoyed after the serious business of living has been concluded. Music scholars, composers, and performers take 'serious' music seriously but sometimes consider it as an autonomous art form—a lofty sphere apart—that has little to do with the nitty-gritty of social life. The leaders of governments and political movements strongly disagree. From Lincoln to Mao to Robert Mugabe, politicians in countless times and places have clearly understood and have effectively harnessed the iconic and indexical power of music to further their own pragmatic ends. For Lincoln, reappropriating "Dixie" *was* serious business regarding what had become, through its multiple and deep indexical connections, a very serious song.

Although sung by Northerners and Southerners with a variety of different texts during the war years (Cornelius 2004:30–37), "Dixie" had become an unofficial anthem of the Confederacy. Lincoln was making a public display of capturing the enemy's flag, but it was more than this. With Lee's surrender, the Stars and Bars had been lowered and the Confederate flag was not to be flown, certainly in Washington, at that time. "Dixie," however, was brought back into the national fold through the White House performance, to be cherished along with Lincoln's hopes for reconciliation. Doris Goodwin writes that in requesting the patriotic song of the South Lincoln remarked, "It is good to show the rebels that with us they will be free to hear it again" (2005:727). But why the song and not the flag? One might begin such an analysis by considering that the flag was an index for the Confederate government and army, while the song's history was more complex. It had been popular before the Civil War, initially in the North, and had been sung and enjoyed with a variety of different lyrics by people throughout the country. During the course of the war "Dixie" came to be closely associated with the South, but the flag was an index for the Confederate state while the song was an index for the people themselves. Lincoln wisely understood the difference.

A central purpose of this book is to suggest new ways to think about the special potentials and functions of music in social life. Nowhere are these connections clearer than in the use of music within political movements, in part because the political uses of music are quite conscious and explicit. In this chapter I discuss two particularly dramatic political cases: music in Nazi Germany and music in the civil rights movement in the United States.

Music in Nazi Germany

In my discussion of participatory occasions and the special semiotic potentials of music to create collective identities, I have emphasized positive community settings among indigenous Aymara peasants in Peru, Shona villagers and the black middle class in Zimbabwe, and middle-class old-time cohorts in the United States. The Nazi case illustrates that the same powers that music has for creating positive community relationships can also be used to villainous ends. As with all human technologies and abilities, darkness, violence, and the guilt of acquiescence stand as an all too present shadow to the brilliant, beautiful, and loving musical achievements of which people are capable.

In American popular culture of the past fifty years, Nazis are the bad guys everyone loves to hate; they are a clear-cut image of evil iconically rendered through Darth Vader's helmet or as the demonic antagonists to the American hero and to God in *Raiders of the Lost Ark*.[1] For many contemporary Americans, World War II was the last conflict that is easy to justify—because the Nazis were so horrific, because Japan struck first, and because we won; Korea, Vietnam, the Iraqi wars were not so easily justified and not so successful. The "popularity" of Nazis in our popular culture may be in part due to the fact that they are comforting in their outrageousness; they direct our attention elsewhere.

The philosopher and novelist George Santayana has said, "Those who do not remember the past are condemned to relive it." This applies to understanding our own history so as to move the government and civil society in more positive future directions. It also applies to understanding what happened in the Third Reich, and especially how it was possible that normal German people—cultural differences aside, people like you and me—could have knowledge of, carry out, or at least condone the atrocities of the holocaust in which millions of people, mainly Jews, were exterminated. It is not just Hitler who is condemned by history but the German people as well. Why do people follow leaders whose actions clearly contradict their own sense of human decency and morality? How is insanity made normal and acceptable? To use Adam LeBor and Roger Boyes's phrase (2000), how did Hitler *seduce* the German people?

Hitler was chosen to lead Germany in November 1933, at a time when the country was still reeling psychologically from its defeat in World War I and from the economic hardships resulting from the 1919 Treaty of Versailles (loss of territories, reparation payments) and widespread economic depression after 1929. In 1921 the mark slid to seventy-five to the dollar, and by November 1923 it took four billion marks to buy a dollar. German currency had become worthless, people's wages and life savings were reduced to nothing, people were going hungry. The new democratic Weimar Republic established in 1919 was blamed because it had accepted the Versailles treaty (Shirer 1959:61). Hitler used the chaos and hopelessness of

---

1. At one point in the third Indiana Jones movie this all-American hero remarks, "Nazis, I hate those guys." A few scenes later he machine-guns down a few of them without remorse and, it is assumed, without any remorse on the part of the viewers.

this time to build support for his vision of a renewed Germany and what became the National Socialist (Nazi) Party.

Before he moved to Munich, Hitler spent his early twenties in Vienna. The young German-Austrian had developed strong nationalist sentiments about the superiority of the German people. By the turn of the twentieth century, the German-Austrian hold on the Austrian empire had been challenged by demands for national autonomy by various groups, including the Czechs, the Slovaks, the Serbs, and the Croats. In his classic work *The Rise and Fall of the Third Reich,* William L. Shirer observes, "To [Hitler] the empire was sinking into a 'foul morass.' It could be saved only if the master race, the Germans, reasserted their old absolute authority. The non-German races, especially the Slavs and above all the Czechs, were an inferior people. It was up to the Germans [Hitler felt] to rule them with an iron hand" (1959:21–22). Hitler came to feel that 'Germans' scattered in different places must be united. During this period he began to analyze political movements, and he concluded that the Social Democrats, although much too liberal, were successful because they knew how to create a mass movement, they had mastered the art of propaganda among the masses, and they knew the value of what he called "spiritual and physical terror." It was also during his Vienna years that the young Hitler began to develop his rabid racism against Jews, sentiments that were widespread in that place and time. As expressed in his own book *Mein Kampf (My Struggle),* these aspects of his thinking were to come back to haunt the world after the Nazis came to power.

In the period between World War I and Hitler's dictatorship, a plethora of small political parties and organizations vied for power over their regions and among special interest groups within the weak Weimar Republic. After returning to Munich from World War I, Hitler joined and then took dictatorial control over one such group first known as the German Worker's Party. A failure in everything he had tried previously in civilian life, he found that he had ability (some have called it genius) for political organizing and maneuvering. He also discovered that he had an ability to "speak"—to win people with his words—and a sense of how to build a mass movement through the use of rallying emblems and propaganda. Shirer remarks that during this period, when the Nazi Party was rising,

the first signs of his peculiar genius began to appear and make themselves felt. What the masses needed, he thought, were not only ideas— a few simple ideas, that is, that he could ceaselessly hammer through their skulls—but symbols [read *signs*] that would win their faith, pageantry and color that would arouse them, and acts of violence and terror, which if successful, would attract adherents (were not most Germans drawn to the strong?) and give them a sense of power over the weak. (1959:42)

Through violence (breaking up competing parties' meetings), threats of violence against opposition on the street, and the skillful use of signs in speeches, emblems, and political events, Hitler took over the party and built a mass following. This backing combined with political conditions in 1933 set the stage for Hitler's dictatorship—he dismantled the 1919 Weimer Republic and made the state synonymous with the Nazi Party and ultimately with the Führer himself. LeBor and Boyes describe Hitler's victory in 1933 in the following terms:

The concern was that the mass unemployment of 1932–33 would sweep the Communists into power and unleash a red revolution. Social Democrats, conservatives, big business and estate owners, and ultimately Hindenburg himself came to see a Chancellor Hitler as a less dangerous option than the postponement of new elections. Postponement of elections would have violated the [1919] constitution while nominating Hitler stuck to the letter of the law. Hitler chose the correct words, promising work and bread to the unemployed, the elimination of class warfare (and its "parties"), and a "new German Reich of greatness and honor." (2000:17)

While the Nazi Party did not come close to holding a majority, the forces allied against it were weak and were competing internally. Because of the Nazi minority in the cabinet, big business and the conservatives thought they could control Hitler, and so on January 30, 1933, President Hindenburg entrusted the chancellorship to Hitler. All too soon they were to learn their mistake.

Once in power, Hitler and his relatively small political cohort began to transform German society and the broader cultural formation in fundamental ways. It was Hitler's invasion of Poland in September 1939, unprovoked and rationalized by lies, that led England and France to honor their treaty with Poland and finally oppose Hitler, thus beginning World War II. There was no jubilation at the time; members of the military recognized that Germany was not yet prepared for a war with England. As an eyewitness, William Shirer describes the reaction of German people on the street: "I was standing in the Wihelmstrasse before the Chancellery about noon when the loudspeakers suddenly announced that Great Britain had declared herself at war with Germany. Some 250 people—no more—were standing there in the sun. They listened attentively to the announcement. When it was finished there was not a murmur. They just stood there. Stunned. It was difficult for them to comprehend that Hitler had led them into a world war" (1959:615). Obviously, their attention had been diverted from what had been going on around them since 1933.

The Semiotics of the Nazi Movement

The famous Italian social theorist Antonio Gramsci emphasizes the cultural and educative dimensions of political movements. He notes that it is important, and ultimately more economical, for leaders to gain the consent of their populations through practical concessions (e.g., providing jobs, better wages, and consumer goods), as well as by ideological means—convincing people, through imagery and discourse, of the leadership's legitimate right to lead. Gramsci uses the term *hegemony* to refer to this gaining of consent and stresses that it is a temporary condition that has to be actively maintained through ongoing negotiations and concessions, as well as ideologically through public imagery, discourse, and education. While requiring a good deal of attention and effort, maintaining hegemony is preferable to continually having to use the police, prisons, and the military to maintain control of a state's population; in fact the need to use coercion is a clear sign that consent has faltered. The ultimate goal of a political movement or a state is to have the population actually internalize the leadership's vision, goals, and actions—its right to lead—as being part of the natural state of things, beyond question and questioning, so they become "common sense." Gramsci notes that even when consent is strong, hegemony is always backed by the potential of force. In Hitler's Germany, propaganda and concessions, violence and fear were used in tandem. Our main interest here is how the Nazi leaders used music as an important component of the ideological front to "win hearts and minds" within the context of other semiotic practices and against the backdrop of intimidation and violence.

The idea of using nonverbal signs, expressive cultural practices, and rituals to bind people to the state has been around for a long time. In his study *Ritual, Politics, and Power,* David Kertzer discusses an ancient Confucian philosopher who advised that rulers should always avoid giving commands, . . . for commands, being direct and verbal, always bring to the subject's mind the possibility of doing the opposite. But since rituals are non-verbal, they have no contraries. They can therefore be used to produce harmony of wills and actions without provoking calcitrance; if a man finds himself playing his appointed part in *li* [ritual] and thus already—as it were *de facto*—in harmony with others, it no more occurs to him than it occurs to a dancer to move to a different rhythm that that being played by the orchestra. (1988:13–14)[2]

Kertzer's and the Confucian's point about rituals echoes a suggestion that I made in chapter 1 about the different functions of icons and indices on the one hand and symbols on the other. Symbolic propositions, statements *about* other things, often call forth an analytical state of mind; that is, they readily inspire the listener to symbolically assess the truth or falsity of the claim being made with the possibility of finding the statement faulty. Icons and especially indices partake *of* the things they signify, through either resemblance or cooccurrence, and thus seem more natural, real, and hence unquestionable. Hitler was conscious of the fact that he should present only a "few simple ideas" to hammer into the skulls of the populace; like the Zimbabwean nationalists discussed in chapter 5, he was more concerned with creating indexical imagery and pageantry that would attract Germans to his movement and inspire them with emotion to action.

Already in 1920, Hitler was conscious of the need to provide emblems that would attract people, and he hit upon the ancient form of the swastika. Through placement on storm trooper armbands and, in black against a red and white background, on the Nazi flag (combining the old empire's colors with the Nazi insignia), this sign became an central index for the party, the Leader, and, with their ascension, Germany as a whole. Ever present at Nazi events throughout the 1920s, the sign grew in ubiquity and thus in indexical potency. The Nazis also paid attention to everyday social practices and used them to their advantage. "Heil Hitler" and the Nazi salute were instituted as the basic form of greeting in Nazi Germany. Supporters of the party were proud to use this greeting. People who privately disapproved of the Nazis still felt they had to use this style of greeting in

Sign / Symbol of the Swastika

2. Quotation taken from J. G. A. Pocock, "Ritual, Language, Power: An Essay on the Apparent Meanings of Ancient Chinese Philosophy," *Political Science* 16 (1964): 3–31.

public for fear that if they did not it might be noted and they would come under suspicion.

Why bother with such details of mundane life? David Kertzer analyzes the effects of the Nazi greeting through the concept of *cognitive dissonance*, which he says occurs when our perception of events in the world conflicts with our beliefs about those phenomena (1988). Kertzer writes that the stronger the cognitive dissonance the greater the effort to reduce it in some way. Peirce makes the same argument about doubt in general; he observes that doubt creates discomfort and people will seek to reduce it whenever possible. Kertzer suggests that cognitive dissonance is particularly strong when a person's beliefs conflict with those of the majority of people around her, especially socially important people. Little cognitive dissonance is experienced, however, if people's beliefs are held in common with those around them, even if those beliefs conflict with what might be observed in the outside world. In short, the easiest path to reducing cognitive dissonance or doubt is to conform to majority thinking; it takes a particularly strong person to trust her own positions and observations in opposition to majority views. This idea goes a long way to explain social conformity and how illogical ideas like racism can become common sense. Kertzer quotes Bruno Bettelheim regarding the effects of the Nazi greeting style:

> To Hitler's followers, giving the salute was an expression of self assertion, of power. Each time a loyal subject performed it, his sense of well-being shot up. For an opponent of the regime it worked exactly opposite. Every time he had to greet somebody in public he had an experience that shook and weakened his integration [i.e., there was cognitive dissonance]. More specifically, if the situation forced him to salute, he immediately felt a traitor to his deepest convictions. So he had to pretend to himself that it did not count. Or to put it another way: he could not change his action—he *had* to give the Hitler salute. Since one's integration rests on acting in accord with one's beliefs, the only easy way to retain his integration was to change his beliefs. (quoted in Kertzer 1988:98)

It was precisely the fact that this Nazi ritual took place in a *constantly repeated* mundane facet of social life that made it so powerful. It functioned to constantly erode opponents' sense of self and notions of right and wrong tied up with their opposition to the Nazis. Repeated enough, it might become habit, and the beliefs that chafed with every greeting might begin to fade.

Redundancy is the central mechanism for creating new social habits of thought and action—making them cultural common sense and a core aspect of individuals. Just as repetition is basic to the practicing of any musical instrument, art, or sport to create the basic habits necessary for successful performance, redundancy is basic to the shaping of collective thinking. Redundancy is used in a variety of ways in political movements. As we know from advertising, the constant repetition of a certain cluster of words, images, and ideas ("a few simple ideas pounded into people's skulls") indexically links those images or symbols *with each other,* making their fit seem true or natural, even if they are not. These *indexical clusters* of formerly (and perhaps logically) unrelated signs begin to be organically connected through the repeated experiencing of them together.[3] Connections *among the signs* become *fact* in our experience and begin to be taken for granted, ultimately going unnoticed, regardless of whether there are real connections among the objects of those signs. This is precisely the goal in directing people's thinking and shaping common sense.

Indexical clusters are a basic tool for political rhetoric and propaganda. For example, the Nazi leaders repeatedly linked "German greatness and unity," "Jewish degeneracy," "work," "bread," "freedom," and "militancy" with the party and Hitler in speeches, songs, writing, and films. Similarly, in the months leading up to the invasion of Iraq, George W. Bush repeatedly linked the signs "9/11," "terrorists," "Al Quaida," "weapons of mass destruction," and "Saddam Hussein" in his speeches, and these connections were constantly echoed in the mass media and even country songs. This new indexical cluster was so effective that even after it was demonstrated and publicized that there were no such "weapons of mass destruction" in Iraq and that there was no direct link between Hussein and 9/11 or Al Quaida, some Americans I spoke with still felt that the war was justified because of these connections.[4] Through constant repetition, especially by socially important or powerful people and media, indexical clusters come to be *felt* as true and do not tend to elicit the analytical assessment inspired

3. The concept of indexical clusters should not be confused with the snowballing effect of indices (chapter 1). *Indexical clusters* refers to the repeated grouping of a set of signs such that the signs become indexically tied to each other in one's experience; *snowballing* refers to a single index's acquiring a series of potential associations through different experiences with the sign over time.

4. Note that after it came out in the media that no weapons of mass destruction or links between Hussein and 9/11 were found, the Bush administration gradually changed its justification of the war to be the spreading of 'democracy' and 'freedom'— an old tried-and-true indexical cluster.

by symbolic propositions and arguments. In fact, when logical argument is avoided in public discourse, it is likely that the premises underpinning an indexical cluster are spurious.

Racism is always based on faulty premises—for example, the premise that the members of any group are essentially the same. Nonetheless, racism was a central pillar of Nazi Aryan nationalism. By demonizing 'non-Aryans,' Hitler bolstered Germans' sense of self-worth. Even if a 'true German' was poor, he was still better than Jews, Negroes, Czechs, communists, homosexuals, people with physical disabilities—the list goes on. Such a message was welcomed by many Germans in the face of the humiliations suffered after World War I. Hitler did not invent anti-Semitism, for it was already widespread; he simply tapped into a popular sentiment and pushed racism to its logical extreme—murder.

Jews were displaced from their businesses, which were taken over by 'true Germans'; thus racism had a direct economic benefit, which is usually the case. Moreover, the Nazis provided cheap consumer goods for 'Germans'—very important for winning the hearts and minds of a population—by looting Jewish homes. The demand for consumer goods increased with the improvement of the economy under the Nazis: in January 1932–33 there were six million unemployed, but by 1936 there was fewer than a million.[5] Public auctions of Jewish goods were held in Hamburg every working day between February 1941 and April 1945. LeBor and Boyes paint a dark picture:

> The contents of 72,000 apartments in the East—Jews sent to Auschwitz—were loaded onto trains and sent to central collection points in German cities. Jewish slave laborers sorted through the property and then sent it for auction around the country. Essen received 1,928 freight wagons, Cologne 1,457, Rostock 1,023, Hamburg 2,699. . . .
>
> Frank Bojohr, who has researched the "Aryanization" of Hamburg, calculates that more than a hundred thousand people in the city alone, "ordinary Germans," directly profited from the Holocaust. The Hamburg librarian Gertrud Seydelmann remembers how Germans felt as if they had won the lottery: ration cards were still being honored, there were no serious shortages, husbands were returning from the East laden with meat, wine, and clothes, and then luxury goods were offered at basement prices. "Simple housewives were suddenly wearing fur

5. LeBor and Boyes (2000:30) say there was full employment; Shirer (1959:258) states that there were fewer than a million unemployed.

coats, dealing in coffee and jewelry, had fine old furniture," recalls Seydelmann. "It was the stolen property of Dutch Jews who, as I found out after the war, were already on their way to the gas chambers. I didn't want anything to do with it." (2000:24)

Another way that redundancy works to shape common sense is by presenting the same images and ideas in all realms of life so that in a particular field of practice there will not be conflicting views of reality that might raise doubts or create *heterodoxy*. In demonizing Jewish people to create an image of 'German' superiority and to justify theft and extermination, the Nazis had to deny Jewish humanness and any contributions Jews might make to society. To admit that non-Aryans could produce good art or anything else of worth would be to admit that they might be valuable human beings after all, and this the Nazis could not do. "In the first year of the Third Reich, 1933, [Jews] had been excluded from public office, the civil service, journalism, radio, farming, teaching, the theater, the films; in 1934 they were kicked out of the stock exchanges, and though the ban on their practicing the professions of law and medicine or engaging in business did not come legally until 1938 they were in practice removed from these fields by the time the first four-year period of Nazi rule had come to an end" (Shirer 1959:233). Thus the same message came through again and again across all fields of practice: Jews are inferior, degenerate, not to be trusted or included in civil society—views sanctioned by the law of the land. They were displaced from their homes by force and were constantly demeaned in public before the period of mass extermination—making the image of their inferiority and weakness a common sight in the streets.

This brings up a third type of redundancy, that is, across sign types and modes of experience. Symbolic statements about Jewish degeneracy, weakness, and alien status—in speeches as well as popular and scholarly writing—came to contextualize and define people's indexical experiences with the "weakness" of Jews as they bowed to German violence in the street and to their general exclusion from civil society; symbols were used to generalize and justify what people were seeing and experiencing all around them. Different types of signs were operating to get the same message across in different ways, each fortifying the others to strengthen a particular view of reality.

The twin side of the Nazi racist coin of Jewish inferiority was German Aryan 'racial' superiority and strength. These two ideas were repeated again and again through various types of signs and expressive cultural practices and were acted upon in all fields of social life, thus helping create the belief that they were true. Such redundancy in public imagery and policy is possible only when the state or elites are able to effectively control all realms of social life and public discourse. Immediately in 1933 the Nazis began to assume such control, which affected all realms of musical life. Because of its power to bond communities and its special place in German society, the Nazi leaders used music in a variety of pointed ways.

Classical and Popular Music in the Third Reich

Germans were particularly proud of their musical heritage. The "three Bs," Bach, Beethoven, Brahms, at the center of the cosmopolitan classical canon were German (defined, as the Nazis did, broadly) and were a source of the national and 'racial' pride that is so important to nationalist movements. Indeed, in 1938 Joseph Goebbels, the Reich minister of public enlightenment (sic) and propaganda, proclaimed that music was the most glorious art of the German heritage (Potter 1998:ix). Throughout the Nazi period state-sponsored international tours of German orchestras were intended to demonstrate their superiority in this art and to deflect charges of barbarism aimed at the regime. In all identity formation, people often highlight aspects of the self or group that are identified as special by others, and such was the case of Nazi nationalism and German classical music. The irony here is that Nazis denigrated cosmopolitanism as a diluted, false cultural position while at the same time their selection of musical indices was influenced by the stature of German composers in cosmopolitan circles.

Already in the 1870s the German composer and writer Richard Wagner had promoted the somewhat self-serving idea that the essence of Germanness was to be found in music. Wagner's nationalistic, racial definition of German identity as transcending state and regionally defined boundaries fit well with Hitler's conceptions and expansionist plans, and Wagner became a pillar of Nazi musical nationalism and a favorite of Hitler. Michael Meyer notes that in the last three decades of the nineteenth century, music "had become inextricably tied to the ideological milieu which also produced National Socialism via the cultural nationalists who had opposed Bismarck. The entry of German music as a superior artistic achievement into national consciousness coincided with the victory of German arms and the creation of the Reich, whose export articles included Wagner's music, thus reinforcing Germany's claim to cultural superiority. Wagner and the Reich complemented one another" (1991:8).

Only months after Hitler came to power, in November 1933 a new law was passed that replaced all of the cultural organizations of the Weimar Republic with the Reich Chamber of Culture (*Reichskulturkammer*) under Goebbels. The law made it compulsory for everyone in Nazi Germany who was involved in the

> "creation, reproduction, intellectual or technical preparation, dissemination, preservation, sale or procurement of cultural goods and assets" (section 1) to belong to one of the seven specialist sections of the *Reichskulturkammer*, which ranged from the Reich Chamber of Music and Chamber of Theatre to the Chamber of Broadcasting and Film. Thus even the practitioners of popular music, band leaders and composers of hit songs, found themselves automatically subject to the organization and control apparatus of, in their case, the Reich Chamber of Music. (Wicke 1985:150)

William Shirer writes, "The new Nazi era of German culture was illuminated not only by the bonfires of [banned] books . . . but by the regimentation of culture on a scale which no modern Western nation had ever experienced" (1959:241).

As might be guessed, one of the first activities of the Chamber of Music was to purge Jews from their professional music positions, opening new slots for 'German' musicians, conductors, composers, critics, and scholars. With the help of music critics and musicologists, the chamber set about defining and promoting genuine German music as separate from degenerate, destructive musical influences associated with Jewish composers and musicians, whose music was officially banned, along with 'Negro' jazz, quite popular in Europe at the time, and other non-Aryan musics. This was a contradictory and complicated process for various reasons, not the least being that it was impossible to objectively define good and bad music or musical essences in racial terms beyond the indexical associations with the people themselves, since 'race' itself is a bogus ideological construct. Nonetheless, to purify German culture, the state sponsored research of musicians' genealogies and published works like *The Lexicon of Jews in Music* to help identify whose music should be shunned.

The cosmopolitan stature and popularity of certain German classical music composers who also happened to be Jewish, such as Felix Mendelssohn, Giacomo Meyerbeer, and Gustav Mahler, created the need for special explanation. It was argued that their stature was strictly due to the backing of their 'racial comrades' and that the music of Mendelssohn was a cheap and fraudulent imitation of true German romanticism. Meyer writes that Mendelssohn was

> the main target of Nazi criticism, for the reason of having received the greatest acclaim. He also was denied the possibility of ever having reached German depth. Instead of treating him as a German, he was regarded as an intruder who had been celebrated as "substitute of German masters," at times even placed above Beethoven. All his most celebrated works were violently attacked, his violin concerto, the *Midsummer Night's Dream,* his Octet for Strings, all of which "lacked German soul." If he had had soul [the Nazi argument went], he would have composed pure Jewish Music. (1991:270–71)

This type of hollow, circular reasoning is the necessary product of an argument based on faulty racist premises and *essentialist* conceptions of a given subjectivity. The case of the great Viennese waltz composer Johann Strauss underlines the arbitrariness of Nazi racial musical policy. According to Peter Wicke, Strauss was accepted by the Nazis as an example of 'true German nationality' in music. In 1938 it was discovered that he was one-quarter Jewish and thus warranted banning. The Reich Genealogical Office was apprised of this and the report was passed on to Goebbels, who immediately confiscated and classified—i.e., buried—the damaging documents (Wicke 1985:151).

If Mendelssohn was a problem, jazz was even more so because of its broad popularity. As discussed earlier, to be successful political movements must attract as well as compel or coerce. As with Strauss, the popularity of an artist or style carries its own force and attractions for politicians if they can link that popularity to their programs. Within capitalist societies, popularity also carries a different type of force; that is, popular musicians are powerful as commodities for making money. As useful as popularity is for both politicians and businesspeople, problems can emerge if a given artist "won't play ball" or if, as with jazz in Nazi Germany, artists or styles conflict with the core political ideology.

After World War I, jazz and other forms of U.S. popular culture took Europe by storm. Like 'Jewish music,' 'jazz,' often defined broadly to include other types of American popular music, was banned in the Third Reich because of its associations with African Americans and Jewish songwriters such as Irving Berlin and George Gershwin: "jazz is Negro music, seen through the eyes of these Jews."[6] As stated by the Nazi national director of broadcasting, "The elimination of nigger jazz was not a matter of beat or syncopation, but of whether a people of Germany's high cultural level can allow itself indefinitely to look for sustenance from a Hottentot kraal without doing damage to its soul" (quoted in Wicke 1985:152). In spite of this official position, German orchestras continued to play light swing-derived dance music at clubs and on the air in the Third Reich; Goebbels was a practical man who was willing to compromise to keep Germans on the home front happy.[7]

As the country began to gear up for the war, Goebbels increasingly favored light popular music, dripping, in Wicke's phrase, with "sentimentality and high pathos," as a harmless form of escape to divert attention from hardships. Goebbels was also concerned that Germans stay tuned to the radio stations that his ministry controlled. So while American- and cosmopolitan-influenced popular music was not ideologically pure, its very popularity made it useful. Using statistics from 1938, Wicke shows that militaristic and folk music—types favored in Nazi nationalist discourse— made up only 2.5 percent of all radio programs, with 8 percent being devoted to classical music (the German Art!) and 60 percent being dance and light music; the remaining 29.5 percent of airtime involved talking. Economic elites often have close alliances with political leaders, and compromises of official ideology are made for the benefit of both. Thus the German Lindström Record Company made a tidy profit during the war years by distributing original American jazz recordings throughout the occupied countries while these very recordings were illegal in Germany (Wicke 1985:153).

Under the 1939 ban on tuning in to foreign radio stations, listening to the original jazz and swing records that were broadcast from the Allied countries carried a risk of imprisonment of five to ten years. Yet this law was commonly disobeyed, and the BBC, which played a good deal of jazz

6. Quoted from the prestigious German music journal *Melos*, 1930, by Wicke (1985:152).

7. Examples of swing-inflected music played by German orchestras during the 1937–44 period, such as Erhard Bauschke und sein Orchester, can be heard on disc 1 of the box set *Swing Tanzen Verboten! Swing Music and Nazi Propaganda Swing during World War II*, Proper Records, Properbox 56. The notes to the recordings suggest that these orchestras may have played "hotter" versions of swing music live but were required to tone it down for recordings. My thanks to David Patterson for introducing me to this collection.

and swing music, was especially popular. Germans who were caught listening to foreign broadcasts may have occasionally gotten off because of a sympathetic Gestapo man. Mike Zwerin recently interviewed an ex-Gestapo member, who told him, "In 1941 there was a national SS seminar in Berlin on the subject of how to enforce the banning of jazz. Different officers from different cities had different ideas. I was for leniency. I saw no real harm in it. I like jazz. I like to dance with my wife. Though jazz was banned there were no strict rules about its definition. It was up to each officer to interpret just what was jazz" (2000:90). While this may be face-saving reminiscing long after the fact, it at least suggests that even the Gestapo was not a homogeneous group. It also seems realistic. Musicologists cannot always clearly delimit or define jazz, and so it is not surprising that the Gestapo had similar difficulties. Hence there was room for individual interpretation; leniency and undeserved punishment were both possibilities.

Following the formula of British broadcasts, which 'sandwiched' news between the playing of popular music, the Reich Propaganda Ministry began to use (officially banned) American swing and popular songs for propaganda broadcasts aimed at the Allied countries. The German ensemble Charlie and His Orchestra released "You're Driving Me Crazy" in 1940. Standard love lyrics made up the first verse, "You're driving me crazy, / what did I do to you," but spoken dialogue over a swinging instrumental piano accompaniment, and rendered in a particularly sarcastic voice in English, followed:

Here is Winston Churchill's latest tear jerker:
"Yes, the Germans are driving me crazy.
I thought I had friends, but they shattered my plans.
They built up a front against me, it is quite amazing,
above in [?] the skies with their planes.
The Jews are the friends that are near me who cheer me,
believe me they do,
but Jews are the kind that hurt me, desert me,
and laugh at me too.
Yes the Germans are driving me crazy, my last chance I'll pray
to get into this muddle is the U.S.A.

This new pact also is driving me crazy,
Germany, Italy, Japan, it gives me a pain.
I'm losing my nerves. I'm getting lazy. A prisoner lost [?]
to remain in England to reign.
The Jews are the friends who are near me, they still cheer me,

believe me they do,
but Jews are not the kind of heroes who would fight for me,
now they are leaving me too.
Yes, the Germans are driving me crazy,
by Jove I pray, come in U.S.A."

All of this is followed by a light swinging instrumental chorus of the tune, adding to the mocking tone, at the end of the recording.[8]

The Nazis and Participatory Music

The number of musical organizations inherited by the Third Reich Chamber of Music from the Weimar Republican era was vast; Germany had a particularly rich and active musical life. Quoting early twentieth-century German musicologist H. J. Moser, Pamela Potter estimates that there were 50 opera houses and 150 ranking symphony orchestras supported by the state, and 100 string quartets, 50 piano trios, 25 chamber music groups with winds, and at least 15 oratorio quartets and madrigal groups that worked professionally on a freelance basis.

The real surge in musical activity, however, occurred in the realm of amateur choruses and participatory musical activities in the growing youth movement. Potter writes, "At a time when Germany seemed ever more politicized and disjointed, communal music making promised to promote solidarity. Participation, it was hoped, would not only instill community spirit and goodwill but would also restore music's power to unify, which had been lost in the bourgeois era." For 1929, she lists 13,000 amateur choirs with 1.3 million members belonging to the German Singers' League. Choral singing was also associated with major political movements such as the Social Democratic Party and the Communist Party, and by 1928 the German Workers Singers' League had 440,000 members (1998:4–6).

Around the turn of the century a youth movement began to emerge which, by the 1920s, grew beyond its middle-class roots. The growth of this movement has been attributed to young people's response to the political fragmentation and bleak economic conditions plaguing Germany. Youth music organizations promoted values that were directly opposed to elite musical aesthetics. Potter reports that these organizations "eschewed anything they regarded as musical manifestations of bourgeois individualism, art for art's sake, and the cult of the genius." Instead they pursued

8. *Swing Tanzen Verboten!* disc 2, cut 1.

participatory music making that "could bond the entire community." To this end they emphasized German folk songs, pre-1700 polyphony, and work songs written explicitly for the youth movement. They rejected commercial forms of music and jazz, associating them with American business and Jews, and even traditional concerts because they bred passivity (1998:7). Early on in its development, the Nazi Party inherited all these participatory activities and community-building ideas and began turning them to its own political ends.

Hitler paid a good deal of attention to German youth and to education. As in most nationalist and political movements, education was seen as the key for molding new citizens—and soldiers—and tying them to the party and the state. Hitler took such measures to the extreme. After 1933 all textbooks were Nazified, and Jewish teachers were purged. If they wanted to remain, teachers had to support the cult of the Führer, and *Mein Kampf* became the new intellectual guide. Elite schools were set up for talented young people, who were trained to take leadership roles in the party and military. Once their children were enrolled, parents could not remove them from these schools. Vacations for home visits were highly restricted, and letters from home were strictly rationed. "Step by step, mothers and fathers were banished from the lives of their children and familial loyalty was transferred to the teacher, to the school, and to the Fuehrer" (LeBor and Boyes 2000:53). Although the goal was never completely achieved, after 1936 all German boys were supposed to join Hitler Youth, and the parents of those who refused could be punished. "At ten, after passing suitable tests in athletics, camping and Nazified history, [a boy] graduated into the Jungvolk ('Young Folk'), where he took the following oath:

> In the presence of this blood banner, which represents our Fuehrer, I swear to devote all my energies and my strength to the savior of our country, Adolf Hitler. I am willing and ready to give up my life for him, so help me God. (Shirer 1959:253)

There was a separate organization for Young Maidens, who also received physical and ideological training in camplike settings; the emphasis was on their future roles as healthy mothers of healthy 'Aryan' children. Girls fourteen to twenty-one became members of the League of German Maidens. Young women were obliged to do a year of service on a farm or in an urban household, and girls' camps were often located near labor service camps for young men. Parents began to complain that their daughters were becoming pregnant in these situations. Shirer reports, "On more than one occasion I listened to women leaders of the [League of German Maidens] . . . lecture their young charges on the moral and patriotic duty of bearing children for Hitler's Reich—within wedlock if possible, but without it if necessary" (1959:254). Turning the Nazi slogan, "Strength through Joy," on its head, the saying "I lose strength through joy" became a common joke among young men who were probably only too happy to fulfill this duty to the Reich.

In relation to the youth movement as a whole, Shirer's eyewitness account is again valuable:

> In such a manner were the youth trained for life and work and death in the Third Reich. Though their minds were deliberately poisoned, their regular schooling interrupted, their homes largely replaced so far as their rearing went, the boys and girls, the young men and women, seemed immensely happy, filled with a zest for the life of a Hitler Youth. . . . No one who traveled up and down Germany in those days and talked with the young in their camps and watched them work and play and sing could fail to see that, however sinister the teaching, here was an incredibly dynamic youth movement. (1959:256)

Coming out of a period when there was not much hope for the future, Hitler gave the youth something to believe in and helped them believe in themselves. The Nazi youth programs created communal, peer-based, participatory activities in camplike settings that bonded these young people to each other; a genuine happiness often results from such bonding experiences regardless of the underlying motivations. In a 1933 speech, Hitler said, "When an opponent declares, 'I will not come over to your side,' I calmly say, 'Your child belongs to us already. . . . What are you? You will pass on. Your descendants, however, now stand in the new camp. In a short time they will know nothing else but this new community.'" In the youth camps and meetings, as well as in many other public activities, collective singing was a prominent tool for Nazi education and for creating feelings of social unity, pride, and strength.

In his article on Nazi music, Vernon Lidtke suggests that there were three distinct phases in the development of Nazi music and songs. In the first stage, before 1933, songs were used to win people to the party and publicize Nazi ideas. During this "period of struggle," the storm troopers and Hitler Youth were the most active singers. Few new Nazi songs were composed. Rather, the bulk of songs had preexisting tunes from a variety of sources with altered or new texts. Pointedly, melodies from Social

Democrat or Communist workers' songs were used to set Nazi lyrics. This was a type of *creative indexing*. The melodies were familiar and indexed old party loyalties, while the texts included Nazi indices and images. Creative indexing was intended to fuse old feelings of loyalty to the Nazi party. World War I soldier-song, popular song, and 'folk' song melodies were also widely used. Lidtke remarks that Nazi lyrics "stressed combat, struggle, revolution, brutality, anti-Semitism, blood, and loyalty to Germany; but always fighting, fighting, fighting" (Lidtke 1982:169). As another example of creative indexing, the tune of the beloved labor song "The International" received new lyrics to attract workers to the Nazi Party:

> Arise, Hitler men, close your ranks,
> We are ready for the racial struggle,
> With our blood we consecrate the banner,
> The symbol of a new era.
> On its red and white background
> Shines our black swastika bright.
> Victory sounds are heard all over,
> As the morning's light breaks through;
> National Socialism
> Is the future of our Land.
>
> (quoted in Lidtke 1982:174)

As discussed in chapter 1, while all symbols involve language in the linking of sign and object, not all words always function as symbols. This is certainly true of literature, poetry, and song texts. While obviously expressed in words, this Nazi text combines the semiotic potentials of icons, indices, and symbols. The text juxtaposes the images of the flag and the swastika, central indices of the party; the iconic metaphor "Hitler men"; and "blood," a metonymic index for life and being; and the symbolic proposition "we are ready for the racial struggle."[9] The stanza ends with the metaphoric icons "victory sounds" and "morning's light breaks through" for the projected possible "future of our Land" (symbol), which is indexically linked, through juxtaposition in the text itself, to "National Socialism." Through repeated performances, songs are an ideal vehicle for cementing new indexical clusters that typically involve the combining of iconic,

---

9. A *metaphor* is a special type of icon that asserts a resemblance between the objects of two or more linguistic signs. A *metonym* is a special type of index in which the part stands for the whole.

indexical, and symbolic signs to link people's senses of the actual, the possible, and constructed symbolic abstractions (e.g., "racial struggle").

The first Nazi songbook appeared in 1923 with only a dozen texts, but the number increased dramatically after 1933; separate songbooks were needed in the second phase for specific Nazi organizations including the Hitler Youth, the League of German Maidens, the Strength-Through-Joy (subsidized recreation), and the Labor Service, among many others. Lidtke remarks that lyrics in the second phase emphasized "community, the regeneration of Germany, and the protective and sacred power of the Fuehrer" (1982:186). Professional writers, poets, and musicians were hired by the state to compose the wealth of new songs that were required. After the Nazis had gained control over all realms of social life, the collective singing of Nazi songs became a prominent part of public holiday celebrations and political rallies and at meetings of all types of social organizations. Communal singing was the focus of state-sponsored "Evening Song weeks" among workers. Collective singing was also instituted as a basic activity before and/or after a day's work in factories. Singing had become a "political task," and it was meant to create a sense of German community and as a way to implant Nazi ideology in people's minds through ceaseless repetition. And what was sung?

> Our flag flutters before us,
> We enter the future man for man.
> For Hitler we march through night and need,
> With the flag of youth, for freedom, for bread.
> Our flag flutters before us,
> Our flag is the new era.
> It leads us into eternity.
> Our flag means more to us than death!

and

> As one man, we, both young and old,
> Embrace the swastika flag.
> Farmers and burghers and workers
> Are wielding both hammer and sword.
> They fight for Hitler, for labor, and bread.
> Germans, wake up! And death to the Jew!
> Folk, take arms!
>
> (quoted in Lidtke 1982:197, 192)

209

Unison singing in plain voices and in simple style was emphasized so that all could participate equally without distinguishing those with more musical experience. As can be witnessed in Hitler's propaganda movie *Triumph of the Will* from the early 1930s, thousands upon thousands of people sang together at political rallies.[10] The effect of mass singing on an individual's consciousness can only be guessed, but raising one's voice in unison with so many others is typically a powerful emotion-producing experience. When the emotion felt is indexically tied to the words sung and the meaning of the event itself, it can be a highly effective political tool. Lidtke remarks, "Through singing communal songs individuals would be swept up by the totality, would lose their sense of self-identity and be merged, momentarily at least, with the organic wholeness of the German *Volksgemeinschaft* (national-racial community)" (1982:187–88). Such was the conscious goal of Nazi participatory music programs: that the German people might be willingly led anywhere and to do anything. As I have been suggesting throughout this book, music is a particularly powerful resource for building and bonding communities. While community solidarity is usually thought of as positive for individual and social life, the powerful semiotic potentials of music can be used in mass movements for dangerous ends.

Music and the Civil Rights Movement in the United States

If Nazi Germany is one of the darkest moments in human history, the civil rights movement of the 1950s and 1960s in the United States is one of the brightest, filled with heroism, dignity, and intelligence expressed through the actions of extraordinary "average" African American citizens seeking decency and justice. Tales of African Americans' personal sacrifices and chilling feats of bravery in the face of white supremacy—schoolchildren and seamstresses willingly going up against snarling police dogs, fire hoses, and baseball bats—during those years seem almost surreal from a contemporary vantage point, a vantage point made possible by the civil rights movement itself. In some ways there have been major changes. Americans no longer require two of everything: water fountains, lunch counters, hotel accommodations; public murders of African Americans

---

10. This film by Leni Riefenstahl records and idealizes the 1934 Nuremberg Nazi Party Congress. In the long opening sequence, Hitler slowly descends in his airplane like the Messiah coming down from the clouds.

are not so easily condoned. Yet black teenagers are still trained by their mothers to keep the receipts for expensive items in case of visits from the police (chapter 4), and economic disparities and percentages of youths in prison can still be plotted along color lines. As recently as June 2005, Congress finally passed a federal antilynching law—something proposed and defeated earlier in the twentieth century with the same states' rights argument that had fueled the Civil War. Congress issued the new law with an apology, and so it should have. By now "the Movement" has dissipated, but much of the same work remains to be done. The decade of 1955 to 1965 provides a glimpse of what is possible when "average" people in great numbers come together for a just cause.

'Race' Relations in Postwar America

Like the nationalist movements against colonialism in Africa, the civil rights movement was partially a response to World War II. The viciousness of Hitler's racism was repugnant especially among the Allied powers, and this helped liberalize attitudes toward colonial peoples who had been kept in a dominated position largely because of European ethnocentrism and racist attitudes. The war had its effects among African Americans as well. African American soldiers who had fought against Hitler's racism did so in a segregated U.S. military. They returned home after freeing Europe to find that they were still not free or equal in their own country. But here too things were beginning to change. In 1948, President Truman issued an executive order that the armed forces be integrated as rapidly as possible, although it took more than a decade to complete the process. U.S. politicians from Truman to John Kennedy were becoming increasingly conscious that racism in the United States made the country look bad abroad. This was of particular concern in the cold war period of the 1950s and 1960s, as the U.S. government sought to spread capitalism around the world under the banner of freedom and democracy in competition with the Soviet Union. Civil rights leaders would come to use this to their advantage.

Although the Fourteenth Amendment of 1868 provided 'equal protection under the law' to all citizens of the United States, the 1896 *Plessy v. Ferguson* Supreme Court case allowed for 'separate but equal' race relations. The idea of 'separate but equal' legitimated segregation in almost everything: eating facilities, public transportation, water fountains, hotels, housing, and schools—with an emphasis on *separate* rather than *equal*. In 1954, the NAACP brought a series of cases before the Supreme Court that challenged segregation in public schools. In *Brown v. Board of Education of Topeka, Kansas,* the court found that segregation generated feelings of inferiority among African American schoolchildren, that it was harmful, and that segregated institutions should be integrated "with all deliberate speed." In spite of the federal ruling, state and local officials and citizens blocked school desegregation, often violently (Dierenfield 2004:27). In September 1957, President Eisenhower was finally compelled to send in federal troops to stop mob violence and enforce desegregation in Little Rock, Arkansas, yet the battle had to be fought over and over on a case-by-case basis, and it is estimated that 75 percent of southern school districts still remained segregated in 1965.

The Fifteenth Amendment of 1870 had guaranteed the vote to African American men (notice that women's rights were not even considered). Yet they were disfranchised in different states (beginning with Mississippi in 1890) through the use of poll taxes, literacy requirements, and bogus examinations not required of white voters. Where these measures failed, intimidation and threats of violence kept African Americans away from the polls and segregationists in political power.

Just as colonial Zimbabwe (Rhodesia) was officially divided into 'African' and 'European' areas and Africans could not own homes or land in places designated as white (chapter 5), so too Birmingham, Alabama, was legally zoned along color lines. Glen Eskew reports, "The adoption of a general zoning code in 1915 and its revision into a comprehensive zoning ordinance in 1926 initiated a process of prohibiting African Americans from living in certain areas of Birmingham, a spatial manifestation of white supremacy" (1997:54). As the need for more housing arose in the postwar period, African Americans in Birmingham appealed to a 1917 Supreme Court decision that outlawed residential segregation. They also simply began to spill over the official color line into white neighborhoods. The white response? Between 1947 and 1965 approximately fifty African American homes were dynamited, and no culprits were ever apprehended by the police. The city became known as Bombingham, and one contested neighborhood became known as 'Dynamite Hill.'

Racism, like many long-held and deeply entrenched habits of thought and practice, changes at a snail's pace. By the mid-1950s, average African Americans were growing weary of waiting. The bus boycott of 1955–56 in Montgomery, Alabama, is often considered the beginning of the civil rights movement, yet there were precedents. A similar boycott led by Reverend T. J. Jemison had already occurred in Baton Rouge, Louisiana, two years previously. In 1941 A. Philip Randolph, head of the Pullman Porters Union and founding father of the civil rights movement, threatened a mass march on Washington, forcing Roosevelt to ban discrimination in the war industries.[11] In 1933 there was a "Don't Buy Where You Can't Work" movement. The Montgomery boycott, however, brought greater countrywide attention to the fight for equal rights, and it was there that Martin Luther King Jr. began to assume a leadership role in what would become a more unified mass movement.

Overcoming former reluctance and fear to oppose white segregationists, African Americans of Montgomery walked miles to their jobs in all kinds of weather or formed car pools, and black cab drivers lowered their fares. Money was raised for the MIA to buy fifteen station wagons for transporting people. Bruce Dierenfield notes that the unity of the black community behind the boycott raised people's confidence levels; he quotes a Montgomery janitor as saying, "The world knows we are right, and we is gonna win our cause. . . . White folks don't scare us no longer" (2004:47). The bus company and city businesses lost a million dollars, yet company and city officials refused to negotiate, fearing that compromise on this issue would threaten the very fabric of their society. Opposition to the boycott turned violent; King's parsonage was bombed with his wife and daughter inside. Whites threw eggs and balloons filled with urine at black pedestrians walking to work. Car-pool stations and black churches were bombed. In November 1956, the U.S. Supreme Court ruled that Montgomery's segregation laws were unconstitutional, and after 381 days of sacrifice and intimidation, a vote was held to end the boycott. On December 21, King, E. D. Nixon, and Ralph Abernathy sat in the front of the bus.

White resistance and violence continued, but the boycott helped spread the idea that unified mass action could be effective against Jim Crow laws and customs. Other acts of heroism were to follow. On February 1, 1960, four black college freshmen, Joseph McNeil, David Richmond, Franklin McCain, and Ezell Blair, launched the student phase of the civil rights movement with a sit-in at a segregated Woolworth's lunch counter in Greensboro, North Carolina. Sit-ins across the South followed, and televised images of these direct-action protests inspired young people, both black and white, around the country to get involved. The student sit-ins were a model for spontaneous grassroots involvement. The Student Non-violent Coordinating Committee (SNCC) emerged out of the student

11. Larry Tye's *Rising from the Rails: Pullman Porters and the Making of the Black Middle Class* (2004) provides a fascinating account of Randolph's career and African American political mobilization prior to the civil rights movement. My thanks to Karl Kramer for bringing this book to my attention.

sit-ins and served as an umbrella for community organization. Following King, they advocated nonviolence but added a more uncompromising direct action approach than that of King's organization, the Southern Christian Leadership Conference (SCLC), which had mainly been working on voter registration drives.

The biggest sit-ins took place in Nashville, Tennessee, where a group of students already had been training themselves for such protests through role-play, workshops, and lectures on the nonviolence philosophies of Jesus Christ, Gandhi, and Martin Luther King, ideas that had become central to the movement during this phase. James Lawson, a divinity student and one of the leaders in Nashville, was involved in training protesters in nonviolent methods, "You have to do more than just not hit back," he told them. "You have to love the person who's hitting you" (Dierenfield 2004:54). The first wave of peaceful protesters were pulled off the lunch-counter stools and beaten by thugs before being dragged off to jail on trespassing and disorderly conduct charges. A new wave of sit-ins followed the next day with the same results, followed by another wave. The Nashville students adhered to a new strategy of 'jail no bail'—the idea that keeping so many people in jail would tax the white power structure financially and in terms of space. In Nashville, the students inspired the entire black community to boycott downtown businesses, and when a bomb destroyed the home of Alexander Looby, the students' defense lawyer, four thousand African Americans marched on city hall in what Dierenfield calls the first large-scale march of the civil rights movement. Confronted by the marchers, the mayor conceded that discrimination was morally wrong, and several weeks later Nashville became the first major southern city to begin desegregating its lunch counters.

The stories of valor go on and on: the "freedom rides" of 1961 to protest segregation of interstate buses; black students' attempts to enter segregated schools and universities at great personal risk; the long campaign in 1963 headed by Fred Shuttlesworth to end segregation in Birmingham. The Birmingham protests brought some of the staunchest segregationists of the South, such as Bull Connor, to the verge of capitulation but for an untimely compromise by Martin Luther King, who was being pressured by President John Kennedy and U.S. Attorney General Robert Kennedy to end the protests.[12] The more conservative middle-class leaders of the movement were not always in step with the masses they claimed to lead,

12. Glenn Eskew's brilliant book *But for Birmingham* chronicles this campaign in great detail and is highly recommended for anyone who wants to understand the com-

but the masses had certainly been aroused to action. According to Justice Department records, there were more than a thousand different demonstrations around the country during three months in 1963 alone.

The Freedom Songs of the Civil Rights Movement

Where was the music in all of this? The answer is everywhere (see Johnson Reagon 1983). Almost all commentators suggest that mass singing was one of the primary forces that helped unite people to action and bolster courage in the face of white oppression and violence during the first decade of the movement. The black churches were the focal points for mass grassroots organization and action, and consequently hymns, gospel, and spirituals were a primary source for civil rights music in the early phase. Another source was leftist labor songs, sometimes introduced to the movement by white folksingers and political activists such as Guy Carawan and Pete Seeger. In their book *Freedom Is a Constant Struggle,* witnesses and participants Guy and Candie Carawan write,

> Since 1960 singing has been important to the movement. People sang on demonstrations and at mass meetings, in paddy wagons and jail cells, to bolster spirits, to gain courage and to bring people together. Every new chapter of the struggle produced its own songs. . . .
>
> The Selma March in the Spring of 1965 brought attention to a growing movement in the black belt of Alabama. The fifty mile march was very conducive to the spontaneous improvisation of verse after verse after verse. Many songs got started there and carried elsewhere by the 40,000 marchers from all across the country. The march ended in front of the state capitol in Montgomery in a powerful show of "black and white together . . . we shall overcome" and will surely go down as a turning point—perhaps the last time that such a scene will be witnessed in this country for some time to come. (1968:8)

The sit-in demonstrators in Nashville sang one song over and over:

I'm gonna do what the spirit says do,
If the spirit says sit in, I'm gonna sit in.
If the spirit says boycott, I'm gonna boycott.

plexity of the civil rights movement, class-based conflicts within its leadership, and the economic basis underpinning segregation in the South; see especially 283–89.

If the spirit says go to jail, I'm gonna go to jail.
I'm gonna do what the spirit says to do.

(quoted in Dierenfield 2004:55)

The schoolchildren who became the primary protesters in the marches in Birmingham after most of the adults in the movement had been locked up hit the streets singing.

The Birmingham movement's sixty-person gospel choir electrified mass meetings with call-and response songs such as this one:

Lead Singer:	**Choir:**
I've got a job	I've got a job
And I want you to know	You've got a job
All of God's children	All of God's children
Surely	Surely got a job
We've got a job	We've got a job to do

We can't get freedom 'til we get through
Carryin' the cross of our Lord.

. . . .

We are fight for	Freedom
Come on, you might not hear us	Freedom
One time for Bull Connor	Freedom
One time for Mayor Boutwell	Freedom
One time for Governor Wallace	Freedom
One time for the city jail	Freedom
One time for the city hall	Freedom

The constitution of the United States	
Says that we're due freedom	Freedom
Freedom	Freedom (8×)
Justice	Justice (4×)
Yes, Lord	Yes, Lord (4×)
Freedom	Freedom (4×)
We've got a job	We've got a job to do

We can't get freedom 'til we get through
Carrying the cross of our Lord.

(quoted in Carawan and Carawan 1968:22–23)

The basic function and effects of the mass singing of such songs were the same as for those sung at Nazi nationalist rallies, although the message was certainly different. The very fact of many voices sounding together creates the experience of unity, directly and concretely felt. The call-and-response structure of this and so many gospel songs, like all interlocking practices in participatory music, both articulate and are the result of social coordination and unity. The constant repetition of a few simple ideas in the texts cement them in people's minds as truth, and thus help generate courage to act on that truth in the face of opposition.

[handwritten margin note: power & unity of participatory singing]

Dorothy Cotton, SCLC member and participant in the St. Augustine, Florida, demonstrations of 1964, commented on the power of singing: "This was about the roughest city we've had—forty-five straight nights of beatings and intimidation. We marched regularly at night. We kept being ordered not to march especially at night because it was so dangerous. We sang every night before we went out to get up our courage. The Klan was always waiting for us—these folk with the chains and bricks and things—Hoss Manucy and his gang. After we were attacked we'd come back to church, and somehow always we'd come back bleeding, singing 'I love everybody'" (quoted in Carawan and Carawan 1968:25). This adapted spiritual associated with the SCLC repeats the words "I love everybody, I love everybody, I love everybody in my heart," with substitutions such as "I love Hoss Manucy, I love Hoss Manucy, I love Hoss Manucy in my heart," "You can't make me doubt Him, You can't make me doubt Him, You can't make me doubt Him in my heart," and "The Klan can't make me doubt Him," etc.

Speaking to the power of repetition, Cotton goes on to say, "It was hard to sing 'I love Hoss Manucy' when he'd just beat us up. . . . So we sing it, and the more we sing it, the more we grow in ability to love people who mistreat us so bad" (in Carawan and Carawan 1968:27). Here is the exact opposite image of Nazi songs that repeated the hateful message "Death to the Jew" over and over, yet the function of the songs and the power of singing were the same—to get people to think the unthinkable, internalize those thoughts, and then act on them. Cotton's is surely a powerful testimony about the power of group singing to strengthen resolve and a particular way of being in the world.

Speaking of her experiences as a singer and activist in the Albany movement, Bernice Johnson Reagon notes,

I sang and heard the freedom songs, and saw them pull together sections of the Black community at times when other means of commu nication were ineffective. . . . In Dawson, Georgia, where Blacks w 75 percent of the population, I sat in a church and felt the chill tha through a small gathering of Blacks when the sheriff and his deputies walked in. They stood at the door, making sure everyone knew they were there. Then a song began. And the song made sure that the sheriff and his deputies knew we were there. We became visible, our image of ourselves was enlarged when the sounds of the freedom songs filled all the space in that church. (1983:28)

Songs have the capacity to condense huge realms of meaning in an economical form through layered indexical meanings as well as the juxtaposition of varied ideas as indexical clusters without the requirements of rational ordering or argument. Through indexical snowballing (chapter 1), a song can also become associated with various social movements through time and so index earlier aspirations and struggles. This was precisely the Nazis' goal for creative indexing when they used the tunes associated with earlier political movements to set Nazi lyrics. Similarly, Johnson Reagon (1983:28) considers the use of the old tune "Old Time Religion" with new words:

We are moving on to victory
We are moving on to victory
We are moving on to victory
With hope and dignity
We will all stand together
Until we all are free.

She notes "These transformed songs, used in conjunction with older songs, effectively conveyed the message that the Black struggle had a long history" (1983:28).

"We Shall Overcome," the anthem of the civil rights movement during its pacifist phase, had a variety of associations over time, as explained by Ron Eyerman and Andrew Jamison (1998:2–4). The tune was apparently related to several African American religious songs of the late nineteenth century. In 1901 Charles Tindley published the spiritual "I'll Overcome Some Day." In the 1940s the song was sung by members of the (African American) Tobacco Workers Union in the South; the title was changed to "We Will Overcome," and the tempo slowed down. From there it was diffused as a union song from the Highlander Center, an institution outside Knoxville that had supported a variety of progressive political movements since the 1930s. Eyerman and Jamison write:

Zilphia Horton, the music director at Highlander, had heard the song being sung among black workers, and it soon became one of her favorites and was taught and sung in the cultural programs that she had initiated at Highlander. Symbolically, the title was altered to the more grammatically correct "We *Shall* Overcome," probably by the Harvard dropout Pete Seeger, then active at the Center. . . .

In 1959 at the end of a [civil rights] workshop at Highlander the local police burst in, and somebody stared to hum "We Shall Overcome." In the heat of the moment, a young female high school student from Montgomery, Alabama, began to sing a new verse, "We are not afraid," and, according to Bernice Johnson Reagon, this helped give the song "new life and force." It soon became what Reagon calls the "theme song of the [civil rights] Movement, it was used wherever Movement activities were carried out." (1998:3–4)

In the same way that flags and anthems function for nationalist movements, this anthem came to concretely index a whole range of beliefs, attitudes, and aspirations of the civil rights movement during its first decade. Through its history of black religious roots, associations with both black and white political and labor movements, and as a favorite in a political-activist center, "We Shall Overcome" was well positioned to become the anthem of the civil rights movement. The text economically crystallized the ideas of fortitude and bravery, patience, unity, Christian faith, faith in justice, and racial reconciliation and partnership, all core aspects of the movement's ideology during this phase:

We shall overcome,
We shall overcome,
We shall overcome someday.
Oh, Deep in my heart
I do believe,
We shall overcome someday.

We are not afraid
We are not afraid
We are not afraid, today.
Deep in my heart
I do believe
We shall overcome someday.

The Sound of Black Power

On August 28, 1963, Martin Luther King gave his famous "I Have a Dream" speech during the March on Washington. On September 15 that year, four little girls were senselessly murdered in the vigilante bombing of a Birmingham church.

The civil rights movement had never been unified, there had always been disagreements about strategy and tactics, and there had always been compromise: between local middle-class and grassroots African American leaders and between local movements and countrywide umbrella organizations such as King's SCLC. There had also been African American spokespeople, such as Malcolm X, who did not agree with the 'I love everybody' philosophy of the SCLC. In a speech in Cleveland in 1964, Malcolm stated, "We will work with anybody, anywhere, at any time, who is genuinely interested in tackling the problem [of African American rights] head-on, nonviolently as long as the enemy is nonviolent, but violent when the enemy gets violent" (Malcolm X 1965, see 23–44). In a Harlem speech in 1964 Malcolm suggested, "You'll get freedom by letting your enemy know that you'll do anything to get your freedom; then you'll get it. . . . When you stay radical long enough and get enough people to be like you, you'll get your freedom" (quoted in Zinn 1999:461). Malcolm and others were critical of the black middle-class leaders, represented by King, because they saw them as too willing to compromise with and be co-opted by white politicians.

Increasingly Malcolm and others such as Huey Newton and the Black Panthers shifted the language from 'ethnic' assimilation into the American Dream to separatist nationalism. Point 10 of the Panthers' founding document (October 1966) states:

> We want land, bread, housing, education, clothing, justice, and peace. And as our major political objective, a United Nations–supervised plebiscite to be held through the Black colony in which only Black colonial subjects will be allowed to participate, for the purpose of determining the will of Black people as to their national destiny. (quoted in Dierenfield 2004, appendix)

The Panthers' use of nationalist discourse instead of the concept of ethnicity is important here. As discussed briefly in chapter 4, 'nation' is a type of identity unit that, as constructed through nationalist discourse itself, is linked to the idea of political and territorial sovereignty and independence; that is, according to the premises of nationalism, a social group is defined as a *nation* in relation to having or aspiring to having its own state. The concept of 'ethnicity,' by contrast, is defined within nationalist discourse as a subnational social group, a 'minority' group that is part of, and belongs to, a larger national unit. The Panthers were fully aware of this distinction and so called on the United Nations to mediate between the U.S. government and their *nation*—suggesting that African Americans should be considered on separate but equal footing with the U.S. nation-state.

Meanwhile northern cities across the country exploded in violence—belying the smug idea among northerners that "the race problem" was restricted to southern states.[13] Discontent over poverty, police brutality, and employment inequality led to major race riots in Harlem in 1964 and elsewhere for five consecutive summers—the worst being in the Watts neighborhood of Los Angeles (August 1965), westside Chicago (1966), Newark (July 1967), and Detroit (July 1967). Smaller battles were being waged in U.S. cities throughout these years. In the summer of 1968, I was teaching music in a city children's program in Louisville, Kentucky, and remember driving to work between buildings lined with riflemen. The country really appeared to be entering a period of armed revolt. Congress responded with the Civil Rights Act of 1968, which strengthened the laws against depriving people of their civil rights and violence against African Americans. But as Howard Zinn notes, the bill also contained a section prohibiting interstate travel or activities that would instigate a riot; ironically, the first person prosecuted under the 1968 Civil Rights Act was H. Rap Brown, a SNCC leader who had made an angry speech in Maryland.

For some involved in the continuing struggle against racism, music was simply becoming irrelevant, or at least the old freedom songs certainly were. Expressing this sentiment in the October-November 1966 issue of the liberal folksong magazine *Sing Out!* Julius Lester wrote:

> Now it is over. America has had chance after chance to show that it really meant "that all men are endowed with certain inalienable rights." America has had precious chances in this decade to make it come true. Now it is over. The days of singing freedom songs and the days of combating bullets and billy clubs with Love. We Shall Overcome (and

13. King moved his SCLC staff to Chicago early in 1966 to work for economic improvement in the northern slums and to spread his philosophy of nonviolence. Their reception in white working-class neighborhoods led King to comment that he had never encountered such hate—not in Mississippi or Alabama—as he saw in Chicago.

we have overcome our blindness) sounds old, out-dated and can enter the pantheon of the greats along with the IWW songs and the union songs. As one SNCC veteran put it after the Mississippi March, "Man the people are too busy getting ready to fight to bother with singing anymore."

For the growing number of people who had become radicalized, angry, and cynical about the possibility for peaceful social change, the old freedom songs became indices of their frustration and disillusionment—potent signs of the futility of pacifism. Musical meaning is strongly indexical, and it is the nature of indexical signs to take on new meanings as the events with which they are associated change.

While some people in the civil rights struggle had begun to deny the power of music, or at least turned away from the old freedom songs, others created new music to express the new mood. Otis Redding recorded a powerful, soulful performance of Sam Cooke's anthem "A Change Is Gonna Come." Gil Scott-Heron recorded a biting message of black independence and power in "The Revolution Will Not Be Televised" in proto-rap style. The music of Black Power was spearheaded by James Brown, whose "Say It Loud, I'm Black and I'm Proud," sung in call and response with children, became an articulation and an anthem of the new phase. The song begins with a sharp drum introduction and Professor Brown's knife of a voice calling out, "Say it *loud*," and the children's defiant voices answering "I'm *Black* and I'm *Proud*!"

> (*verse two*)
> I worked more jobs
> With my feet and my hands.
> You know all the work I did
> Was for the other man.
> Now we demand a chance
> To do things for ourselves.
> We're tired of beatin' our heads against the wall
> And workin' for someone else.
>
> J. BROWN: Say it *Loud*!
> CHILDREN: I'm *Black* and I'm *Proud*! (4×)
>
> Now we demand a chance
> To do things for ourselves

We're tired of beatin' our heads against the wall
And workin' for someone else.
Lookie here there's one more thing I got to say.
We're people, we like the birds and the bees,
But we'd rather die on our feet,
Than livin' on our knees.

The message of the text is certainly clear, but beyond this, the recording is a brilliantly rendered icon of how the message should be spread; strong, no-nonsense elders must directly teach their young to stand up for themselves. This effect of the song is supported by Brown's hard-edged vocal timbre, which functions as a dicent index of a powerful man (at least *I'm* convinced). The qualities of toughness, no tolerance of nonsense, and leadership ability are also rendered through the sparse, tightly controlled, percussive parts played by the horns, guitar, and drummer; this dicent indexical effect is partially framed by Brown's general reputation as a strict band leader. Vocal timbre emphasizes tough determination in the young voices answering Brown, with their unified accents on *black* and *proud*. The effect of this aspect of the performance, for me as a listener, however, is as an icon for the *possible* rather than as a dicent index. The children seem overly coached, not themselves, making the overall effect of their performance a suggestion of the possible—this is what the children *should* feel in the best of possible worlds.

In spite of Julius Lester's observation that singing had become irrelevant, people concerned with civil rights and Black Power continued to use music as a potent vehicle to imagine and realize the possible. As always, people continued to use songs to express their deepest sentiments in particularly condensed and powerful form, to create icons of what should be, and to say things that would be difficult to say otherwise:

Your dove of peace with bloody beak sinks talons in a child
You bend the olive branch to make a bow, and then with a smile
You string it with the lynch rope you've been hiding all the while
That's why we keep marching on.[14]

---

14. "The Movement's Moving On," tune of "John Brown's Body," words by Len Chandler Jr., Fall River Music, 1965, quoted in Carawan and Carawan 1968:223.

A couple of years ago I was playing an old Folkways recording of "We Shall Overcome" for my students in a class and, with some surprise and embarrassment, found that my eyes had filled with tears. It was the type of immediate emotional-energetic response that I have suggested often occurs in reaction to complex indexical signs. If I were to analyze my own response, I might say that the voices, recorded during the early 1960s, carried all the hope, bravery, and idealism of the movement at that time. But this layer of meaning was compounded by other associations, especially my feelings about racism and the knowledge that so many of the hopes of the people singing so beautifully on that recording still remain unfulfilled. And there is probably more to it. I had been reading intensely about the civil rights movement around that time and was alternatively proud, disgusted, and frustrated by what I read of my fellow countrymen and women. The sound of that melody and those voices condensed all of this, and perhaps more, but I did not think out my reaction at the time; I was simply moved without wanting or expecting to be. Such is the power of music.

8   For Love or Money

Recently I was invited to speak to a group of undergraduate students in a music business course at a nearby university. I opened by asking them if there were realms of life that people in the United States were reluctant, or might even feel were immoral, to associate with money. At first there was an embarrassed silence, as if the question was too obvious or too obscure—I couldn't tell. Finally, a young woman spoke up, "Love," then another quietly, "Friendship." An uncomfortable silence fell again, and I queried, "Spirituality?" They nodded in agreement. "What else?" I urged, but we got no further.

I then began to explain that there are places in the world where people would not associate music and dancing with money any more than we would associate love or friendship with it and that, in fact, in these places music and dance are very much about love, friendship, and spirituality, or in a word, about *connecting*.

I told them about participatory musical events in Peru and in Zimbabwe and the values, priorities, and practices that make these activities very different from the ways we often conceptualize and value music in the United States. I suggested that one of the useful social functions of fields like ethnomusicology and anthropology is to learn and teach about radically different ways of conceptualizing the world so that we might have more models to think with and act from. It is generally accepted that a diversified gene pool has greater evolutionary potential; I made the case that the diversified habits of thought and practice shared among different groups of people—'cultures'—follow the same biological law, 'culture' being a central component of human evolution.

At this point, a student identifying himself as an international business major spoke up. He told us that students in his field are taught that 'global culture' is a good thing, certainly for the expansion of markets. He seemed to assume the reality of 'global culture' and its natural association with the spreading of capitalism. "Given that we now live in a global world," he asked, "what is the future for a diversified culture pool and for the types of musical and cultural situations that you have described?"[1]

This, of course, is the key question. I answered that while the forces behind capitalist expansion are particularly strong and the media blitz that is naturalizing the idea of 'global culture' is affecting our views of reality, there are still many places and people out there who operate according to different values and worldviews—who are not part of this so-called global culture. I argued that even where capitalism has made major inroads into other cultural formations, people are critical and creative and do not just accept what is handed to them.

Driving home thinking about my response to this young man, I was not so sure. I felt that my presentation had failed to address his real concern and the similar concerns of other students who spoke to me after class. Young college-age students seem worried, and they have a right to be.

While one of the potentials of fields like ethnomusicology and anthropology is to draw attention to different lifeways and modes of thought, the dangers of exoticism and distancing are pronounced. It is all well and good for Shona or Aymara peasants in Never-Never-Land to bond through participatory music and dance; they have grown up with traditions that make such joys possible. But the students seemed to be asking, "What about us? What can we do?" The very social and cultural differences that I typically emphasize make these alternative models of practice seem impractical and unlikely in the students' own lives. So what *do* people who are attracted by ideas of fashioning a different type of social and economic life here at home do?

The answer is decidedly *not* simply to learn to play the mbira or the panpipes or the banjo, although getting deeply involved with an instrument or a style of music is certainly wonderful and enriching in its own

1. The term *global world,* which I have heard a number of people use, at first seems redundant until one realizes that *global* in this context is functioning as a metonymic index for the larger discourse involving neoliberalism and the spreading of capitalism. Through placement in a variety of indexical clusters, *global* has come to serve as a synonym for *capitalist,* and this discourse serves to naturalize the spread of capitalism.

right. Part of the beginning of an answer is for people to begin where they are, both literally and figuratively, and yet to learn about, think about, and perhaps start to really internalize fundamentals of different value systems, priorities, and habits that underlie those styles of music making and styles of life. I developed the four-fields framework precisely as a way of talking about different values, goals, conceptions, and modes of musical practice. Hopefully I have offered enough examples of participatory performance to suggest that its potentials—for social bonding, for integration of individual selves, for imagining the possible, for experiencing the actual, and for flow—are available to anyone through a wide range of activities. It is not playing the mbira or panpipes or banjo that makes the difference; it is the *whys* and *hows*, the values and practices underpinning alternative modes of performance that are important for devotees and 'multicultural educators' to understand, experience, and teach.

The concerned students who populate my classes have grown up in a cultural formation in which economic competition favors continual growth in capital accumulation, the size of enterprises, hierarchy, and specialization. As Marx suggested long ago, this system creates greater and greater distances between individuals and the forces that direct their lives as well as the activities that constitute their lives. Students feel the distance, and some, perhaps rightfully, feel that their best shot is to join in as well as they can, but they are worried. For example, what happens to a way of life that is largely dependent on a nonrenewable energy source that is running out, an energy source that will cause major climatic changes before it runs out? Some remain confident that the specialists will find a way so that growth can continue unabated and the system can remain intact. Others are worried that it is this very habit of thought that has got us in the fix that they feel we are in. Maybe it will take a real crisis in the wealthy countries to instigate fundamental social change, but maybe the people who are concerned can get started before that happens and be ready if it comes.

Small Is Still Beautiful: Cultural Cohorts and Formations

I return to the notions of *cultural cohorts* and *cultural formations* as tools for thinking through the way choices might be available for alternative lifeways here at home. Students' feelings of helplessness stem from the size, power, and intangibility of 'the system' they want to oppose. If they can't alter the whole thing, they will only be applying Band-Aids, they say.

A good balance of arrogance and modesty might help—individuals can make an important difference, but it can only begin as a small difference, and it can only begin where they are and with the people around them. Those who feel that prevailing macro trends are wrongheaded can come together around certain activities and ideas to forge cohorts as the seeds of alternative communities. The 1960s back-to-the-land, civil rights, and women's movements are positive examples in the United States of what people can do. Grounded in different but sympathetic cohorts, these social movements had, and continue to have, effects within the broader formation. In chapter 6 I tried to suggest that the most important effects of new cohorts result in the generations subsequent to the founders. Taking the long view is helpful because social habits change and new ones develop solidity at glacial speed. Patience is often incompatible with youth, but it is young people who believe in themselves and who can glimpse and patiently work toward their visions of alternative futures that we need.

In spite of the emphasis in earlier nationalist and now globalist discourses on the value of cultural homogeneity within ever larger social units, there is nothing that says mass movements are the only path to viable social change. Capitalist economics and cultural values favor ever-increasing size—of corporations, of markets, of resource extraction. From another point of view, massive size is part of the problem, not part of the solution. In fact, while the rise of the Nazis points to the impact a small political cohort can have, especially in times of crisis, it also underlines the dangers of mass movements that become monolithic. Even if it were possible, overturning one increasingly monolithic cultural formation with another is not the best objective; a dictatorship of the Green Party, or the Amish, or the Goths, or the Rotarians is not what I have in mind.

In keeping with the principle of a diverse culture pool, an expansion of the number of smaller cultural formations is a more practical and positive goal. This does not imply 'preserving' the myriad small-scale indigenous cultural formations that still exist in the world. This is not work that cosmopolitans can do anyway, although they might support movements that oppose, and lifeways that do not hasten, the destruction of other ways of life. What I am suggesting is that the 'culture pool' is *not* a nonrenewable resource. A more practical goal is the development of new formations, beginning with grassroots cohorts, with the "wheres" and "whos" people happen to be. I want to stress the potential of cohorts and the issue of *time*.

Cultural cohorts are pluralistic by nature, because people are. Left to their own devices, individuals emphasize different concerns, interests, and talents, and groups of individuals typically form cohorts around different foci and so generate diversity as a matter of course. Cohorts operate on different geographical scales, but they are usually grounded in the local and in the face-to-face. If developed over generations, they can also provide the seeds for a diversity of small-scale cultural formations within a given state. There are often links, or at least sympathy, among the cohorts working on particular types of issues, and thus there is potential for flexible networks of support and coordination. The development of sympathetic networks is another mode through which cohorts begin to lay the foundations for new cultural formations.

These processes are already happening at a grassroots level. Small-scale organic farms and food co-ops exist throughout the United States, run by people concerned with producing healthy food locally so that dependence on fossil-fueled transportation is reduced. People are working locally on issues of water quality and renewable energy sources. Groups exist for the sole purpose of cleaning up and protecting rivers, forests, and prairies. Others are experimenting with new building materials, such as straw bale, and energy efficiency for the construction of ecologically sound housing. Others are working on making urban spaces more human or developing neighborhood solidarity. Others throw their energies behind community art centers or hip-hop clubs, or organizing local contra dances and dance weekends. The list goes on.

I can hear the voices now: "But these activities are just a drop in the bucket given the corporate power behind the destruction of the rain and hardwood forests, the pollution of the oceans, the production of greenhouse gases, and the control of popular culture!" I respond to this valid objection in several ways.

The view that small-scale cohorts are insignificant is partially created by the mass media, through their very lack of coverage of such movements. One of the goals of this book has been to theorize and illustrate how different cultural visions of reality are created and directed for particular agendas. In the United States, importance, prestige, and viability are indexed by major media coverage, which is increasingly controlled by a few corporations. Reading *Yes*, a magazine dedicated to covering alternative social movements, rather than watching CNN or reading *Time* would create a different impression of the abundance and viability of different socially concerned cohorts. This shift in perception would consequently help the viability of the social movements that already exist. There is a parallel here to people's reluctance to vote for candidates not affiliated with the two major parties. The mass media create the sense that only major-party candidates are viable and hence the idea that a vote cast otherwise will be wasted, even if the voter prefers an alternative candidate. In a self-fulfilling way, the corporate media don't just objectively report 'reality' but have an important role in fashioning our reality—democracy is dismantled in the process.

People who become passionate members of a particular cohort don't need the mass media to tell them about the importance or viability of the given focal activity in their own lives; they know it from experience. Although accomplishing this is not so simple, they simply need to separate themselves from the prestige system of the broader formation to fully credit those experiences and to encourage others to get involved. Believe it or not, mass publicity and mass popularity need not be important except to the mass popularizers. In fact from the basis of a different value system, small-scale local activities, organizations, and movements might be deemed more prestigious and valuable because of their effects on the places and people one knows firsthand. Who are you going to dance with? Whose reality are you going to believe?

My second response to the viability question is that any concerned individual has the choices of doing something or doing nothing, of doing a little or doing a lot. An all-or-nothing attitude regarding social change gets us nowhere. An individual opposed to the capitalist system, for example, is not going to overturn it singlehandedly nor completely purify her life of all its traces. But walking or riding a bike rather than driving a car whenever possible makes a difference; organizing block parties in one's neighborhood makes a difference; investing in responsible companies makes a difference; singing in a community chorus makes a difference; building Habitat for Humanity housing two days a month makes a difference; starting a volunteer after-school program to help working mothers makes a difference; working for a political party makes a difference.

One attraction of cultural cohorts for instigating individual and social change is that they are partial, at least initially. Cohorts articulate with certain aspects of the self and one's life without requiring a transformation of everything at once. In the description of the old-time music cohort it was mentioned that a number of people got into the music to imagine a simpler rural life without, as they put it, having to get up at six in the morning. Yet others started by imagining through the music and then actually moved to rural areas and began working in crafts and agriculture. Cohorts allow people to begin where and with the "whos" that they are and, if so inclined, to begin working toward their vision of a satisfying life "part time," supported by others of like mind. People may find that the gradual changing of one set of habits may lead to other changes of the self and therefore to other activities, priorities, and modes of life. The model for cultural formations outlined in chapter 4 begins and ends with individuals. It follows that social change must begin with individuals as well.

The 'culture pool' is not a nonrenewable resource; we do not have to pretend to go back in time or imitate Shona spiritualists. People adapt and invent new cultural practices, traditions, and cohorts all the time. The power and meaning of these inventions, however, depend on two things: participation and time. People develop a deeper sense of engagement and investment through direct participation in contrast to simply being a spectator or consumer. Longevity is necessary for the richness of indexical meaning that comes through repeated performance in a variety of instances over time—a lifetime and better still across generations. Participation over time is fundamental to deeply integrating new habits of thought and practice as parts of the self and integrating them with other parts of the self, a movement toward coherence that will happen because of people's desire to reduce cognitive dissonance. Nostalgia (a longing for some idealized past) and exoticism (idealizing other societies) may be points of departure for the processes of new habit formation, but in and of themselves they will probably not be very satisfying ultimately. A bold and creative orientation to present and future possibilities based on who, where, and what we are and know now would seem to have more potential. Ethnomusicology and anthropology have augmented what we know and can think, but in my opinion they serve best as points of departure for our own dicent creativity. If we understand ourselves and our social formations in relation to habits and grasp how discourses function to construct our realities, then we gain a new freedom to shape our habits and visions of the world.

Who Cares about Music? Issues of Value

Given the enormity of young people's concerns, who cares about music? Why do I harp on this aspect of life? In this book I have tried to emphasize the range that music and dance have to offer and, further, have emphasized the value of participatory music and dance as, by design, the most potentially available to the most people. So who cares?

One of the first things adults in the United States ask when they initially meet is "What do you do?" and they expect to hear about professional occupation, not the fact that you are an avid tennis player, gardener, kayaker, contra dancer, or garage-band guitarist if the activity is not the means of your livelihood, even if it is at the center of your life. *Work* is considered serious, important, and basic to identity; *leisure*, by definition, is less important and to be fit in around work. These two culturally relative concepts strongly shape how people in the capitalist cosmopolitan formation spend, conceptualize, and value their time, which is to say, their lives.

The ethics that promote economic competitiveness as the key to success deemphasize another necessary side of being successful and happy: the social bonding, nurturing, and cooperation upon which adult as well as infant survival depends. There is a saying in the United States that "few people on their deathbeds wished they had spent more time in the office." Yet many people do not live day to day with this thought in mind, and the underlying confusion of exchange value with *value in general* powerfully influences many fields of social practice. It is striking how few aspects of life the music business students were able name that should not be associated with money.

By contrast, Anthony Seeger (1979) describes how the Suyá of the Amazon rain forest are able to meet their subsistence needs in relatively few hours a day and how they spend a large portion of their time in ceremony, music making, dancing, and other social activities. Nonprofessional, nonspecialized music making, dancing, sports (e.g., log rolling), and ceremonies are centrally important *occupations* in this society, reversing the "living to work" ethos to one of working so that they can live expressive social lives. In the Aymara peasant communities of Conima, Peru, reciprocity rather than competition constitutes a foundational habit of thought that influences many fields of social practice. Acts of reciprocity and the idea of cause and effect in relation to the Earth,[2] spiritual forces, and other community members pervade daily social life. For Aymara peasants, daily life is hard, but this is balanced with festivals on the average of once a month in which communal musical performance and dancing are highly valued activities that bring joy and excitement to life.

As people in the capitalist cosmopolitan formation choose or are forced to rethink their priorities for satisfying and sustainable ways of living, they might begin by reconsidering their conceptions of the importance of 'work' and 'leisure' as well as the types of activities that currently constitute leisure. Because of the priority placed on occupation and work within the capitalist formation, it is mainly professionals who are considered seri-

2. For example, the Andean saying "If you do not give to the Earth she will not give to you."

ous or 'real' musicians. It is not that the Suyá, the Shona, or the Aymara inherently have more artistic and ceremonial activities available in their societies; it is that these activities are not devalued as *merely* leisure and that everyone's participation in these activities is valued as central to social life and personal well-being. The important models offered by these societies are not captured simply by learning to play their instruments and music. The real importance for me comes from learning this deeper value orientation, which can be applied to all the activities we already have here at home. Putting it another way, it is coming to *really* know that a neighborhood softball game is as valuable as the World Series.

Following Bateson, Csikszentmihalyi, Peirce, and my Peruvian and Zimbabwean teachers, throughout this book I have tried to show how and why music making, dance, and the arts are valuable activities for personal integration and wholeness, which, in turn, is necessary for social and ecological survival. Using Peirce's semiotic terminology, I have suggested that to achieve integration it is important to balance activities that emphasize the different sign types, since these different signs activate different parts of ourselves and bring those different parts into relation with each other. Just as academic or theoretical activities emphasize symbolic thought *about* and are necessary to generalize and make sense of specific experiences, artistic activities emphasize imagination of the possible and connection to the actual through icons and indices—signs *of* imagination and direct experience. Music making, dancing, drama, painting, literature, sports, games, and ceremonies, in conjunction with symbolic thinking and dialogue, are universal and necessary because, balanced together, they make us whole.

Following Bateson, by connecting and integrating the different parts of the self we are better able to connect and integrate with others and our environment. In addition, Csikszentmihalyi tells us that the arts, games, and with the right attitude many other types of activities can facilitate flow or optimal experience by offering the proper balance of skill and challenge, clearly bounded activity, and immediate feedback. For the reasons discussed, music-dance performance is particularly well suited to provide the conditions that facilitate flow. Csikszentmihalyi asserts that flow experiences result in both a temporary transcendence and a cumulative expansion of the self.

In chapter 4, I proposed a model of the self as comprising constellations of habits that lead to situationally relative cultural affiliations and identity cohorts all the while being fundamentally guided by the tendencies of one's cultural formations, typically including the family, regional, countrywide, and cosmopolitan levels. This multifaceted, situationally guided model of the self suggests that different people will approach and fulfill the same basic needs for integration and transcendence in a multitude of ways. Thus, in elaborating four fields of music making, I suggested that each field serves different types of needs and personalities. Studio audio art provides a space for individual control over artistic media, giving broad range to the imagination and pushing artistic boundaries in sound. Presentational performance spotlights individuals' accomplishment without the safety net of editing and retakes that are possible in high fidelity recordings—recordings that are valuable for their idealized, repeatable representations of musical presentations and that make wide diffusion possible. Participatory performance provides a space for direct, intimate, *dicent* social connection and experience and provides the potential for flow experience that is readily accessible to anyone. The four fields were proposed as a model to suggest that music is not a single art form or type of activity. Each field offers different potentials for creativity and being human, and each offers its own constraints.

Chapters 5 and 7 analyzed how the specific semiotic potentials of music serve social and political movements and how participatory music, in particular, is a powerful political tool. While much of the discussion of the participatory field emphasized positive small-scale community building, the same potentials have served mass movements for good and evil. In both the U.S. civil rights movement and Nazi Germany, the redundant singing of songs helped people internalize new indexical clusters that, in turn, influenced their cultural views of reality and their personal views of what is possible. What is striking is that in one case singing "I love everybody" helped people face bricks and bats with courage and love, whereas in the other, singing "Death to the Jew" fostered participation in, or acquiescence to, mass murder. These two examples alone are convincing evidence of the power of music as a social force and as key resources for transforming individual subjectivities. How these powerful resources are to be harnessed—for individual growth and fun, for community building and bonding, for imagining the possible and experiencing the actual, for love or money—remains for each person to decide.

Glossary

capital (Bourdieu). Anything controlled or possessed by a person that is of consequence to the other actors in the particular social field in question and that can serve as a basis of power or exchange for other types of capital. Virtuoso guitar ability is capital in the presentational rock field; money and land are capital in the field of capitalist economics; academic degrees and publications are capital in the field of higher education.

cosmopolitan. A *type* of transstate cultural formation dispersed among a number of countries and often including only certain segments of the population, among whom immigrant status and an original homeland source are not criteria for identity and meaning (see *diaspora*).

cultural cohorts. A cultural/identity unit based on a restricted number of shared habits and parts of the self—for example, gender cohorts, age cohorts, occupational cohorts.

cultural formations. Cultural groups on a variety of nested levels, ranging from the family to transstate formations, that are united by the primary models for socialization and shared habits among members.

diaspora. A *type* of transstate cultural formation dispersed among a number of different countries, the members of which trace their origin to a 'homeland' and maintain practical and/or ideological links to the homeland as well as to other sites in the diaspora.

dicent (Peirce). A sign that is affected by what it stands for and is thus interpreted as causally linked to its object: a weathervane is a dicent because the wind direction (its object) points it.

discourse (Foucault). A system of premises and terms about a particular realm of life or social field; the premises and terms bring each other into existence and sustain each other: nationalist discourse, racial discourse, ethnomusicological discourse.

essentialism. The highlighting of a restricted number of aspects of the selves constituting an identity unit, and the assertion that those aspects are fundamental or immutable for the purposes of unification (strategic) as well as for 'othering' or subjugation (e.g., racism).

fields, social (Bourdieu). A realm of social practice defined by the nature/purposes of the activity, types of roles, relations between and status of roles, and types of capital valued.

frame (Bateson, Goffman). An indexically cued mental framework for interpreting a particular slice of experience: joking frame, theatrical frame, casual greeting frame, science fiction frame, everyday life frame. All interpretation is framed in some way.

harmony. Pitches heard together; in tonal music, a system that designates functions and greater importance to certain chords, especially the first pitch/chord of the scale (tonic), the fifth pitch/chord (V), and the fourth (IV).

hegemony (Gramsci). Gaining consent to lead through the granting of concessions to and 'educating' the led.

heterophony. A texture in which two or more performers render the same melody simultaneously with slightly different rhythmic attacks or pitch choices, adding density and interest.

homophony. A texture in which a single melody is accompanied by chords, be they played on a guitar or sung by the altos, tenors, and basses of a chorus.

icon (Peirce). A sign that stands for something else through some type of resemblance between sign and object.

identity politics. Struggles over who has the right to define and publicly represent a particular group as well as the use of identity unification for the purposes of political power.

index (Peirce). A sign that comes to stand for something else because sign and object are experienced together (cooccurrence), usually repeatedly.

indexical clusters. The redundant grouping of preexisting signs, such that they come to be indexically associated with each other and this relationship takes on the 'naturalness' or 'reality' of indexical relations, creating a new context for interpreting the original signs. Musical canons are a subset of indexical clusters.

interlocking. A manner of performance in which performers place their pitches/accents/body movements in the spaces or "rests" of other performers' parts.

internal context. All past experiences, memories, dispositions, and habits of an individual that influence the interpretation/reception of signs.

interpretant (Peirce). The effect of the sign-object relation in the perceiver.

metaphor, linguistic. A type of iconic relation in which some type of resemblance is asserted between the objects of two or more linguistic signs: "My wife is a pearl."

metonymy. A part standing for the whole; this is a subset of indexical relations, since parts cooccur with their wholes: in "the crown of England," part of the king's attire stands for the whole of the king.

monophony. A texture designation for a single melody regardless of how many voices or instruments render it together (in unison).

motive (music). A small structural melodic unit: for example, the first four notes of Beethoven's Fifth Symphony.

object (Peirce). That which is stood for by a sign, be it an abstract idea or an actual object (e.g., a rock) out in the world.

ostinato. A repeated musical motive, phrase, melody, chord progression, or rhythmic figure; when continual repetition of the musical unit in question serves as the basic structure of a piece, it may be termed *ostinato form*.

primary process (Bateson). The passing of imagery/ideas from the subconscious to conscious awareness without the filtering, reordering, or domestication of 'rational' or symbolic thought.

semantic snowballing. The potential collecting of multiple layers of indexical meanings around the same sign vehicle due to cooccurrences of the same sign vehicle and different objects in varied contexts over time, but with potential traces of, combinations with, past associations.

semiotic density. The relative numbers of potential signs that coexist simultaneously in an art form or communicative act. A written text is less dense than someone speaking the text, where tone of voice, rhythm, and tempo of speaking, along with facial expressions and gestures, add more signs that occur simultaneously with the words spoken. Songs are denser still with the addition of melody, instruments, harmony, etc., to the sung text.

semiotics (Peirce). The theoretical study and analysis of signs. When used as an adjective, the term refers to events, actions, and forms in which signs are operative.

sign, sign vehicle (Peirce). Something that stands for something else to someone in some way.

symbol (Peirce). A sign that is connected to its object through linguistic definition and agreement. It is a general sign that has symbols (other general signs) as its object.

texture (music). Relationships of musical sounds experienced together in time: e.g., *contrapuntal texture* refers to two or more melodies played at the same time which compete for the listener's attention, as in a Bach fugue; other examples include *heterophonic texture* and *homophonic texture*.

timbre (music). Tone quality.

References and Recommended Reading

Allen, R. Raymond. 1981. "Old-Time Music and the Urban Folk Revival." *New York Folklore 7.*

Anderson, Benedict. 1983. *Imagined Communities: Reflections on the Origin and Spread of Nationalism.* London: Verso.

Bateson, Gregory. 1972a. "Style, Grace, and Information in Primitive Art." In *Steps to an Ecology of Mind,* 128–52. New York: Ballantine.

———. 1972b. "A Theory of Play and Fantasy." In *Steps to an Ecology of Mind,* 177–93. New York: Ballantine.

———. 1979. *Mind and Nature: A Necessary Unity.* New York: Bantam.

Bealle, John. 2005. *Old-Time Music and Dance: Community and Folk Revival.* Bloomington: Indiana University Press.

Benedict, Ruth. 1973 [orig. 1934]. "The Integration of Culture." In *Highpoints in Anthropology,* ed. Paul Bohannan and Mark Glazer, 174–83. New York: Alfred A. Knopf.

Benjamin, Walter. 1969. "The Work of Art in the Age of Mechanical Reproduction." In *Illuminations,* ed. Hannah Arendt, 217–52. New York: Schocken.

Bennett, H. Stith. 1990. "The Realities of Practice." In *On Record: Rock, Pop, and the Written Word,* ed. Simon Frith and Andrew Goodwin, 221–37. New York: Pantheon.

Berliner, Paul. 1978. *Soul of Mbira.* Berkeley: University of California Press.

Blacking, John. 1992. "The Biology of Music-Making." In *Ethnomusicology: An Introduction,* ed. Helen Myers. London: Macmillan.

Bourdieu, Pierre. 1977. *Outline of a Theory of Practice.* Cambridge: Cambridge University Press.

———. 1984. *Distinction: A Social Critique of a Judgement of Taste.* Cambridge, MA: Harvard University Press.

———. 1985. "The Social Space and the Genesis of Groups." *Theory and Society* 14:723–44.

Buchanan, Donna A. 2006. *Performing Democracy: Bulgarian Music and Musicians in Transition.* Chicago: University of Chicago Press.

Caplow, Theodore, Louis Hicks, and Ben J. Wattenberg. 2001. *The First Measured Century: An Illustrated Guide to Trends in America, 1900–2000.* Washington, DC: American Enterprise Institute for Public Policy Research.

Carawan, Guy, and Candi Carawan. 1968. *Freedom Is a Constant Struggle: Songs of the Freedom Movement.* New York: Oak.

Chester, Andrew. 1990. "Second Thoughts on a Rock Aesthetic: The Band." In *On Record: Rock, Pop, and the Written Word,* ed. Simon Firth and Andrew Goodwin, 315–19. New York: Pantheon.

Conway, Cecelia. 1995. *African Banjo Echoes in Appalachia: A Study of Folk Traditions.* Knoxville: University of Tennessee Press.

Corbett, John. 1990. "Free, Single, and Disengaged: Listening Pleasure and the Popular Music Object." *October* 54 (Fall): 79–101.

Cornelius, Steven H. 2004. *Music of the Civil War Era.* Westport, CT: Greenwood.

Csikszentmihalyi, Mihaly. 1990. *Flow: The Psychology of Optimal Experience; Steps Toward Enhancing the Quality of Life.* New York: HarperPerennial.

Csikszentmihalyi, Mihaly, and Isabella Selega Csikszentmihalyi, eds. 1988. *Optimal Experience: Psychological Studies of Flow in Consciousness.* Cambridge: Cambridge University Press.

Denisoff, Serge R. 1971. *Great Day Coming: Folk Music and the American Left.* Urbana: University of Illinois Press.

De Turk, David, and A. Poulin. 1967. *Dimensions of the Folk Song Revival.* New York: Dell.

Dierenfield, Bruce J. 2004. *The Civil Rights Movement.* Harlow, UK: Pearson/Longman.

Eskew, Glen T. 1997. *But for Birmingham: The Local and National Movements in the Civil Rights Struggle.* Chapel Hill: North Carolina University Press.

Eyerman, Ron, and Andrew Jamison. 1998. *Music and Social Movements: Mobilizing Traditions in the Twentieth Century.* Cambridge: Cambridge University Press.

Fales, Cornelia. 2005. "Short-Circuiting Perceptual Systems: Timbre in Ambient and Techno Music." In *Wired for Sound: Engineering and Technologies in Sonic Cultures,* ed. Paul D. Green and Thomas Porcello, 156–80. Middletown, CT: Wesleyan University Press.

Fehrenbach, T. R. 1983. *Lone Star: A History of Texas and Texans.* New York: American Legacy.

Feld, Steven. 1988. "Aesthetics as Iconicity of Style, or 'Lift-Up-Over-Sounding': Getting into the Kaluli Groove." *Yearbook for Traditional Music* 20:74–113.

Feldman, Heidi Carolyn. 2006. *Black Rhythms of Peru: Reviving African Musical Heritage in the Black Pacific.* Middletown, CT: Wesleyan University Press.

Filene, Benjamin. 2000. *Romancing the Folk: Public Memory and American Roots Music*. Chapel Hill: University of North Carolina Press.

Frith, Simon. 1987. "Towards an Aesthetic of Popular Music." In *Music and Society: The Politics of Composition, Performance, and Reception*, ed. Richard Leppert and Susan McClary, 133–50. Cambridge: Cambridge University Press.

Geertz, Clifford. 1973. "Thick Description: Toward an Interpretive Theory of Culture." In *The Interpretation of Cultures*, 3–28. New York: Basic Books.

Gelman, Susan A. 2003. *The Essential Child: Origins of Essentialism in Everyday Thought*. New York: Oxford University Press.

Goffman, Erving. 1974. *Frame Analysis: An Essay on the Organization of Experience*. New York: Harper Colophon.

Goodwin, Doris Kearns. 2005. *Team of Rivals: The Political Genius of Abraham Lincoln*. New York: Simon and Schuster.

Graves, James Bau. 2005. *Cultural Democracy: The Arts, Community, and Public Purpose*. Urbana: University of Illinois Press.

Green, Archie. 1965. "Hillbilly Music: Source and Symbol." *Journal of American Folklore* 78, no. 309: 204–28.

Green, Paul D. 2005. "Introduction: Wired Sound and Sonic Cultures." In *Wired for Sound: Engineering and Technologies in Sonic Cultures*, ed. Paul D. Green and Thomas Porcello. Middletown, CT: Wesleyan University Press.

Green, Paul D., and Thomas Porcello, eds. 2005. *Wired for Sound: Engineering and Technologies in Sonic Cultures*. Middletown, CT: Wesleyan University Press.

Gura, Philip F., and James F. Bollman. 1999. *America's Instrument: The Banjo in the Nineteenth Century*. Chapel Hill: University of North Carolina Press.

Hale, Rebecca. 1997. "The Adaptation of Karaoke as American Nightclub Entertainment." MA thesis, University of Illinois at Urbana-Champaign.

Hall, Edward. 1977. *Beyond Culture*. Garden City, NY: Anchor.

Hall, Stuart. 1996 "Introduction: Who Needs 'Identity'?" In *Questions of Cultural Identity*, ed. Stuart Hall and Paul de Gay, 1–19. London: Sage.

Harris, Marvin. 1979. "Theoretical Principles of Cultural Materialism," Chap. 3 in *Cultural Materialism: The Struggle for a Science of Culture*. New York: Vintage.

Hausman, Carl R. 1993. *Charles S. Peirce's Evolutionary Philosophy*. Cambridge: Cambridge University Press.

Hennion, Antoine. 1990. "The Production of Success: An Antimusicology of the Pop Song." In *On Record: Rock, Pop, and the Written Word*, ed. Simon Frith and Andrew Goodwin, 185–206. New York: Pantheon.

Jamison, Phil. 2004. "Old-Time Square Dancing in the 21st Century: Dare to Be Square." *Old-Time Herald* 9, no. 3 (Spring): 8–12.

Johnson Reagon, Bernice. 1983. "Songs That Moved the Movement." *Perspectives*, Summer.

Kealy, Edward. 1990. "From Craft to Art: The Case of Sound Mixers and Popular

Music." In *On Record: Rock, Pop, and the Written Word*, ed. Simon Frith and Andrew Goodwin, 207–20. New York: Pantheon.

Keil, Charles. 1987. "Participatory Discrepancies and the Power of Music." *Cultural Anthropology* 2, no. 3: 275–83.

———. 1995. "The Theory of Participatory Discrepancies: A Progress Report." *Ethnomusicology* 39, no. 1: 1–20.

Kertzer, David I. 1988. *Ritual, Politics, and Power*. New Haven, CT: Yale University Press.

Klein, Joe. 1980. *Woody Guthrie: A Life*. New York: Delta / Random House.

Koskoff, Ellen. 1989. "An Introduction to Women, Music, and Culture." In *Women and Music in Cross-Cultural Perspective*, ed. Ellen Koskoff, 1–24. Urbana: University of Illinois Press.

———. 2001. *Music in Lubavitcher Life*. Urbana: University of Illinois Press.

Kroeber, A. L. 1963 [orig. 1923]. "The Nature of Culture." In *Anthropology*, 60–69. New York: Harcourt, Brace and World.

Kunstler, James Howard. 1993. *The Geography of Nowhere: The Rise and Decline of America's Man-Made Landscape*. New York: Touchstone.

Lea, James. 2001. "Charles Sanders Peirce: The Extraordinary Moment and Musical Affect." DMA dissertation, University of Illinois.

LeBor, Adam, and Roger Boyes. 2000. *Seduced by Hitler: The Choices of a Nation and the Ethics of Survival*. Naperville, IL: Sourcebooks.

Lidtke, Vernon L. 1982. "Songs and Nazis: Political and Social Change in Twentieth-Century Germany." In *Essays on Culture and Society in Modern Germany*, ed. Gary D. Stark and Bede Karl Lackner. College Station: Texas A&M University.

Lieberman, Robbie. 1989. *"My Song Is My Weapon": People's Songs, American Communism, and the Politics of Culture, 1930–1950*. Urbana: University of Illinois Press.

Linn, Karen. 1990. *That Half-Barbaric Twang: The Banjo in American Popular Culture*. Urbana: University of Illinois Press, 1991.

Linton, Ralph. 1943. "Nativistic Movements." *American Anthroplogist* 45:230–40.

List, George. 1980. *Music in a Colombian Village*. Bloomington: University of Indiana Press.

Livingston, Tamara Elena. and Thomas George Caracas Garcia. 2005. *Choro: A Social History of a Brazilian Popular Music*. Bloomington: Indiana University Press.

Lott, Eric. 1995. *Love and Theft: Blackface Minstrelsy and the American Working Class*. New York: Oxford University Press.

Malcolm X. 1965. *Malcolm X Speaks*. Ed. George Breitman. New York: Grove Weidenfeld, 1965.

Malone, Bill C. 1979. *Southern Music, American Music*. Lexington: University Press of Kentucky.

———. 1985. *Country Music U.S.A.* Austin: University of Texas Press.

Mattis, Olivia. 1992. "Varése's Multimedia Conception of Déserts." *Musical Quarterly* 76, no. 4.

McNeill, William H. 1995. *Keeping Together in Time: Dance and Drill in Human History.* Cambridge, MA: Harvard University Press.

Meintjes, Louise. 2003. *Sound of Africa! Making Music Zulu in a South African Studio.* Durham, NC: Duke University Press.

Merriam, Alan P. 1964. *The Anthropology of Music.* Evanston, IL: Northwestern University Press.

———. 1977. "Definitions of 'Comparative Musicology' and 'Ethnomusicology': An Historical-Theoretical Perspective." *Ethnomusicology* 21:189–204.

Meyer, Michael. 1991. *The Politics of Music in the Third Reich.* New York: Peter Lang.

Mowitt, John. 1987. "The Sound of Music in the Era of Its Electronic Reproducibility." In *Music and Society: The Politics of Composition, Performance and Reception,* ed. Richard Leppert and Susan McClary, 173–97. Cambridge: Cambridge University Press.

O'Brien, John. 2001. *At Home in the Heart of Appalachia.* New York: Alfred A. Knopf.

Parker, Kelly A. 1998. *The Continuity of Peirce's Thought.* Nashville: Vanderbilt University Press.

Peirce, Charles Sanders. 1955. *Philosophical Writings of Peirce.* Ed. Justus Buchler. New York: Dover.

———. 1992. *The Essential Peirce: Selected Philosophical Writings,* vol. 1, *1867–1893.* Ed. Nathan Houser and Christian Kloesel. Bloomington: Indiana University Press.

———. 1998. *The Essential Peirce: Selected Philosophical Writings,* vol. 2, *1893–1913.* Ed. Nathan Houser. Bloomington: Indiana University Press.

Peña, Manuel. 1985. "From *Ranchero* to *Jaiton:* Ethnicity and Class in Texas-Mexican Music." *Ethnomusicolgy* 29, no. 1: 29–55.

Penley, Constance, and Andrew Ross. 1990. *Technoculture.* Minneapolis: University of Minnesota Press.

Peterson, Richard A. 1997. *Creating Country Music: Fabricating Authenticity.* Chicago: University of Chicago Press.

Porcello, Thomas. 2005. "Music Mediated as Live in Austin: Sound, Technology, and Recording Practice." In *Wired for Sound: Engineering and Technologies in Sonic Cultures,* ed. Paul D. Green and Thomas Porcello. Middletown, CT: Wesleyan University Press.

Potter, Pamela. 1998. *Most German of the Arts: Musicology and Society from the Weimar Republic to the End of Hitler's Reich.* New Haven, CT: Yale University Press.

Progler, J. A. 1995. "Searching for Swing: Participatory Discrepancies in the Jazz Rhythm Section." *Ethnomusicology* 39, no. 1: 21–54.

Radano, Ronald, and Philip Bohlman. 2000a. "Music and Race: Their Past, Their Presence." Introduction to *Music and the Racial Imagination,* ed. Radano and Bohlman, 1–53. Chicago: University of Chicago Press.

———. 2000b. *Music and the Racial Imagination.* Chicago: University of Chicago Press.

Randel, Don Michael, ed. 1984. *The New Harvard Dictionary of Music.* Cambridge, MA: Belknap Press / Harvard University Press.

Rosaldo, Renato. 1989. "The Erosion of Classic Norms" and "After Objectivism." In *Culture and Truth: The Remaking of Social Analysis,* 25–67. Boston: Beacon.

Rosenberg, Neil V., ed. 1993. *Transforming Tradition: Folk Music Revivals Examined.* Urbana: University of Illinois Press.

Scales, Christopher Alton. 2004. "Powwow Music and the Aboriginal Recording Industry on the Northern Plains: Media, Technology, and Native American Music in the Late Twentieth Century." PhD diss., University of Illinois at Urbana-Champaign.

Seeger, Anthony. 1974. *Why Suyá Sing: A Musical Anthropology of an Amazonian People.* Cambridge: Cambridge University Press.

———. 1979. "What Can We Learn When They Sing? Vocal Genres of the Suyá Indians of Central Brazil." *Ethnomusicology* 23:373–94.

Shamuyarira, Nathan. 1965. *Crisis in Rhodesia.* London: Andre Deutsch.

Shirer, William. 1959 *The Rise and Fall of the Third Reich: A History of Nazi Germany.* New York: Simon & Schuster.

Small, Christopher. 1987. "Performance as Ritual: Sketch for an Enquiry into the True Nature of a Symphony Concert." In *Lost in Music: Culture, Style, and the Musical Event,* ed. A. Levine White, 6–32. New York: Routledge and Kegan Paul.

Sterne, Jonathan. 2003. *The Audible Past: Cultural Origins of Sound Reproduction.* Durham, NC: Duke University Press.

Stokes, Martin. 1994. "Introduction: Ethnicity, Identity, and Music." In *Ethnicity, Identity, and Music,* ed. Stokes, 1–28. New York: Oxford University Press.

Sugarman, Jane. 1997. *Engendering Song: Singing and Subjectivity at Prespa Albanian Weddings.* Chicago: University of Chicago Press.

Supiya, Stephen T. 1962. "ZAPU Endeavours to Blend the Old and the New." *African Parade,* May, 8, 53, 58.

Thompson, Emily. 1995. "Machines, Music, and the Quest for Fidelity: Marketing the Edison Phonograph in America, 1877–1925." *Musical Quarterly* 79 (Spring): 131–73.

Toll, Robert. 1974. *Blacking Up: The Minstrel Show in Nineteenth-Century America.* New York: Oxford University Press.

Turino, Thomas. 1990. "'Somos el Peru': Cumbia Andina and the Children of Andean Migrants in Lima, Peru." *Studies in Latin American Popular Culture* 9:15–37.

———. 1993. *Moving Away from Silence: Music of the Peruvian Altiplano and the Experience of Urban Migration.* Chicago: University of Chicago Press.

———. 1999. "Signs of Imagination, Identity, and Experience: A Peircean Theory for Music." *Ethnomusicology* 43:221–55.

———. 2000. *Nationalists, Cosmopolitans, and Popular Music in Zimbabwe.* Chicago: University of Chicago Press.

———. 2003. "Nationalism and Latin American Music: Selected Case Studies and Theoretical Considerations." *Latin American Music Review* 24, no. 2: 169–209.

———. 2004. "Are We Global Yet? Discourse Analysis, Cultural Formations, and Zimbabwean Popular Music." *British Journal of Ethnomusicology* 12,, no. 2: 51–80.

———. 2008. *Music in the Andes: Experiencing Music, Expressing Culture.* New York: Oxford University Press.

Turino, Thomas, and James Lea, eds. 2004. *Identity and the Arts in Diaspora Communities.* Warren, MI: Harmonie Park.

Turnbull, Colin. 1962. *The Forest People.* New York: Simon and Schuster.

Turner, Victor. 1969. *The Ritual Process.* Chicago: Aldine.

Tye, Larry. 2004. *Rising from the Rails: Pullman Porters and the Making of the Black Middle Class.* New York: Henry Holt.

Tylor, Edward Burnett. 1973 [orig. 1871]. *Primitive Culture.* Excerpted in *Highpoints in Anthropology,* ed. Paul Bohannan and Mark Glazer, 61–78. New York: Alfred A. Knopf, 61–78.

Welsh-Asante, Kariamu. 1993. "Zimbabwean Dance: An Aesthetic Analysis of the Jerusarema and Muchongoyo Dances." Ph.D. diss., New York University.

West, Cornel. 1994. *Race Matters.* New York: Vintage.

Whisnat, David. 1983. *All That Is Native and Fine.* Urbana: University of Illinois Press.

Wicke, Peter. 1985. "Sentimentality and High Pathos: Popular Music in Fascist Germany." *Popular Music* 5:149–58.

Zinn, Howard. 1999. *A People's History of the United States: 1492–Present.* New York: HarperCollins.

Zwerin, Mike. 2000. *Swing under the Nazis: Jazz as a Metaphor for Freedom.* New York: Cooper Square.

Annotated Discography

Afro-American Folk Music from Tate and Panola Counties, Mississippi. Rounder Records, Rounder 18964-1515-2, 2000. This CD of previously released Library of Congress (1978) recordings includes African American banjo players and fiddlers as well as fife and drum bands, quills (panpipes), and the one-string "bow diddley." This publication contains an excellent booklet by David Evans. Music discussed in chapter 6.

Black Banjo Songsters of North Carolina and Virginia. Smithsonian/Folkways SF 40079, 1998. This is an excellent anthology of African American banjo players as discussed in chapter 6.

Bubba George Stringband, *Live at the Finger Lakes GrassRoots Festival of Music and Dance.* LNK 002, 1999; to order online: http://www.Funkyside.com. This recording provides an excellent sense of old-time string band music as participatory music and is one of my personal favorites; chapter 6.

Bulawayo Jazz, Southern Rhodesia / Zimbabwe, 1950, '51, '52. SWP 032 Biem/Stemaa; International Library of African Music (http://ilam.ru.ac.za). This recording contains classic examples of African jazz from Zimbabwe, such as "Skokiaan" by the Cold Storage Band. Chapter 5.

John Cage and David Tudor, *Cartridge Music,* by John Cage. MS 5015 (vinyl LP). Performed using phonograph cartridges and contact microphones applied to a variety of objects; the recording is a superimposition of four performances. This example of studio audio art was discussed in chapter 3.

Ecuatorial; Déserts; Intégrales; Hyperprism; Octandre; Offrandes; Density 21.5, by Edgard Varése. New York: CDS Masterworks, 1984 (vinyl LP). This anthology includes examples of *musique concréte.* Chapter 3.

The Freight Hoppers, *Where'd You Come From, Where'd You Go?* Rounder 3719. This recording provides an excellent example of the hard-driving old-time style of the Skillet Lickers–Highwoods line of development. Chapter 6.

The Fuzzy Mountain String Band. Rounder CD 11571, 1995. This reissue of 1971 and 1972 recordings includes many of the tunes in the countrywide old-time canon. Chapter 6.

The Heartbeats, *Spinning World.* Green Linnet Records (43 Beaver Brook Road, Danbury, CT 06810), GLCD 2111, 1993. This recording illustrates one of the creative directions that old-time groups have taken. Chapter 6.

The Hollow Rock String Band, *Traditional Dance Tunes.* Country Records, Country-CD 2715, reissued 1997. Discussed in chapter 6.

Alison Krauss and Union Station, *Every Time You Say Goodbye.* Rounder Records CD 0285, 1992. This is one of my favorite bluegrass albums with contemporary compositions as well as a bluegrass rendition of the old-time standard "Cluck Old Hen" (track 4). Chapters 2 and 6.

Thomas Mapfumo and the Blacks Unlimited, *Chamunorwa.* Mango Records 162 539 900-2, 1991. This recording exemplifies Mapfumo at the height of his career and includes songs that have been in his repertory since the 1970s ("Hwa Hwa"), classical mbira pieces ("Chitima Ndikature"), a guitar-band version of jerusarema ("Muramba Doro"), and the indigenous hunting/war song "Nyama Yekugocha." Chapters 2 and 5.

Minstrel Banjo Style. Rounder Records, Rounder CD 0321, 1994. This recording, featuring performances by Joe Ayers, Clarke Buehling, Bob Carlin, Bob Flesher, Tony Trischka, and Bob Winas, presents a series of minstrel pieces reconstructed from nineteenth-century banjo instruction/repertory books, as discussed in chapter 6.

Mountain Music of Peru, vol. 2. Smithsonian/Folkways, SF 40406, 1994, recording and notes by John Cohen and Thomas Turino. Tracks 12–29 are from Puno, Peru. Tracks 22–29 are of Aymara music from the district of Conima and the province of Huancané, discussed in chapter 2.

Music of the Andes: Experiencing Music, Expressing Culture. Oxford University Press, 2008. A thirty-four-track CD of Peruvian music largely recorded by Thomas Turino between 1977 and 1988 is included with this book. There are a number of selections of Aymara music from Conima included on this CD and analyzed with time charts in the book. Chapter 2.

Say It Loud! A Celebration of Black Music in America. Rhino Records, R2 76660/ A53894, 2001. Disc 4 of this six-CD box set contains two speeches by Martin Luther King, a speech by Malcom X, and a speech on civil rights by John Kennedy. Disc 4 also includes two songs mentioned in chapter 7: James Brown's "Say It Loud" and Otis Redding's "Change Is Gonna Come." Disc 5 includes Gil Scott-Heron's "The Revolution Will Not Be Televised." Other songs relevant to the civil rights movement are also included. Chapter 7.

Sing for Freedom: The Story of the Civil Rights Movement through Its Songs. Smithsonian/Folkways, 1992. Recorded and produced by Guy Carawan. Notes by Guy and Candie Carawan. This collection of freedom songs recorded in civil rights events in Alabama, Tennessee, Georgia, and Washington, DC, during the early 1960s includes classics such as "Keep Your Eyes on the Prize" and "We Shall Overcome." Chapter 7.

The Skillet Lickers, *Old-Time Fiddle Tunes and Songs from North Georgia*. Country Records, Country-CD 3509, 1996 (originals late 1920s, early 1930s). This group represents a primary model for old-time music revivalists. Especially evident is the dense, driving fiddle sound. Chapter 6.

Soul of Mbira. Nonesuch Records H-72054. This is a CD reissue of Paul Berliner's excellent recordings of Shona mbira music that accompanied his book of the same name. Chapters 2 and 5.

Swing Tanzen Verboten! Swing Music and Nazi-Propaganda Swing during World War II. Proper Records, Properbox 56. This is a four-CD box set including the propaganda swing and a variety of German swing bands of the World War II era. The notes are excellent on the place of this music and the musicians in Nazi Germany. Chapter 7.

The Young Fogies. Rounder Records, Rounder CD 0319, 1994. This is perhaps the best single anthology to accompany the text of chapter 6. It includes selections of many of the groups discussed, including the New Lost City Ramblers, the Hollow Rock String Band, the Highwoods String Band, and the Horseflies along with many others. Other recordings by the New Lost City Ramblers can be found on the Smithsonian/Folkways Web site. Chapter 6.

Index